Children's Health in America

A History

Twayne's History of American Childhood Series

Series Editors
Joseph M. Hawes, Memphis State University
N. Ray Hiner, University of Kansas

DATE DUE

DATE	ISSUED TO

DEMCO

Children's Health in America

A History

Charles R. King

Twayne Publishers • New York

Maxwell Macmillan Canada • *Toronto*
Maxwell Macmillan International • *New York Oxford Singapore Sydney*

Children's Health in America: A History
Charles R. King

Copyright © 1993 by Twayne Publishers

Twayne Publishers
Macmillan Publishing Company
866 Third Avenue
New York, New York 10022

Maxwell Macmillan Canada, Inc.
1200 Eglinton Avenue East
Suite 200
Don Mills, Ontario M3C 3N1

Library of Congress Cataloging-in-Publication Data

King, Charles R. (Charles Richard), 1947-
    Children's health in America : a history / Charles R. King.
        p. cm.
    Includes bibliographical references and index.
    ISBN 0-8057-4101-1. — ISBN 0-8057-4111-9
    1. Child health services—United States—History. 2. Child health services—social aspects—United States—History. 3. Pediatrics—United States—History. 4. Pediatrics—United States—Philosophy—History. I. Title.
    [DNLM: 1. Child Health Services—history—United States. 2. Child Care—history—United States. 3. Child Welfare—history—United States. 4. Pediatrics—history—United States. WA 11 AA1 K5c 1993]
    RJ102.K46 1993
    362.1'9892'000973—dc20
    DNLM/DLC
    for Library of Congress   93-6756
                                                                                                                      CIP

10 9 8 7 6 5 4 3 2 1 (hc)
10 9 8 7 6 5 4 3 2 1 (pb)

Printed in the United States of America

for
Rich, Jason and Seth

Contents

Illustrations

Introduction

Most people live their lives within the loosely woven fabric of everyday life. This work-a-day world of factory, home, playground, and school looms even larger for children. The heroic events of history—elections, military campaigns, and the deeds of mighty people—pale in comparison to the influence of parents, food, shelter, and the minutiae of daily life on the growth and development of children. An essential feature that permits the maturation of the child is health, that is, the natural, normal, and proper functioning of body and mind. This freedom from death and disease (the impairment of natural function) is situated within the fabric of daily life, not in the political arena, not on the battlefield, and not even within the technology of modern medicine. To understand the history of children's health in America we must move beyond political campaigns, industrialization, and even the startling science of the physician and instead emphasize the home and the hearth as much more dramatic determinants of children's health.

Poor health and disease have devastated humanity since its inception. Just as children have been forgotten or ignored by historians, so the importance of children's health has often been neglected. Before the twentieth century, nearly one-half of all live-born children died before they reached adolescence. An understanding of the history of children's health in America is of necessity based on death records, recorded conversations of the participants, and the political rhetoric of the day. Such a reconstruction is not an attempt to consider all children, white or minority, urban or rural, all doctors, famous or infamous, all diseases, rare or common, all treatments, heroic or futile, nor all the effects of therapy, positive or negative, but rather an effort to understand from the colonial era to the modern world the nature of children's health and disease and the social, cultural, professional, and lay influences on it.

Initially, the health care of children in America was influenced by three major ideologic factors: religion, science, and philosophical thought. From the seventeenth-century Puritans to the First Great Awakening to the rise of the progressive movement to the words and actions of contemporary Christian Scientists, religion has provided a fundamental basis for thought about children's health. Disease was often viewed as a product of divine intervention with no real basis for human action; however, human action and intervention were deemed appropriate by some groups for the solution of humanity's problems. Beginning in the eighteenth century, rising in the nineteenth, and peaking in the twentieth century, scientific medicine has provided tools—stethoscopes, scalpels, and x-rays—and ideas—the localized concept of disease and the germ theory—by which both parents and practitioners understand, explain, and treat the diseases of children. The acceptance of the germ theory of disease, the surgical treatment of illness, and the prevention of childhood lead poisoning are three examples of this process. Finally, from the physician and philosopher John Locke to the psychiatrist Sigmund Freud, European thought and ideas have revolutionized American medical thought and practice and provided a nucleus for American thinking about children's health. From Cotton Mather to Benjamin Spock, American physicians have often used a European theoretical framework in their efforts to improve the health care of America's children.

The medical care of children, and adults as well, was a major part of the broader fabric of seventeenth-century colonial life. The foundation of a new nation created health problems and concerns that were foreign to emigrating Europeans. At the same time continental thinkers—Locke, Rousseau, and Calvin—provided a philosophical framework within which the health care of many colonial American children was provided. The Puritan worldview that "fixed their eyes on a heavenly goal, which directed and informed their lives"[1] was representative of Calvin's view of the divinely predestined nature of human life. Locke's concept of a "Happy State in this world" was also based on "a sound mind in a sound Body."[2] The combination of these perspectives enabled colonial parents, ministers, governors, and physicians to provide medical and spiritual attention to sick children. In 1693, when Cotton Mather's daughter Katharine was "taken so dangerously sick," the Boston minister "cast [him]self at the Feet of His Holy Sovereignty," prayed, and read the Bible. His daughter recovered, according to Mather, by God's will.[3] In spite of this submission to God's will, and its implication that death was expected, the Puritan fathers clearly grieved for their deceased children. As Samuel Sewall recorded following the birth of a stillborn son, "I was grievously stung to find a sweet desirable son dead, who had none of my help to succor him and save his life."[4]

In the early eighteenth century, European thought continued to influence colonial American life and medical practices. The encyclopedic systems of medical thought championed by the physicians Herman Boerhaave and Thomas Sydenham were widely employed in America; yet most medical care for children and adults was provided by nonphysicians. Early English texts of pediatrics, like Michael Underwood's *A Treatise on the Diseases of Children* (1773), were popular in this country. Even though written by a physician, this text "carefully avoided all technical terms, or has so explained them, and so enlarged on the nature of diseases, and the doses of medicines, that parents and others not versed in the practice of physic, may find all common directions sufficiently explicit."[5] In 1713, Cotton Mather wondered about a project he later completed, "whether I may not do well, to print a little sheet, of advice for sick persons and Houses."[6] Benjamin Franklin wrote with the aid of the English physician William Heberden a pamphlet justifying the routine inoculation of children against smallpox.[7] Parents, educated laypersons, clergy, midwives, and physicians all played important roles in the health of colonial children, and all employed comparable pills, potions, and elixirs in the treatment of disease.

Contrary to the Calvinist view of human nature, Rousseau argued that children were born innocent, with a capacity for reason, and that parents served only to develop their natural virtues.[8] While Mary Wollstonecraft vigorously attacked Rousseau in her *Vindication of the Rights of Woman,* she strongly agreed with the Frenchman that reason promoted child rearing and children's health.[9] American parents, preachers, and physicians increasingly applied reason and analysis to the solution of the problems of children's health. In the process they expanded and codified empiric observation into a burgeoning science, based on the observation, analysis, and study of the natural world as judged against an accumulated and increasingly formalized body of medical knowledge and customs.

By 1800 the health of American children was still very poor in comparison to modern standards. Too many families recorded the deaths of their children, as did Francis and Rebecca Hardy of Boston: "Francis, died October 26th, 1807, aged two months. John died August 28th, 1808, aged two days. Margaret, died September 16th, 1809, aged six weeks."[10] While medical science did not provide remedies for most of the health problems of children, increasingly mothers promoted child health with the growing aid of lay and medical practitioners. Ideal mothers sacrificed their "good health and personal comfort as the price that had to be paid to attain the honorable and powerful position of mother."[11] This personal, biological, and social responsibility of motherhood caused one mother to conclude "what a delicate office is that of a mother!"[12] A 23-year-old South Carolina mother more explicitly concluded: "I am resolved to be a good mother to my children, to pray for them, to set them good examples, to give them good advice, to be careful both of their souls and bodies, to watch over their tender minds, to carefully root out the first appearings and buddings of vice and to trouble to do them good, to correct their errors what ever uneasiness may give myself and never omit to encourage every virtue I may see dawning in them."[13] Motherhood was seen as a natural and patriotic duty for women, and the central means by which American society dealt with the issues of children's health.

From the colonial era to the twentieth century, in addition to mothers and physicians, other lay healers, especially midwives, tended, soothed, and healed ailing children. Midwives and other wise women attended their sisters, neighbors, and friends in childbirth. The midwife's duties generally extended beyond birthing and often included assisting new mothers with the daily duties of feeding, clothing, and caring for their children. They were advisers about breast feeding, nutritional recommendations, health practices, and disease treatment. They dispensed elixirs and other remedies that were traditionally compounded and administered by families and laypersons and formulated in recipe and domestic advice texts throughout the eighteenth and nineteenth centuries. In fact, midwives and lay healers played at least as important a role in the health care of American children as more formally trained medical practitioners.

Although children sickened and died, and parents, layhealers, and physicians treated their ailments, throughout the first two-thirds of the nineteenth century medical discourse largely ignored the unique nature of the health care of children. Most medical schools did not have courses in the diseases of children until after mid-century, and most practitioners were unable to adequately explain the diseases of children. Many agreed with William Dewees, Philadelphia physician and specialist in the diseases of women and children: "The belief that the diseases of children almost constantly present nothing but perplexing obscurity or embarrassing uncertainty, has much retarded the progress of inquiry, by engendering doubts of their susceptibility of successful investigation, lucid explanation, or useful arrangement, and of course, that every prescribed remedy has but an uncertain aim, and consequently, a contingent or doubtful effect."[14] A broader base for scientific inquiry and the growing recognition of the importance of childhood disease, based on successful treatment of childhood diseases in Europe, helped create the American science of pediatrics. The importance of this effort was noted by its central figure, Abraham Jacobi (1830–1918): "The young are the future makers and owners of the world. Their physical, intellectual and moral condition will decide whether the globe will be more Cossack or more Republican, more criminal or more righteous."[15] In Jacobi's view, the "pediatrist" was responsible for all aspects of children's health, not merely the treatment of disease. Importantly, Jacobi recognized the central influence of social factors, as well as medical factors, on children's health.

The combination of the emerging science of pediatrics and the social goals of motherhood, including not only successful child rearing, but also the instillation of moral values and a sense of national spirit, as fostered in the nineteenth-century child-protection movement, promoted the establishment of orphanages, foundling homes, and hospitals for children. Women, generally white, middle-class, Protestant mothers, led this moral and social campaign for children's aid programs. An important feature of these efforts was moral reform as a part of the aid of poor, orphaned, delinquent, or sick children. Child placement efforts, led by Charles Loring Brace and others, dramatically sought to promote children's health by transferring children from the destitute tenements of New York City to upstate farms and the Midwest heartland. Not all efforts were equally effective. In 1876, the *New York Times* reported the deaths of infants "crudely neglected" at a foundling home, where the infants were fed flour and water rather than milk. When autopsies were performed for two of the children, their stomachs were "empty and not a trace of food."[16] Recognition of these problems rapidly expanded the role for both government and private institutions in the health care and protection of children and, importantly, in the regulation of the methods of its provision.

The progressive movement spawned a rise in journalism, social work, sociology, psychology, and, most important for this discussion, interest in sanitation, children's health, and preventive medicine. A religious revival and a concern for humanity fueled these efforts, which applied the expanded scientific knowledge of the late nineteenth century, especially the germ theory and improved methods of sanitation and communicable disease control, to the prevention and control of disease. Science became "a goal as well as a procedure, which gave it the authority of higher law and removed it from criticism."[17] In the process both public and private efforts promoted children's health and reduced the pain and suffering of American children.

Science formed the foundation for the twentieth-century medical care of children. It became the basic method that reduced infant mortality, provided pure milk, and expanded the study of the normal child. The advice of experts had replaced maternal instinct and customs as the foundation for child health.[18] Professionals, especially physicians, became the official advisers to American parents. Infant care manuals abounded, baby fairs were held, and baby welfare consultations performed. One mother concluded that if the Department of Agriculture educated farmers with technical bulletins, then mothers had "a right to know the scientific reasons which underlie [infant] feeding."[19] By 1921 more than a million and a half copies of the Children's Bureau publication *Infant Care* had been distributed throughout the country.[20] American mothers and physicians formed an essential alliance that benefited the nation's children.

Comparable efforts were launched to provide pure milk for infant feeding. During the first decades of the twentieth century, the high rate of infant mortality (20 to 40 percent of live births) resulted largely from improper, inadequate, and unsanitary methods of infant feeding. Scientific studies that identified bacteria in milk were followed by public health measures that supplied pure milk through municipal milk stations and eventually promoted the pasteurization of the general milk supply. By 1907 the New York Milk Committee was formed for "the reduction of infant mortality and the improvement of the milk supply of New York City."[21] In four years there was an eightfold increase in the number of milk stations and a 27 percent decrease in infant deaths. These initially successful efforts against infant mortality provided impetus for the first major piece of federal social legislation that benefited the health care of American infants and children—the Sheppard-Towner Act of 1921. This program sponsored by the Children's Bureau provided matching federal funds that promoted maternal and children's health. Public education, prenatal clinics, and well-baby programs were a few of the successful projects sponsored by this funding.

During the current era those scientific and institutional programs that promoted children's health early in the century have been dramatically expanded. Pediatric science has grown from studies of milk composition to the molecular genetic analysis of cystic fibrosis. The diagnosis of disease is no longer based at the child's bedside, but on the laboratory analysis of blood and urine, cerebrospinal fluid, and bone marrow, providing evidence of leukemia, cocaine addiction, or cytomegalovirus infection. Sulfanilamide has been replaced by antibiotics too numerous to name, and immunization against poliomyelitis has replaced the iron lung. Freud and Spock have scientifically analyzed the child's mind[22] and in the process have emphasized the importance of a healthy mind in a healthy body. Increasingly, parents, politicians, and medical professionals jointly attacked the economic, social, physical, psychological, and spiritual causes of childhood death and disease.[23] The result has been a growing recognition of the importance of children's health in America. And, while significant progress has been made, the health problems of American children remain incompletely resolved and, in the opinion of many, inadequately addressed.

Today, pediatricians, legislators, and parents utilize the sociocultural model of pediatrics, originally proposed by Jacobi, and promoted in the early twentieth century, as the essential basis for an understanding of the broad implications of children's health. Since children were, and are, situated within the social fabric of American life, and since disease attacks a child within a specific family and social setting, it was natural that this evolution from the treatment of children as miniature adults should occur. As a result previously neglected issues of children's health, like child abuse, learning disabilities, and delinquency, were defined as medical problems. In spite of the emphasis upon the science of medical practice, the health care of children remains a problem rooted in daily life. As more practitioners broadened their understandings of children's health, fewer American children died, and those who became ill experienced less pain and suffering. The relief that malaria-stricken, 13-year-old Hannah Hawkes[24] felt when a nineteenth-century neighbor carried "fresh water" to her was not necessarily different from the comfort that a contemporary child with leukemia experiences from the visit of Ronald McDonald. Quinine for the treatment of malaria or cytosine arabinoside for leukemia may provide the medical cure, but the recovering child recalls the soothing hands of another, not the science expressed in a medical textbook.

Before the twentieth century, in colonial New England, along the trans-Mississippi West, and in the crowded tenements of New York, Philadelphia, and Chicago, childhood death was common in American families.

1

Physician to Body and Soul

On the night of 17 October 1637, Mrs. William Dyer of New Exchange (Massachusetts Bay Colony) gave birth to a "monster." The stillborn female infant was born "about two months before the just time" and was turned from the "hiplings" position by the midwife in attendance. The child had "a face, but no head, and the ears stood upon the shoulders and were like an ape's; it had no forehead, but over the eyes four horns, hard and sharp." More incredible were talons on the feet, scales over the breast and back, and the presence of two mouths. These findings were confirmed five months later when the "much corrupted" body was exhumed and examined by Governor John Winthrop and several of the magistrates and elders of Boston. These efforts were necessary because the Dyers were said to be "notoriously infected with Mrs. Hutchinson's errors."

This inquiry into children's health in America commences with the birth of infant Dyer, for this incident dramatically illustrates the state of American children's health in the seventeenth century. Medicine was hidden within the theological discourse of the day, and disease, as exemplified by the anomalous birth of infant Dyer, was seen as the result of supernatural forces. God was responsible for death and disease, and He in turn provided the necessary healing absolution. It was no accident that the infant was female, as were Mrs. Hutchinson and other midwives, who "went out of the jurisdiction"[1] and were accused of being witches. The premature, breech birth was also a portent of the distress of nature. Clearly, these forces were beyond human control, yet the inquiry of Governor Winthrop (1588–1649) and his colleagues was an indication that reason and rational analysis offered a new means for the understanding of human illness. Importantly, this inquiry was directed not by physicians, but rather by educated laymen and the clergy. Medical practice was enmeshed in the fabric of daily life, where educated

laymen and midwives provided medical attention on a par with more formally educated physicians.

This early seventeenth-century event provided a bridge between the theological discourse of the day and the emerging philosophical thought of the
Enlightenment. A monstrous birth, as Samuel Sewall noted nearly a century
later, was a time for reflection on "the Mercies of my Birth, and of the Birth
of Mine! Laus Deo!"[2] God was held responsible for what the human mind
could not explain. Often such events were seen as the products of the black
forces of witchery, but within the framework of seventeenth-century religious
thought it was believed, especially by New England Calvinist Protestants, that
God's supernatural powers ultimately controlled the health and lives of his
creatures.

The reaction to unusual births illustrates how theology was used to
explain children's illness and death in colonial America. Human curiosity
about natural events, including abnormal births, death, and disease, was not
new, but the exhumation of a body for physical examination, as much for
theological as for medical reasons, was not commonly performed. The
examination of infant Dyer by the leaders of Boston was noteworthy
because it occurred at all, but more important, it made the laity—not the
clergy—the explicators for an anomalous birth. This was graphic evidence
that empiric secular inquiry, a traditional means of understanding the world
and one championed by the English philosopher and physician John Locke
(1632–1704), and not theological dogma alone, formed a basis for explaining childhood death and disease. Over the next 400 years this tension
between a traditional religious perspective and the emerging secular scientific approach to health in general, and children's health specifically,
became one of the central themes in the development of the medical care of
children in America.

From New England to New Spain to New France, colonial Americans
based their understanding of health and disease on both the formal medical
knowledge and the folklore and traditions of their European countrymen.
Medicine, whether practiced by physicians, clergymen, midwives, governors,
or laypersons, was based on the ideas and practices that early Americans
brought with them from Europe. From this philosophical framework, the
essentially pragmatic colonists, who generally lacked time, facilities, and
sponsors for speculative inquiry, erected a system for health care that was
both practical within the world of its day and based on the larger framework
of colonial society and institutions.[3]

Childhood Death and Disease in Colonial America

Anomalous births were not frequent in colonial America, but infant and childhood deaths were widespread. Estimations of the magnitude of childhood death from this era are difficult, since vital statistics were incomplete, stillbirths were often not recorded, children, especially infants, were informally buried, and the high frequency of such deaths made their occurrence unremarkable. Nonetheless, as Ross Beales concluded in his summary of the literature, nearly 10 percent of seventeenth-century New England children died during infancy, and along the Chesapeake perhaps one of every two live-born children died before they reached 20 years of age.[4] Today fewer than one in 100 American infants die, and this dramatic contrast provides evidence of the hardships of colonial life compared with contemporary America.

Cotton Mather (1638–1728) noted that a dead child was "a sight no more surprising than a broken pitcher."[5] Most childhood illnesses did not have a fatal outcome, but potentially serious problems, such as the now preventable smallpox and diphtheria, often ended in death. Many parents and practitioners of the day recognized physiological changes, like teething, as diseases; however, most did not go as far as the seventeenth-century practitioner Robert Pernell, who concluded that "among all the diseases that children are subject to there is none more serious or troublesome to them than the pain in breeding of their teeth."[6] It was not known until the late nineteenth century by physicians, and perhaps the twentieth century by many parents, that acute infectious diseases, like measles or scarlet fever, and not the eruption of new teeth, were responsible for deaths.

For immigrants, disease often did not begin in the new world. Some immigrants left Europe in a diseased state, and death and disease were common on the voyage across the Atlantic. Poor diets, leading to scurvy and nutritional deficiencies, and inadequate sanitation, resulting in common infectious diseases like dysentery, typhus, typhoid fever, and smallpox, were frequent. The Palatine Gottlieb Mittelberger on his way to Philadelphia in 1750 reported that many died "miserably" from "many kinds of sea sickness, fever, dysentery, headache, heat, constipation, boils, scurvy, cancer, mouthrot, and the like."[7] Children were not spared the dangers of the voyage. Mittelberger noted that children less than eight years of age rarely survived. Many parents (Mittelberger observed 32 such instances) were "compelled to see their children miserably suffer and die from hunger, thirst and sickness, and then to see them cast into the water." In 1729, the *Boston Weekly Newsletter* reported a ship from Ireland off Martha's Vineyard on which more than half of the passengers starved to death. Only 1 of 30 children survived.[8]

Although the voyage to the New World was uncertain because of death and disease, some promoters of colonial settlement advised prospective immigrants that "no one became ill in America."[9] One observer concluded that the air in the new world was "medicinal," especially for those with a "cold, melancholy, Flegmatick temper of body." For one New Yorker, this healthfulness was the "maine blessing of God."[10] While these statements include a measure of hyperbole, they also include an element of truth. Tabulations by modern historians indicate that while infant death in the colonies was frequent (10 to 30 percent of all liveborn infants did not survive to one year of age), death was more common in London and many of the other continental urban centers. In addition, probably because of less crowded living conditions and a more abundant food supply, seventeenth- and eighteenth-century rural colonists and their children had a lower death rate than more crowded urban colonial families.[11] Nonetheless, infant deaths along the seventeenth-century Chesapeake, as estimated by Ross Beales, were evidence that despite apparently better living conditions and nutrition, infant and childhood death was all too common. As late as 1841, the frequency of early death led New Bedford's Samuel Rodman (1792–1859), who had just entered his 50th year to conclude: "It seems a matter of surprise that I have lived so long, and without yet any material change. I have actually passed beyond the period of youth and middle age and may justly be classed among the old."[12] Rodman and many other Americans who survived the periodic epidemics and repeated illnesses of early childhood reached advanced age. However, the possibility of old age did not reduce the pain and sorrow that accompanied the death of child relatives.

Nearly all observers reported that death in the New World was common. Dr. Samuel Fuller, who arrived in Massachusetts in 1630 with Governor Winthrop, reported the "sad news" that "many are sick and many are dead." As a physician Fuller's ability to help was limited because drugs, facilities, and "things fitting to work with" were lacking.[13] Although the exact frequency of childhood death may never be known, many colonial children died.[14] Deaths were probably more frequent in the seventeenth than the eighteenth century, especially in the Chesapeake Bay area. Although incomplete records limit available conclusions, in New England mortality may actually have been lower in the seventeenth century than in the eighteenth century, when urban crowding and limited public sanitation enhanced an already high death rate. When colonial stillbirths, infant deaths, and early childhood deaths are totaled, at least one of every four Americans born in the seventeenth and eighteenth centuries died in infancy or childhood.

For individual families, more precise estimates of the frequency of infant and childhood death are possible. The tragedy that these families experienced may not have been typical of all colonial families, but such personal accounts graphically illustrate the magnitude of infant death in some early American households. Samuel Sewall (1652–1730) had 14 children with his first wife. One was stillborn, seven died before two years of age, and only six reached adulthood. This 50 percent death rate continued for Sewall's grandchildren as well.[15] Cotton Mather's wives bore 16 children over 26 years, but during only two of those years were more than two children under the age of five alive in the household at the same time.[16] A Virginia father who had buried three wives recorded the personal agony of the death of his seven-year-old daughter. "Her face, feet and hands were all cold and her pulse quite gone and reduced to the bones and the skin that cover them and dying very hard . . . [a] severe stroke indeed to a man bereft of a Wife and in the decline of life."[17] This child died of malaria, a condition so common in colonial Virginia that it was dubbed a "seasoning," part of the adaptation that nearly all European immigrants to the colony experienced.

Children in the colonies, as well as their modern counterparts, experienced rare and common diseases and died from disease, accidents, and injury. Children died with convulsions, tumors, fevers, agues of being "Cutt for the Stone"[18] (the surgical removal of a bladder stone), and hydrophobia (rabies), even when "bitten five months before."[19] But infant feeding problems, which were compounded by the inability to treat the dehydration that accompanied the vomiting and diarrhea of gastrointestinal illnesses, were much more frequent causes of death. The effects of such problems were especially threatening with the increased temperatures of the summer and thus were often described as "summer complaint." These "fluxes" (diarrheas) included more severe problems, such as dysentery and typhoid fever, which were spread as one early Virginia resident noted in 1610, by the "brackish River" that served as a local water supply.[20] Few remedies for these problems were available, and in the absence of an understanding of the germ theory, the means of prevention by improved sanitation were limited. It was small consolation, and probably unrecognized by colonial Americans, that although infant death was common in the New World, it was also frequent in London.

Accidents, injuries, even poisonings were common for colonial children. Among the first reports of such problems was from Governor White of the ill-fated Roanoake Colony, who reported that during the summer of 1587, English children on St. Croix ate the poisonous Manchinee. These small green apples caused their mouths "to burn, and their tongue swelled to such a size that many of them could not speak."[21] Mothers reported ingestions of snuff, gun powder, spirits, home remedies, and a myriad of other agents. Physical agents also caused injury. Elizabeth Drinker of Philadelphia reported that her three-year-old daughter placed a piece of nutshell up her nose. Several physicians unsuccessfully attempted to remove the foreign object. After two weeks "her nose was offensive," and her father attempted with a

"silver hook, to no purpose but to make her nose bleed, she screaming violently all the time. It being a case of so much consequence he was loath to
give out, and with three to hold her fast down, tried again and was favour'd
to relieve the dear child. He brought away with the hook half of a ground
nutshell."[22] The frustration that this father felt at his inability to resolve his
daughter's problem can be appreciated by all parents. In all likelihood colonial physicians would have been no more successful at relieving this young
girl's pain and fear.

Accidents and burns from firearms were frequent as well. In 1642,
Richard Sylvester's middle son was playing with a fowling piece that "went
off, and shot the child into the mouth and through his head."[23] Not surprisingly, the child died. As is often the case today, the parents were away from
home when the event occurred. Samuel Sewall recorded not once, but twice,
the death of a friend's son, who "was drown'd in a Tub of Suds."[24] Burns
from open hearths, candles, and other fires were common. Within the first
two months of 1699, two of Cotton Mather's daughters were burned. In
February, his eldest, Katy, was carrying a candle into the cellar, when "her
muslin Ornaments, about her Shoulders took Fire from it, and so blazed up
as to set her Head-gear likewise on Fire. By the wonderful and merciful
Providence of God her Shriek for Help was heard; and by that Help the Fire
was extinguished." Unfortunately, she was "horribly burnt, and she was
thrown into Exquisite Misery."[25] Physicians and parents had few means with
which to reduce the pain and suffering of their burned, maimed, and injured
children.

Accidents involving horses, wagons, and other livery vehicles were also
common. Broken bones and musculoskeletal injuries from such events often
led to deformity, if not death. Governor Winthrop reported an eight-year-
old child who was playing about the "hinder end" of a cart, when it fell
upon the child. An iron from the cart pierced the child's skull and "drove a
piece of the skull before it into the brain, so as the brains came out, and
seven surgeons . . . did all conclude that it was the brains . . . and that there
was no hope of the child's life."[26] With the aid of "earnest prayers" the child
"recovered perfectly." Within the context of the day, this outcome was surely a miraculous event. Survival despite such apparently fatal injuries, when
counter to the predictions of physicians of the day, not only provided an
inaccurate prognosis, but must have made many colonists question the advice
that their physicians dispensed. At the same time the clergy did not fail to
remark upon such a miraculous event.

The horror and dread with which epidemic infectious disease was
viewed by the colonists can hardly be appreciated by the modern observer.
These problems ranged from the nearly universal "seasoning" by malaria of
new arrivals to the mid-Atlantic and southern colonies to widespread attacks
of dysentery, measles, whooping cough, diphtheria, and, most dreaded of all,

smallpox. Today all these conditions are treatable or preventable, but during the colonial era none was understood as an infectious disease, and only smallpox was preventable by inoculation or, by 1800, by vaccination with matter from the cowpox.

Colonial children also experienced what we consider the common and usually nonfatal childhood diseases—measles, mumps, and chickenpox. During the second decade of the eighteenth century the population of New England suffered from the measles. In Boston every member of Cotton Mather's family except himself had the disease. Some of the family received "a gentle Visitation" of the disease, but daughter Nibby, who was "lying very sick" of the disease, daughter Jerusha, and a pair of newly born twins, who died of the disease, had more severe cases. Many adults were not spared either: Mather's maid died with a "malignant fever," and perhaps most tragically for Mather, his "dear, dear, dear Friend," his wife, died as well. Throughout all this personal tragedy Mather continued to attend his congregation. He visited the sick daily and provided what spiritual comfort he could. He preached sermons, reprinted a pamphlet, "Wholesome Words," which he had previously written for families of the sick, and newly penned a letter to families afflicted with this "heavy Calamity." He was especially concerned about poor families where disease added "exceedingly to the Difficulties" of their lives.[27]

Similar outbreaks of the disease followed in the other colonies over the ensuing decades. In New York during 1729, James Alexander reported to Cadwallader Colden that there was "never so great a mortality" as was then occurring.[28] Many of these measles-related deaths were caused by secondary infections and pneumonia. Concern about this high mortality gave pause for self-reflection. An 11-year-old boy began his diary with such a report: "A fever attended with the Meazells, and after that with great weakness and infirmities as also great pain, which set me upon thinking upon what would be the estate of my soul after my Dissolution, which was apprehended by all to be Nigh, often in my Mind repeating the Psalmists words Blessed is he whose Transgressions is forgiven . . . Heartily wishing and praying . . . promising also that if God would in his great Mercy Spare my life I would spend it more to the Glory and praise of his great Name."[29] For the clergy, children, and their parents, the healing of both body and soul was essential for a complete return to health.

If measles was a dangerous disease for colonial Americans, diphtheria was even more lethal. During the New England diphtheria epidemic of 1735–40, more than 5,000 colonists, mostly children, died. This wave of death, which descended from the "frown of Providence," began in Kingston, New Hampshire, where the first 40 residents with the disease died; ultimately, one-third of the children of the community succumbed. The following year in Haverhill, Massachusetts, among 1200 residents, 23 families were left childless from the disease.[30] By the fall of 1735 the disease, or at least one that local physicians diagnosed as the "throat distemper," had entered Boston. By the end of the decade deaths from the epidemic had occurred from Maine to New Jersey.[31]

Physicians, surgeons, the clergy, and the laity all agreed on the cause: "God hath been provoked to visit this People with sore and grievous Calamities."[32] The "breach of [God's] laws," just as in other ages, had brought this "plague" upon the people. Repentance and prayer were called for by the clergy and governors alike. Healing of the soul was the only resort when the "Doctor's Art" and all the "Doctor's skill" were "in the dark" and unable to suggest a cause, cure, or healing therapy for the disease.[33] In 1740 Jonathan Dickinson, a New Jersey clergyman, Yale graduate, and practicing but formally untrained physician, provided perhaps the best colonial description of the disease by carefully observing and recording what he saw. The first family he observed with the disease already had one dead child when he arrived. This occurrence "gave me the advantage of a Dissection, and thereby a better Acquaintance with the Nature of the Disease, than I could otherwise have had."[34] While his theological and medical colleagues debated the divine causation and cure of the throat-distemper, Dickinson looked within nature for the cause and an understanding of the disease. These observations, and perhaps more important the physical and intellectual dissection of the body by a practitioner without formal training, suggested that new understandings of human disease and its treatment were possible.

The Practice of Medicine

The ability of medical practitioners (layhealers or those more formally trained) to effectively diagnosis and treat disease was limited. Neither measurement of body temperature nor listening to the heart (except with the ear crudely applied to the chest) were routinely practiced. The nature of disease was only partially appreciated. This confusion was well stated by the Revolutionary era physician Benjamin Rush (1745–1813), in his "Dissertation on the Spasmodic Asthma of Children." "How often do we mistake causes for effects and effects for causes of diseases. It is hard to tell where the one ends and the other begins. Sometimes they are so complicated together, that it is difficult to say which was the cause and which the effect."[35] Many Americans accepted a role for divine intervention in the cause of death and disease, and few parents or practitioners had practical evidence that dismissed such an interpretation.

In an era when God was recognized as the true healer, the healing of the soul often took precedence over the mere physical healing of the body. Both public and private efforts were undertaken to this end. In May 1693, when the measles attacked Virginia Colony, Governor Andros declared a "Day of Humiliation and Prayer" to atone to Almighty God for the pestilence "where of several have dyed."[36] Privately, Cotton Mather regularly recorded the therapeutic efficacy for his sick children of his prayers and devotion to the Lord. In June 1699, his daughter Nanny was despaired of by the physicians, yet Mather maintained his faith. Within days he reported divine healing for "behold the Effect of Prayer and Faith! On this very day, the child began to recover. A sensible and marvelous change this day came upon the Child; and from this very Time, its Recovery went on most comfortably."[37] While few other colonial Americans expressed their thoughts on this subject as eloquently as Mather did, most acted as he did. They prayed for their children's health and recovery from disease, and as Mather regularly recorded in his diary, they also dosed their sick children with traditional potions that experience convinced them were effective.

Before 1800, few effective medications beyond the Peruvian bark that William Byrd (1674–1744) of Virginia called a "Sovereign Remedy" for malaria, opiates for pain, and digitalis for dropsy (edema) were available. On the other hand many medications, such as the mercury in calomel, were toxic. Most methods of healing were based on a theory of bodily homeostasis maintained by a balance of the traditional four humors—blood, phlegm, black bile, and yellow bile. Treatment in turn was directed at balancing the humors with the heroic efforts of bleeding, puking, purging, and blistering. Not surprisingly, these remedies were accompanied more often by adverse effects than therapeutic success. For example, Governor Winthrop in 1647 observed an "epidemical sickness" among the Indians and Europeans. Those treated by heroic means with bleeding and other forceful measures died, while "those who took comfortable things, for the most part recovered and that in a few days."[38] Of course many colonists, as well as Europeans, recognized these limitations of the medical profession and sought advice from lay practitioners. The physicians of the day had far less formal training than their modern counterparts, and, relatively speaking, most educated colonists had some medical knowledge. Individuals, such as Governor Winthrop in the seventeenth century or Benjamin Franklin in the eighteenth century, were in essence medical practitioners. They diagnosed, prescribed, and advised just as their more formally trained colleagues did. The clergy also filled this role. Cotton Mather's unpublished *Angel of Bethesda* was one of the earliest medical texts in this country. Most of these lay practitioners viewed healing the body as almost equal in importance to healing the soul. For many, successful healing was not possible without attention to both body and soul.

Since formal treatment, as one physician observed, was ineffective and even harmful, it was not surprising that some employed folk remedies or followed the recommendations of lay advisers.[39] Herbs, potions, and other favorite family remedies were often handed down through generations. The compounding of such preparations was also detailed in recipe and cookbooks. *The Compleat Housewife* (1742) published in the Colonies contained 300 "family receipts of medicine; viz. drinks, syrups, salves ointments, and various other things of sovereign and approved efficacy in most distempers, pains, aches, wounds, sores, and etc."[40] Few of these agents, such as rhubarb, penny royal, tansy, and the like, were efficacious, but neither were they accompanied by the toxicity of more formal medical treatments. Spirits, often in the form of rum or whisky, were frequently added to these concoctions, a tradition that continues into the twentieth century in the formulation of contemporary patent medicines. Such elixirs were given to children with chills and fevers, aches and pains, and their effect was perhaps more directly attributable to the sedation from alcohol than the benefit of the other ingredients they contained. Formulation of these diverse preparations into standard formularies, such as John Tennent's *Every Man his own Doctor; or, The Poor Planter's Physician* (1736), were common.[41] Parents who consulted such handbooks benefited from the particular experience of others, and by so doing they often avoided consultation with the physician, who was often not readily available. Not that physicians had remedies and skills more efficacious than those offered by Tennent; they generally did not.

At times therapy was based on fortune-telling and astrological cures such as William Salmon proposed in his voluminous *Medicinae Practica* of 1692. Almanacs defined the timing for planting crops, breeding livestock, and bleeding family members.[42] These texts also included anatomical charts, physiologic advice, and recipes for compounding home remedies. Some families employed horseshoes and other charms as cures and preventives. Necklaces were worn to ward off the evil eye and the diseases it might cause, while bracelets encircled wrists or ankles to prevent the aches and pains of rheumatism.[43] In short, a multitude of traditional remedies that many believed efficacious were available without the aid or advice of physicians. Undoubtedly, many families used these means to treat their sick children.

Colonial Thought about Childhood Death and Disease

Religious division was an important motivating factor for immigration to the New World; but religious conformity based on the teachings of John Calvin (1509–64) and his Puritan disciples was widely accepted, especially in New England. In the words of the historian Edmund Morgan, Puritans in New

England "fixed their eyes on a heavenly goal which directed and informed their lives."[44] God healed, while New Englanders lived their lives under the shadow of death. Illness, according to Calvin, was merely a message of death that required believers "to have one foot raised to depart when it shall please God."[45] Or, as Cotton Mather concluded: "What are Sickness, but the Rods wherewith GOD counts His own offending Children?" Satan, that is the "Angel of Death," was responsible for disease that arose when "the Humane Body" was put "out of order."[46] The response to this challenge of faith was, as one New England clergyman noted, "if it be God's will I should live, I am willing to live; otherwise, if it be his will I should die, I am willing to die."[47] Christian faith, not reason, was the appropriate method of dealing with the unexplained catastrophes—epidemics, famines, floods—of the physical world. At the same time there was another body of thought, beliefs, customs, and practices in folk medicine, which bordered on magic, that helped explain the world for many colony families.[48]

The Puritan worldview included children and God's interaction with them. Although children were recognized as "Lambs in the fold," their relationship to God and life was more accurately understood as a trial. Samuel Willard in *The Child's Portion* (1684) noted that the reason "God is often angry with [his children], afflicts them and withdraws the light of his countenance from them, and puts them to grief, is not because he loves them not, but because it is that which their present condition requires; they are but Children, and childish, and foolish, and if they were not sometimes chastened, they would grow wanton, and careless of duty."[49] Illness and disease were one such trial commonly experienced by New England children. From a secular perspective the outcome of such confrontation was often childhood death since, as Samuel Wakeman noted in *The Young Man's Legacy* (1673), death was "oftentimes as near the young man's back" as it was "the old man's face."[50] At the same time from a theological perspective death was a "privilege," "an out-let from sin and misery, and an in-let to Glory both in Holiness and Happiness."[51]

New England children suffered from disease and died far too often from its effects. The theological beliefs that their parents accepted "for the Honour and Service of God" at times provided consolation for grieving parents and sick children.[52] Despite such beliefs, or in their absence, infant and childhood death was not always as easily accepted by some colonial families.[53] Shortly before Christmas in 1709, Cotton Mather, faced with the feverous state of his son Nathanael, struggled with his faith. His mind had been overcome with "a strange and sinful stupidity," for Mather had not prayed for his son's life "with such Agony, as I have used for my spared Children. I did not set apart a Day of Prayer for his life, as I could, and should have done. In the Night, and as the Dawn of this Day approached, the Child began to have the evident Symptoms of Death Upon it. I rose, and with several successive Prayers, resign'd it unto the Lord."[54] The outcome of the "Grievous Effects of Sin" was not easily accepted by parents,[55] even when they did not question the theological assumptions upon which their lives were based.

If the cause of disease resided within the spiritual realm, so did the treatment of disease. In New England the daily maintenance of health and the curing of disease were as much a preoccupation of the daily life of a clergyman as were "the duties to his congregation, or the necessities of subsistence farming."[56] God achieved cures that man could not. In 1699 Mather reported a woman from his congregation who was treated by many physicians without success, yet "when she heard of Jesus, she came, and touched his Garment" and was healed.[57] Faith, with a "HOLY and EASY mind," was curative. Not "all the Prescriptions with which all the Physicians under Heaven have ever yet obliged us"[58] were equal to the task. Following a presumably fatal head injury in which her "brains stuck out," and for which seventeenth-century physicians and clergy had no treatment, a Boston girl reportedly recovered without mental loss or other evidence of the injury.[59] Such events could only be described by observers of the day as miraculous in the tradition of New Testament healings.

To further promote healing, the New England clergy preached sermons and wrote religious tracts on the subject. These devotional and often polemic works were generally more pragmatic than theological, and they were often undertaken as much to persuade the faithless to enter the fold or to maintain the faithful within the fold as to physically cure the sick. Cotton Mather preached one such sermon—"What use ought parents to make of Disasters befalling their Children"—after one of his daughters was ill.

> My child fell into a Feavour, and her Neck obliged her to so wry a Posture of her Head, that I was in grievous Distress, whether she would live, or, whether if she did live, there would not be some *visible Mark* of the stroke of the Wrath of the Lord, always upon her. I cryed unto the Lord for the Child, in this my Distress; and I obtained Assurance from Heaven that the Child should not only be shortly and safely cured of her Burning, but that God would make this very Burning, to be the occasion of her being brought more effectively than ever, Home unto Himself, and His Christ.[60]

These efforts were necessary as Mather noted in 1721, while colonial Boston was under siege from the smallpox, to "most plainly and fully Instruct [his congregation] how to get into such Terms with Heaven, that they may be Ready, for whatever Events the Contagion that spreads in the Town may bring upon them."[61] Mather's efforts to heal the soul extended beyond the pulpit. He asked for advice from physicians and the laity and included such recommendations in printed tracts and sermons "of advice for sick persons, and Houses" that were distributed about Boston and the colony.[62] By 1718 local, pious physicians received Mather's "brief and plain Essay," entitled "Raphael. The Blessings of an HEALED SOUL," "entreating them to bestow [blessings] upon their Patients," so that "corporeal and spiritual Healing may go together."[63] The clergy, as agents of God, were seen as more influential than governors, educators, or even physicians in relieving the burdens of the afflicted.

The Enlightenment emphasis on reason and the observation and description of the natural world, especially as espoused by John Locke and Jean-Jacques Rousseau (1712–78), led both physicians and the educated laity to look for natural laws that governed birth, childhood growth, and development. The collection of observations of the world by educated laymen like Benjamin Franklin (1706–90), and later by physicians, and the testing of these against accepted knowledge formed the basis for the development of scientific medicine. During the mid-eighteenth century, Franklin demonstrated this methodology in colonial Philadelphia as he tabulated and analyzed the benefits of inoculation against smallpox.

From a political perspective, John Locke was "America's philosopher,"[64] but he had an equally important influence on the health care of children. In both areas Locke's training as a physician with its emphasis on empiricism and "profitable knowledge" provided a basis for his philosophical view of the world.[65] In fact, Locke undertook his most influential work, which dealt with children, *Some Thoughts Concerning Education* (1693), because "I myself have been consulted of late by so many, who profess themselves at a loss how to breed their Children."[66] Within a century, this work, which was "the most popular book on child rearing in its day," appeared in more than 50 editions in English, French, Italian, Dutch, Swedish, Spanish, and German.[67] It was popular in both the Old World and the New. On the North American continent it was found "on many old library lists . . . and among the few volumes on the single book shelf."[68] Families who did not possess Locke's work undoubtedly borrowed the volume from friends and neighbors and talked among themselves about its contents.

Locke offered advice based in observations of the natural world. His expertise ranged from the care of "great bellied" (pregnant) women to diet, clothing, toilet training, and the rearing of children. Birthing, a natural process in Locke's view, occurred "when the fruit of the womb is full ripe, and if it be let alone till that time, it drops as it were of itself; and is certain it comes easiest."[69] In all matters of health care "useless women," that is midwives, even physicians were wisest when they followed this empiric advice. Likewise, the weak, struggling newborn benefited from the stimulation of "chewed onions and cloves," cinnamon water, blown or "smeared" across the lips and nostrils, or from bathing in a mixture of "water, beer and fresh butter."[70] Few parents, or physicians and midwives for that matter, recorded their use of Locke's methods of infant resuscitation. Although the effects were undocumented, these measures might physically stimulate the child and thus arouse to life a depressed newborn.

Locke, like his theological colleagues, was concerned with both a "sound mind" and a "sound body." His emphasis was "not what a physician ought to do with a sick or crazy Child; but what the Parents without the Help of Physick, should do for the *Preservation and Improvement* of an healthy, or at least, not *sickly Constitution* in their children."[71] To this end he emphasized, as did Calvin, child-rearing practices. Locke concluded that the one "great mistake" of child rearing was that "the mind has not been made obedient to Discipline, and pliant to Reason, when at first it was most tender, most easy to be bowed."[72] Successful child rearing, whether it encouraged "going to stool regularly," obtaining "full satisfaction" from sleep, or controlling the temper, was supposed "to harden and fortify Children against Fear and Danger" and thus "to accustom them to suffer Pain."[73] In short, child rearing based on these principles promoted the development of the child's personality by psychological and social control of the child's world. According to Locke, when parents applied these methods they strengthened their child's body and soul, and presumably promoted health and reduced disease.

Other Enlightenment philosophers, including Rousseau and Mary Wollstonecraft (1759–97), influenced American thought on child rearing and child health. Rousseau's influence was greater upon ideas about women and children than politics.[74] *Emile,* which first appeared in an English translation in 1763, was most influential in this regard.[75] Rousseau, like Locke, was more concerned with educating parents about the natural basis of child rearing than advising doctors. In fact, Rousseau was largely opposed to physicians, declaring that he had never called a doctor for himself and likewise would not do so for his child, "unless his life is in evident danger, for then the doctor can do him no worse than kill him."[76] In an era when medicine in reality offered few benefits for sick children and when the harmful effects of medication were known to both the lay public and the medical profession, this was not an unreasonable notion. In the larger framework of Rousseau's thought, which emphasized the natural processes of nature, child development was also presented as a natural phenomenon with its own peculiar "ways of seeing, thinking and feeling."[77] Entry to this world was not by reason alone, nor by the language of adults, nor by "the sense of the word, but its accompanying intonation [accent],"[78] as every nurse and mother knew, Child health, and more basically communication with children, required an understanding of the world from the perspective of the child. Child health was best promoted when philosophical principles were tempered with an empathetic understanding of the experiences of the child.

By the end of the eighteenth century, Mary Wollstonecraft's works were circulated in the colonies, and like Rousseau's, were shelved in one of every three American libraries.[79] By 1794 *A Vindication of the Rights of Woman* was published in Philadelphia. Although Wollstonecraft attacked Rousseau's view of women, she had views about child rearing that were surprisingly similar to Rousseau's. Wollstonecraft also based her views on the "soundest reason" with the aim of rendering "the infancy of children more healthy and happy." These efforts were necessary since "a third part of the human species" died during childhood, suggesting there was "some error in the modes adopted by mothers and nurses, which counteracts their own endeavours." Wollstonecraft offered middle-class mothers as models of this new "custom" to lower-class women.[80] Because of her untimely death from childbed fever, Wollstonecraft never completed her intended work on child care. Despite the incompleteness of her written views on motherhood and child rearing, Wollstonecraft's ideas and the "plans of Rousseau and other modern reformers" combined so that American women, like Martha Laurens Ramsey, and their physicians, like Benjamin Rush, were "well acquainted" with new and enlightened thoughts about child health.[81]

Colonial Medical Thought and Practice

At the same time that theologians and philosophers expounded upon and promoted child health, seventeenth- and eighteenth-century physicians began the systematic study of the health care of children. Colonial medical practice, whether based in the English colonies, New Spain, or New France, was essentially transplanted from Europe with few changes. Physicians throughout the Americas had similar training, or lack of it, treated similar medical problems with similar drugs, and achieved similar limited results.[82] Their efforts were based on the work of European medical theorists such as the Dutchman Hermann Boerhaave (1668–1738) and London's Thomas Sydenham (1624–89). Although physicians discussed child health and the diseases of children and rare medical texts on the subject had been published, it was another century before physicians recognized, as Rousseau had, that children and their diseases were distinctly different from adults and their health problems. In fact, it was near the end of the seventeenth century before Sydenham first was able to distinguish between two common infectious diseases of the day, smallpox and measles. By so doing he demonstrated, as the Enlightenment philosophers proposed, that observation and accurate recording of natural events enabled a new understanding of the world and in turn a new analysis of its functioning. Many physicians, and others, did not immediately accept either his larger philosophical view of the world or the narrow description of smallpox as a separate disease. The first American publication on child health, Thomas Thatcher's "Brief Rule to guide the common people of New England How to Order themselves and theirs in the Small-pox and measles," concluded in 1678 that these two different diseases were one "disease in the blood, endeavoring to recover a new form and state."[83] In large measure physicians' beliefs about disease and its cause were not important to sick children because, whether measles or small-pox were one disease or two, seventeenth-century physicians lacked effective methods of treatment.

Near the end of the seventeenth century, physicians began to write texts exclusively about children's health and disease. Walter Harris, a London consultant to the king, published *De Morbis Acutis Infantum* in 1689. This work was written in Latin, but it was soon translated, printed in English, and published in America because "that most experienced and accomplished physician, Dr. Sydenham," thought the work "would be of use to others." The appearance of this work in the vernacular provided parents and lay practitioners access to information about the "unbeaten and almost unknown Path" of children's health. Harris was aware of "'treading' upon new territory, for sick Children, and especially infants, give no other light into the Knowledge of their Diseases, than what we are able to discover from their uneasy Cries, and the uncertain Tokens of their Crossness; for which Reason several Physicians of last Rank have openly declared to me, that they go very unwillingly to take care of the Diseases of Children, especially as such as are newly born as if they were to unravel some strange Mystery, or cure some incurable Distemper." Harris correctly recognized the newness of his endeavor, the limitations of his efforts, and the possibility that careful study and analysis might "unravel some strange mystery,"[84] in other words, explain or perhaps cure the diseases of children. Harris provided few therapeutic improvements, but the recognition that childhood illness deserved special medical attention was an important step toward the nineteenth-century development of pediatrics as a medical specialty.

Throughout the next century many texts on children's diseases were written by midwives or physicians who practiced midwifery. Such was the case for Michael Underwood, who attended the Princess of Wales at the birth of Princess Charlotte in 1796. Underwood, like Harris before him, wrote "for the sake of public utility," a process he facilitated by avoiding or explaining "all technical terms." As a result parents found "all common directions sufficiently explicit" to initiate therapy themselves. When unable to do so they were advised "that the care is too difficult" and other presumably professional advice was needed.[85] More experienced practitioners, including folk healers, midwives, wise women, and physicians, had few proven remedies that were not available to colonial parents. Nonetheless, Underwood offered eighteenth-century parents the idea of the expert consultant, a role that more physicians accepted in the nineteenth century, and one that became the standard in the twentieth century.

The works of English authors such as Sydenham, Underwood, Harris, and many other important European medical writers of the seventeenth and eighteenth centuries, were reprinted in the United States. In effect, they became for patients and physicians the first popular texts on child health and disease. As a result new generations of children's health and advice books filled the shelves of booksellers and families during the nineteenth and twentieth centuries. These works were written for literate laypersons, but nearly all authors from the seventeenth to the twentieth century recommended more professional advice for unresolved medical problems.

As did many of these authors, Harris identified a unique aspect to children's health. He concluded that even though "infants can give no account of their complaints in the manner [in which] we receive information from adults, their diseases are all plainly, and sufficiently marked by the countenance, the age, the manifest symptoms, and the faithful account given by the parent, or an intelligent nurse."[86] Mothers and nurses not only cared for children, but, from the physician's perspective, were the voice of the child as well. Within a century Abraham Jacobi, and others, used these same ideas to found the nineteenth-century medical specialty of pediatrics.

Midwives, who generally learned their trade by practicing, observing, and assisting more experienced colleagues, including at times physicians, were important care givers for colonial women and children. When Elizabeth Phillips died in 1761, her career had spanned 40 years and included attendance at more than 3000 births. Another New England midwife was reportedly "very helpful in times of childbirth, and other occasions of bodily infirmities and well furnished with means for those purposes."[87] Historian Laurel Thatcher Ulrich has concluded, based on infant and maternal mortality rates, that at least some New England midwives were as skilled and successful as more formally trained colonial physicians.[88]

One New England midwife, Martha Ballard of Hallowell, Maine, left an unusually complete record of the duties of colonial midwives. In addition to assisting 816 birthing women, Ballard noted in her diary (1785–1812) that she dressed wounds, dispensed doses of roots and herbs, and at times merely sat up all night with a neighbor's ailing child. She diagnosed and prescribed for the rashes, coughs, and assorted ills of the children of her friends, neighbors, and acquaintances.[89] In July 1787, amid an epidemic of what one colonial New Hampshire physician called the "Putrid Malignant Sore Throat" (probably strep throat), Ballard brewed hyssop tea for her patients, carried elixirs to feverish children, picked saffron for inclusion with other remedies, attended funerals, pulled flax, and cared for her own family.[90] Ballard not only practiced medicine on a par with the physicians of the day, but she also continued the daily attention to her own family that necessity dictated. In her diary, Ballard recorded not only the ails of New England children, but also the frustrations of practitioners and parents who attended, often unsuccessfully, the sick children.

Colonial mothers were also experienced care givers for their children. Their knowledge was a part of the common lore and oral tradition that had passed among women for centuries and was at least as useful and practical as that offered by physicians of the day. The importance of this female role was often overlooked, and it was not until the nineteenth-century rise of the ideology of republican motherhood that it was emphasized and codified. At times, in the seventeenth century, these special skills, particularly when accompanied by unexpected results, led to charges of witchcraft. The spread of disease was also attributed to such occult means. In 1690 Martha Carrier, whom Cotton Mather dubbed the "Queen of Hell" prior to her 1692 execution for satanic activities, was accused of deliberately creating an epidemic of smallpox. Reportedly, she had "spread the distemper with wicked carelessness." This was not likely, however, since several of her own family died of the disease and since there is no historical evidence that Carrier initiated, caused, or spread smallpox. It is likely that such charges were leveled against her because she did not readily defer to her more prosperous neighbors. As a result of the charges, the nearly destitute Carriers had their community economic support stopped. The theological dogma of the day necessitated Carrier's death and that of at least four of her children.[91] For colonial Americans who accepted the theological basis of disease, these charges and actions were reasonable and the logical result of their understanding of the nature of disease.

Much of the family and child advice literature of the eighteenth century combined the theological views of Calvin with the philosophical views of Locke and Rousseau. While philosophers and theologians might disagree about the moral status of children, both Locke and Calvin offered similar practical advice about child rearing. According to Calvin parents were often required "to use severity and to temper mildness with rigor" lest their children never completely develop. "If a horse is left free in the fields and not in due time tamed, he will hardly ever endure to be pacified, he will always be refractory. Oxen also will never be brought to bear the yoke if they are placed under it only in the sixth or eighth year. We know by experience that it is the same with men." Without adequate guidance children will never "be formed from childhood to bear the yoke."[92] The apparent widespread acceptance of these views of child rearing was reflected in children's books and stories of the era. Children, and their parents who read them stories, heard a common tale of child rearing based upon the model of the attentive, cooperative, dutiful child.[93] Despite the consistency of the narratives they heard, as Samuel Willard concluded in 1684, children were both "childish, and foolish," sometimes necessitating their chastisement.[94] Successful child rearing was hard work for parents and children.

For the seventeenth- and eighteenth-century men and women who could read (about 50 percent of the population),[95] the advice literature of the era reflected the growing influence of Locke's thought on traditional Protestant ideology. In the early seventeenth century advisers agreed with Calvin that children were born depraved, whereas by 1800 only a minority of advisers offered this view, and more than 50 percent now reported that children were born in innocence. Over the same time interval, when seventeenth-century advisers all favored swaddling of the newborn, by 1800 nearly all had replaced this view with Locke's advice on cold bathing to "harden the child."[96] While swaddling might have symbolic meaning for Calvinists, the practical considerations of daily living and child care, in part influenced by Locke's empiric observations, came to represent the predominant view of American child advisers. By the end of the eighteenth century, theological and philosophical advice about children's health and development increasingly was tempered by pragmatic necessities.

An important subject for colonial advisers was infant feeding. In an era without an understanding of the germ theory, no readily available means of refrigeration, and incomplete methods to manufacture artificial feeding implements, breast feeding was favored by colonial advisers, physicians, ministers, midwives, and mothers. In 1785 Benjamin Franklin advised his fellow Americans that "since Rousseau, with admirable Eloquence pleaded for the Rights of Children to their Mother's Milk . . . some Ladies of Quality now suckle their infants and find milk enough."[97] Franklin's comments on breast feeding by the natural mother point out the influence of Rousseau in American child health practices and contrast with the European practice among wealthy women of employing a wet nurse. Maternal nursing was in many respects easier, and it avoided the uncertainty of locating an available wet nurse who had "a good breast of milk."[98] One factor in the rise of maternal nursing was, as an eighteenth-century Quaker woman noted, the recognition that it provided a "close sympathy between mother and child."[99] Perhaps equally important was the practical recognition that lactation provided some measure of contraception to nursing mothers.[100] Moreover, wet nursing potentially spread disease to nursed infants. In 1646 Governor Winthrop reported from Boston 16 cases of lues (syphilis) transmitted by a wet nurse who "had a sore breast."[101] By favoring maternal nursing, advisers and colonial women promoted the importance of motherhood and bonding between mother and child. In the process of solving some of the practical problems of infant care and feeding, these women demonstrated and their advisers supported the ideal of republican motherhood. During the nineteenth century, the view of motherhood both as a patriotic and moral duty and as the basis for child rearing, became the accepted standard for American women.

Few artificially fed, or dry nursed, infants of the colonial era survived. In 1649 Martha Lyon of Stamford, Connecticut, happily reported an exception by noting that her six-month-old daughter was "well in health" and a "thriving child for one bred up without the breast."[102] But, as the British physician and author William Cadogan noted in his "An Essay upon Nursing and the Management of Children from their Birth to Three Years of Age" (1769), one-half of all childhood deaths occurred in the first three years of life. The majority of these deaths arose from feeding problems or nutritional imbalances that followed otherwise nonfatal infectious illnesses. In short, "half the people that come into the world; go out of it again before they become of the least use to it, or themselves."[103] According to Cadogan, who was a physician at the Foundling Hospital in London, successfully breast-fed infants not only died less frequently, but became healthier and stronger children. The practical experience of many mothers demonstrated and many physicians of the day concurred that proper breast feeding was the solution to the problems of infant feeding.

The Introduction of Inoculation and Vaccination

Throughout the seventeenth and eighteenth centuries epidemics of smallpox happened regularly in the New World. As early as 1617 through 1619, 90 percent of the Indian population along the Massachusetts coast died from the disease. In 1633, 20 settlers from the Mayflower and the colony's only doctor succumbed to the disease. Nearly every decade after the 1630s saw a major epidemic of the disease in Boston.[104] At its peak in 1677 the deaths of as many as 20 Bostonians a day were recorded. During this epidemic an estimated 20 percent of Boston's population died from smallpox, causing Cotton Mather to note that "Boston's burying places never filled so fast."[105] In New York City during August 1731, the correspondent for the *Boston Weekly News-Letter* reported that smallpox raged "very violently in Town," and consequently there was "little or no Business, and less Money, the markets begin to grow very thin."[106] This epidemic reportedly attacked one-half of the 7,500 residents of the city, including many infants and children, and caused an estimated 500 deaths.

During the 1721 Boston epidemic, in which one of every two residents became infected with the disease,[107] inoculation against smallpox became a dramatic issue. Inoculation was a process in which a thread containing dried matter from a patient with the disease was placed into a small nick in the skin in order to cause a mild case of the disease in the recipient. Deaths from smallpox sometimes followed inoculation, but less frequently than the natural disease. Importantly, this campaign was championed by learned men,

Cotton Mather in Boston and later Benjamin Franklin in Philadelphia, although it was opposed by most physicians.

Mather apparently learned of inoculation against smallpox from an African slave that joined his household in 1706. Onesimus reported to Mather about "an operation which had given him something of the smallpox and would forever preserve him from it."[108] For Mather, a procedure that might prevent "the grievous Calamity of the Small-Pox"[109] was especially attractive. He had seen the frequent death of family, congregation members, and other Bostonians, and at least two of his children remained at risk for the disease. Faced with the testimony of his servant that these problems were ameliorated by inoculation, Mather reasoned that inoculation offered a means for man to aid God in the elimination of the smallpox. In the spring of 1721, as the disease spread, Mather "procure[d] a Consult of our Physicians" about "how many lives [and souls] might be saved" by the use of inoculation. For the most part Mather's plea fell on the deaf ears of Boston's physicians. Only the Oxford-trained Zabdiel Boylston (1679–1766) respond-ed to Mather by inoculating his own son and two slaves against the "Destroyer." Both Mather and Boylston were attacked by the Boston med-ical community with "furious Obloquies and Invectives."[110] By the fall, Mather reported that "this abominable Town, treats me in a most malicious, and murderous Manner, for my doing as Christ would have me to do, in sav-ing the Lives of the People from an horrible Death; but I will go on, in the Imitation of my admirable Saviour, and overcome Evil with Good."[111] By offering a new remedy that reduced the pain and suffering of children and adults, Mather incurred the wrath of Boston's medical practitioners who not only had no place in their systems of medical thought for Mather's ideas, but also had no alternative methods that benefited their patients who suffered and died from smallpox.

To further his cause not only did Mather enlist God's aid, but he also pub-lished tracts and asked members of his "Flock" who had benefited from inocu-lation to support him. Perhaps most important, Mather demonstrated his faith in the procedure by inoculating his son Samuel, who begged "to have his Life saved, by receiving the Small-Pox in the way of Inoculation." Notably, one of Samuel's school mates died of the disease received in the "common way" that same month.[112] Although most citizens of Boston opposed Mather's views on this issue and actually threatened his life, Mather continued the advocacy of the procedure and the compilation of statistics, which demonstrated that five to twenty times more people died from natural infection than did from inocu-lation. Eventually, Mather's opinion was widely accepted, but not until after his death in 1728. Only 2 percent of Boston's 11,000 citizens in 1721 were inoculated. By 1752 the number had increased a dozenfold, and a decade later more than 85 percent of the population was inoculated.[113]

By the 1750s inoculation was more frequently performed in other colonies. In Philadelphia after his own son died of the disease, Benjamin Franklin also championed inoculation. In fact, in 1759 he coauthored with the English physician William Heberden (1710–1801) "Some Account of the Success of Inoculation for the Small-Pox in England and America." This pamphlet was intended to convince physicians and the public that inoculation against smallpox was better than awaiting the natural infection. Franklin enumerated the successes and failures of the endeavors against the disease in Philadelphia, and he compiled similar reports received from others who forwarded their results to him. Franklin's efforts to attain widespread American acceptance of inoculation were not immediately successful in this country or in England. The seemingly slow, but widespread, acceptance of inoculation improved general health as well as children's health, and during the Revolutionary War there were fewer deaths from smallpox for Americans than the less frequently inoculated British. The acceptance of inoculation based upon the work of Mather and Franklin (neither a trained physician) was evidence that reason, observation, and statistical compilation provided new means for human control of nature and disease. Importantly, it was also evidence that Mather, a Puritan, and Franklin, a Deist, had a common ground for understanding children's health and disease.

Even more dramatic than the success of inoculation was the introduction in 1798 by the English physician Edward Jenner (1749–1823) of vaccination against smallpox.[114] Jenner observed that maids who had contacted cowpox while milking did not develop smallpox. As a result vaccination, essentially inoculation with the cowpox virus rather than the smallpox virus, was possible with virtually no risk. During the summer of 1800, Benjamin Waterhouse, the Boston physician and first professor of the Theory and Practice of Physic at Harvard University, introduced the procedure to this country by vaccinating seven members of his own household. By the end of the year Thomas Jefferson advised the doctor that he had "read with great satisfaction your pamphlet on the subject of the line-pock, and pray you to accept my thanks for the communication of it."[115] Over the course of the eighteenth century the clergy, the public, and physicians had, in the words of a contemporary historian, "withdrawn from the condition of man" one of the most feared, infectious diseases in history.[116] By the late twentieth century the disease would be eliminated throughout the world.

By 1900 a new understanding of smallpox, and particularly the possibility of prevention by vaccination, formed a new basis for medical care, one that combined reason with changing theological beliefs. The largely empiric practices of observation, experimentation, and analysis were incompletely codified as medical science, but they fostered a new interpretation and understanding of health and disease. Physicians, parents, and other care givers were able to offer American children new means of reducing pain and suffering. More careful attention to breast feeding meant that fewer babies died with "summer complaint"; while more frequent vaccination against smallpox meant fewer children experienced the fever, pustules, and the threat of death from an all too common, yet preventable, infectious disease.

Throughout American history, mothers have provided not only the daily nurture of their children, but also medical attention and the regular treatment of childhood ills.

2

Republican Motherhood

When thousands of American troops penned letters to their mothers in May of 1918, they did more than write home. Their action culminated a decade-long campaign by Anna Jarvis to commemorate her deceased mother with a national Mother's Day and crowned a century-long trend toward making the role of mothers central in American home life.[1] The patriotic fervor of the day led Congress to deem mothers our "greatest source of strength and inspiration" and "the fountainhead of the state."[2] Women were encouraged to bear children and replace the war's losses, and the troops and society were encouraged to honor mothers. These actions fueled a campaign that emphasized the biological position of women as childbearers and mothers and, in effect, continued the predominant gender ideology of nineteenth-century America. This codification of women's role in American society was evidence that they played a central role in the health and growth of their children.

In the young republic, as today, motherhood formed the basis for child rearing and children's health in America. Mothers as the "cornerstone of our civilization" had an influence "too vast to be measured" and, according to the Reverend John Wesley Hill of the Metropolitan Temple in New York City in 1909, accounted "for the great things wrought into our National history."[3] These grand achievements, he said, were both based in and responsive to the principles of the Enlightenment. Above all it was reasonable that women played the central role in child rearing and children's health. They bore children and tended them during their growth and development; and they controlled their education and rearing. Mothers had both biological and social powers that provided the "sense" and "independence of mind" necessary for rearing their children and guarding their health.[4]

During the early nineteenth century, the focus of children's health remained in the home. Children were born and died there. Families, at times assisted by physicians, treated common ailments like influenza, measles, whooping cough, and summer complaint. In this environment mothers were the primary healers for their sick children. But more than this, mothers increasingly assumed the role of guardians for the moral development of their children and as a result the nation. Family growth and the health of children, physically, mentally and morally, became the duty of mothers. Mothers were urged to sacrifice their own health and personal comfort to ensure the growth, development, and health of their children. This was the expected price that women paid to achieve the increasingly honorable and powerful position of mother. In the process, women integrated the philosophical ideas of the Enlightenment and the American Revolution into their domestic lives.[5] They became republican mothers, who bore their children based on a moral and patriotic duty and reared them on the same principles as future citizens. As the nineteenth century advanced, women's domestic role became codified as the cult of domesticity.[6] An understanding of this central role for women provides a basis for approaching children's health in the early American republic. This picture of children's health in the early nineteenth century also includes physicians and, unfortunately, frequent death and disease for American children.

Popular Thought about Motherhood

During the early years of the new American republic, the importance of childbearing to the growth of the new nation and the continued emphasis on children caused by the influence of the Enlightenment philosophy of Locke combined to enhance the position of mothers. At the same time the rather negative assessment of women that Rousseau offered was tempered by other philosophers like the Abbé de Condorcet and Mary Wollstonecraft, who concluded that women were "sensible beings," "capable of reason," and possessed of "moral ideas."[7] When women completed their biological duty of motherhood and reared their children based on reason and patriotic necessity, they assumed the power and position of republican mothers. Their attention to reproduction and the daily challenges of domestic life enhanced women's position within the domestic sphere and placed a renewed emphasis upon motherhood that benefited children by emphasizing their nurture and growth.

In addition to the biological functions of motherhood, republican mothers had new moral and social responsibilities that promoted the common good and the continuation of the moral order.[8] These duties were especially important so that the sons of the nation might enter the political arena. The "sacred office" of motherhood, as *Parents Magazine* described it, required a new "commitment of body and soul to the service of offspring."[9]

In exchange, a woman was assured that she held the most powerful role in the world, "the molding of the future, the care of souls."[10] In addition, women assumed a new relationship with their husbands. As mothers gained power in the home, they also raised a stronger voice in family matters and spoke with more authority about domestic duties.[11] As a result mothers tended, pampered, instructed, advised, and healed their children. This attention to the body and soul of their children promoted children's health.

Political and medical observers of the day emphasized the position of motherhood. Timothy Dwight, Yale president at the start of the nineteenth century, concluded that "the mother gives the first turn and cast to the mind. Her province is infinitely more valuable than that of the father."[12] In short, the growth and successful expansion of American society was dependent upon the nation's mothers. According to the physician and politician Benjamin Rush, the natural function of women as mothers necessitated that society "prepare them, by a suitable education, for the discharge of this most important duty. . . ."[13] An adequate education, according to Mary Wollstonecraft, included anatomy and medicine so that women, and mothers in particular, might become "rational nurses" for their infants and children.[14] By attending to the bodies and souls of their children, mothers formed the children's "character" and promoted their health. Mothers achieved these ends by subtle, even "secret and silent influences,"[15] but the end results were profoundly important for the health of the nation and its children.

Fulfilling the tasks of motherhood was a complete occupation. The ideal woman sacrificed her own health and comfort for the "honorable and powerful position of mother."[16] Eliza Pickney, a 23-year-old South Carolina mother, recorded the all encompassing duties of motherhood: "I am resolved to be a good mother to my children, to pray for them, to set them good examples, to give them good advice, to be careful both of their souls and bodies, to watch over their tender minds, to carefully root out the first appearings and buddings of vice, and to trouble to do them good, to correct their errors what ever uneasiness it may give myself and never omit to encourage every virtue I may see dawning in them."[17] When these duties were conscientiously fulfilled, children matured with healthy bodies and minds.

Successful mothering placed women as the "backbone" of American domestic life.[18] Sweeping, washing, cooking, cleaning, as well as "control of the nursery" were the socially dictated and natural functions of true womanhood.[19] Completion of these duties had a moral basis, and its successful practice avoided "the unhappy consequences" of intemperance and errant behavior.[20] Increasingly as the nineteenth century advanced, American society emphasized the moral basis of this duty within the cult of domesticity.[21] The proponents of this ideology believed that not only American society, but children benefited from this emphasis on moral beliefs and actions. As one mid-century woman noted: "O, if mothers did but realize how early, how imperceptibly they begin to impact their own spirit to the little ones whom God has given them, they would be more watchful never to exhibit before them a single unlovely or undesirable trait."[22] Mothers' attention to their moral duty promoted the health of their children from their physical condition to the character of their souls.

Women and their advisers of the early nineteenth century believed that motherhood was in part instinctual and in part learned behavior. At the same time many women received little instruction about reaching the goals of complete motherhood and child rearing. Susan Huntington concluded in 1813 that there was "scarcely any subject concerning which I feel more anxiety, than the proper education of my children. It is a difficult and delicate subject; and the more I reflect on my duty to them, the more I feel is to be learnt by myself."[23] This "extensive" knowledge was essential to "mould the character of the future man." Although many agreed that women were applying "increased intelligence and zeal" to their duties,[24] most concluded with Catherine Beecher and Harriet Beecher Stowe in the *American Woman's Home* (1869) that there was "no point where a woman is more liable to suffer from a want of knowledge and experience than in reference to the health of a family committed to her care."[25] That same year the noted British sociologist Herbert Spencer concluded that it was "an astonishing fact that, though on the treatment of offspring depend their lives or deaths and their moral welfare or ruin, yet not one word of instruction on the treatment of offspring is ever given to those who will hereafter be parents!"[26] While Spencer certainly overstated his case, many mothers in the early nineteenth century had no formal education about child rearing or children's health. What a mother needed, according to Catherine Beecher, were general principles, the "laws of health" about that "perfect and wonderful piece of mechanism committed to her preservation and care." This emphasis on children's health was needed because nearly one-quarter of the race "perish[ed] before attaining one-seventieth part of their natural term of existence."[27] The Massachusetts educator Horace Mann called for the inclusion of such "laws of life and hygiene" within the school curriculum.[28] Ignorance of the essential "laws of life" caused needless death, disease, and suffering for many children, problems that prepared mothers could prevent.

Popular Thought about Children's Health

If detailed medical knowledge and specific parental education about children's health and child rearing were limited, practical methods of its execution were not. In part these efforts were based in a changing view of the child. Increasingly, nineteenth-century Americans emphasized the position and value of children. Not only mothers, but also children had a larger role within the family. Their value increased further as family size decreased and childhood death became less common.[29] Children were seen less frequently as depraved (the traditional Calvinist view) and more frequently recognized as innocent souls that required nurturing. This basic difference in attitudes about the nature of the child was reflected in different methods of child rearing. At one extreme Francis Wayland (1796–1865), the Baptist educator and president of Brown University, concluded that there was "no greater cruelty than to suffer a child to grow up with an unsubdued temper."[30] Wayland achieved this end by isolating and literally starving his 15-month-old son, Heman, into submission. Wayland believed this authoritarian view of child rearing was commissioned by God and nature and was necessitated by the nature of children. Although in his day, Wayland's methods and ideas were controversial, the method was apparently successful, for Heman succeeded in the Victorian world and Wayland widely espoused his beliefs about child rearing.

At the same time, others, including Bronson Alcott (1799–1888), patriarch of one of the century's most famous literary families, accepted a philosophical view that emphasized the innocence of children. Alcott rejected the damnation and "certain depravity" of children by original sin and, in fact, considered that view an "unpardonable" sin. In its place, Alcott offered a new view of the nature of the child, which he said was based in his careful and detailed "Observations on the phenomena of Life, as developed in the Progressive history of an infant, during the first year of its Existence." The nearly 2,500-page study of the development of his daughter Anna commenced when she was nine days old and continued until she was five. From these observations Alcott concluded that "the child must be treated as a free, self-guiding, self-controlling being. He must be allowed to feel that he is under his own guidance, and that all external guidance is an injustice which is done to his nature unless his own will is intelligently submissive to it. . . . He must be free that he may be truly virtuous, for without freedom there is no such thing as virtue."[31] These gentle means of child rearing were based, as Alcott demonstrated, in the observation and understanding of children. Alcott and others applied the lens of enlightenment and romantic thought to America's children. The result was child rearing based on the needs of the individual child and the knowledge and reason of enlightened parents. This phenomenon was dramatically reflected in the subtitle of Jacob Abbot's 1871 *Gentle Measures in the Management and Training of the Young:* "The Principles on which a firm parental authority may be established and maintained, without violence or anger, and the right development of the moral and mental capacities be promoted by methods in harmony with the structure and the characteristics of the juvenile mind."[32] Parental guidance formed the basis for the individual development of the child. While this process was tempered and directed by the "Christian Spirit," its goal was "to fill the empty cup of the child's mind."[33] Enlightened parents, and especially mothers, provided their children with a kinder environment in which to develop a healthful body and soul.[34]

Mothers learned the tools of their trade from other women, family and friends, physicians, and advisers. When such advisers were not readily available, later in the nineteenth century women consulted an increasing number of popular authors that proclaimed the virtues of domestic medicine. These works often contained more information about how to be a good mother and homemaker than specific medical knowledge. This was the case even when physicians were the authors of advice texts. As nineteenth-century doctors professionalized their practices, they recognized that they possessed knowledge that if freely dispensed in manuals of domestic advice, often compromised their financial and professional position. At the same time specific advice about children was often incomplete, and some advisers, including physicians, simply lacked adequate medical knowledge with which to advise their readers. Nonetheless, both women and physicians helped rear the nation's children. In effect, a cooperative relationship developed that promoted the health of the nation's children. Women served as the nearly constant attendants of children, while physicians increasingly served as the episodic expert consultants about children's health.

The Compleat Housewife or the Accomplished Gentlewoman's Companion, published in 1742, remained a popular source of medical information in the nineteenth century. In addition to hundreds of "Receipts in Cookery" for pastry, preserving, pickles, and cakes, the work included directions for medicinal preparations compounded from wine, rosemary, garlic, thyme, crab claws, snake skins, and saffron, among other ingredients. They were reported as useful treatments for the diseases of children and adults.[35] Whether these agents were effective or not (and they generally were not), the existence and continued popularity of this book demonstrated that mothers searched for and found means to minister to their sick children. Parents not only prayed for the survival of their children but also used preparations from this book to heal their sick children. Advisers on children's health, while promoting their own methods, also observed that the health of children benefited from "training him up for God and heaven."[36] Child rearing based on the recommendations of the popular advisers of the day was on the rise, but faith still occupied an important position in the geography of child health.

Women who possessed the *Compleat Housewife* or other similar works might, as Mary Wollstonecraft suggested, aid poorer or less well educated women in the promotion of their children's health. Women offered testimonials to other women about the efficacy of methods of treating childhood disease. Many mothers recognized teething as a disease, as did physicians. One woman confided in her diary that she was "filled with terror" at the prospect of her child's teething.[37] A Boston mother advised her friends and family about the use of a penknife wrapped with thread "all but the point (so that, if my hand slipped, I couldn't cut him), and then, while he slept one day, took him on my knee and lanced his gums."[38] While such measures may seem harsh today, eighteenth- and nineteenth-century mothers believed such actions were reasonable and necessary.

Shortly after the end of the Revolutionary War, Samuel Thomson (1769–1843), who later became an important herbal doctor, noted that near his family's New Hampshire home there was an old woman that provided his family's medical care. There was no physician for more than 10 miles. "The whole of her practice was with roots and herbs, applied to the patient, or given in hot drinks to produce sweating, which always answered the purpose." When Thomson's mother became seriously ill she was carried to the old woman's home, and after several weeks of therapy she recovered and returned home.[39] Undoubtedly, many other families availed themselves of the services of such wise women. In addition many families supplied comparable remedies that were a part of the family heritage passed through the generations. Thomson's family, for example, regularly gathered herbs and other plants for their medicine chest. Thomson estimated that each year the average family utilized one ounce of emetic herb, two ounces of cayenne, one to two pounds powdered bayberry bark or root, one pound poplar bark, and one pound ginger.[40]

The medical practices of Native Americans were another source of medical knowledge for nineteenth-century Americans. The *Indian Doctor's Dispensatory, Being Father Smith's Advice Respecting Diseases and Their Cure* was penned in 1812 by Peter Smith. The author drew on the practices and experiences of his father and based many of his compounds on Indian recipes, noting that "our best medicines grow in the woods and gardens." This readily available compendium contained directions for compounding hundreds of preparations to ease the ills and ails of children and adults. Smith, for example, included remedies for toothache, rheumatism, belly aches, diarrhea, constipation, and catarrh (the common cold) among other conditions.[41]

Midwives also continued to have an important role. Not only did they tend the birth of babies more often than physicians, they also treated children and other family members. They dressed wounds, set broken bones, purged the sick, and dosed a myriad of common complaints from measles to whooping cough. They often ministered to children and the entire family.

Early colonial advisers generally intended the same text for both physicians and laypersons, but by the end of the eighteenth century physicians wrote works specifically for parents who lacked readily available sources of advice. One of the most popular of these texts was the Englishman William Buchan's *Advice to Mothers* (1809). This work was widely available in the New World. It offered advice about diet, dress, feeding, weaning, behavior, and construction of the nursery. Buchan recognized that events during pregnancy

Hundredth Edition, Revised and Enlarged.

GUNN'S

NEW FAMILY PHYSICIAN:

OR,

HOME BOOK OF HEALTH;

FORMING A

COMPLETE HOUSEHOLD GUIDE.

GIVING MANY VALUABLE SUGGESTIONS FOR AVOIDING DISEASE AND PROLONGING LIFE, WITH PLAIN DIRECTIONS
IN CASES OF EMERGENCY, AND POINTING OUT IN FAMILIAR LANGUAGE THE CAUSES,
SYMPTOMS, TREATMENT AND CURE OF DISEASES INCIDENT TO

MEN, WOMEN AND CHILDREN,

WITH THE SIMPLEST AND BEST REMEDIES; PRESENTING A

MANUAL FOR NURSING THE SICK,

AND

DESCRIBING MINUTELY THE PROPERTIES AND USES OF HUNDREDS OF WELL-KNOWN

MEDICINAL PLANTS.

By JOHN C. GUNN, M. D.,

AUTHOR OF "GUNN'S DOMESTIC MEDICINE."

WITH SUPPLEMENTARY TREATISES ON

Anatomy, Physiology, and Hygiene,

ON

DOMESTIC AND SANITARY ECONOMY,

AND ON

PHYSICAL CULTURE AND DEVELOPMENT.

NEWLY ILLUSTRATED, AND RE-STEREOTYPED.

CINCINNATI:
MOORE, WILSTACH & BALDWIN,
25 WEST FOURTH STREET,
1864.
SOLD TO SUBSCRIBERS ONLY.

In addition to physicians, domestic advice books were popular sources of traditional home health knowledge. By the end of the nineteenth century, Gunn's text had been reprinted more than 200 times.
Collection of the author.

and the health of the mother influenced children's health. He also recorded the "inestimable value" of the mother's services. Buchan's objective was
not to "excite terror" about the dangers of death and disease, but rather to
teach mothers "how to prevent diseases that are almost always the consequences of mismanagement; to inspire them with the fullest confidence in
proper nursing, and with strong prejudices against the use of medicines,
which do mischief twenty times for once that they do good." Not only
could medicines do harm, but also all "the skill of the physician is exerted
in vain to mend what she [the mother], through ignorance or inattention,
may have unfortunately marred."[42] While there is no evidence that childhood deaths were less frequent, the cooperation of mothers and physician
advisers was expected to promote a healthy body and a healthy soul for
America's children.

Throughout the nineteenth century, and even today, manuals of domestic
medicine were popular. Increasingly these works, like Gunn's *New Family
Physician*,[43] published in more than 200 editions, expanded beyond general
medical problems and included more specialized tomes on maternal and children's health. These works, like the botanic physician Thomas Hersey's *The
Midwife's Practical Directory* (1836),[44] continued Buchan's emphasis on children's health. They were written, as another author concluded "for mothers
in the common walks of life." "Intelligent home treatment" not only promoted health and saved lives but avoided "a large doctor's bill" as well.[45] Many
advisers also solicited letters and questions from their readers. One New York
professor even offered a "question blank arranged so comprehensively that
when the symptoms have been filled in and returned to me, I shall be enabled
thereby to make out and forward by mail an accurate statement of the nature
of the disease." Presumably if the doctor was unable to answer the question,
he consulted his wife, who had offered "many valuable suggestions" during
the preparation of the original text.[46] Clearly, children's health was strongly
influenced by mothers and their traditional knowledge, even when written by
physicians.

Breast Feeding in the Nineteenth Century

The importance of one subject was universally recognized by advisers and
mothers alike. This was infant feeding, and all agreed that breast feeding was
the only successful method. Nearly all mothers, at least those in "perfect
health," were advised to undertake maternal breast feeding. The natural
mother was "sure to take more care than a nurse, who has no other view
than interest; besides the milk which a mother gives her own child, must
needs be more proper and agreeable to him, by reason of the near similitude
there is between it and the blood with which he was nourished while in the

womb."[47] This focus on maternal breast feeding not only emphasized its function as a duty, but it also promoted the role of motherhood as an essential function for women. Further, according to the popular adviser Mrs. Lydia Child, "the nourishment" that the mother provided "conveyed into his soul some portion of the moral qualities" that the woman possessed.[48] Thus, according to the best advice literature of the day, both the physical and the moral development of the child were fostered by maternal breast feeding.

Women themselves demonstrated the importance of the subject of breast feeding. They hoped and prayed for each other's success at this essential womanly art. One woman wrote to her recently confined sister, "I hope you are well and will have plenty of nourishment for your child." In spite of such encouragement, new mothers often worried about their successful completion of the biologic and social roles of motherhood. A frontier woman was "delighted to find that the milk has returned in abundance, so much so, that the baby has a great deal more than he can make use of."[49] Some women were not this successful and, like Elizabeth Phelps, "had but little milk for my child, I had to feed him soup."[50] Others succeeded, but only with difficulty. The physical problems of feeding, breast tenderness, infections, and cracked nipples, were often compounded by the social pressures to succeed at this seemingly simple task. One woman recorded the difficulties of her efforts. She had "great soreness of the muscle between the arm and the breast, and the operation of nursing dear little Mary drew tears almost every time."[51] Yet, she was compelled by biology and society to complete her assigned role of mother.

If maternal nursing was not possible, then the services of a relative, family friend, or a "healthy and judiciously fed nurse" were, for many, the only acceptable substitute.[52] Wet nurses were often obtained by advertising, by word of mouth (especially in working class neighborhoods), or, increasingly as the nineteenth century advanced, by soliciting the patients of lying-in hospitals. In 1859 a Charleston, South Carolina, family requested in the *Daily Courier* the "immediate" services of a wet nurse, "white or colored, without a child. Good recommendations would be satisfactory."[53] Such pleas were common throughout the nation, since without such services infant death was nearly universal. Some postpartum women at nineteenth-century lying-in hospitals were found to be of good moral character by families searching for wet nurses and, with the favorable references of the matrons of such facilities, were hired. Near mid-century at the New York Asylum for Lying-In Women, wet nurses were commonly requested by families in need of a source of adequate nutrition for their children. "Indeed such has been the preference for nurses from the Asylum, from the confidence in the community that none will be recommended who are not virtuous and healthy, that they are frequently engaged previous to their confinement."[54] A quarter of a century later, to help provide capable wet nurses, the New York physician

Out of necessity, most American children have been nourished by breast feeding. Only with the development of adequate means of artificial feeding in the early twentieth century did regular survival of artificially fed infants become possible. Collection of the author.

and specialist in the diseases of children L. Emmett Holt (1855–1924) established the Practical Training School for Nursery Maids. He furthered the
skills and knowledge of these care givers by publishing a question-and-
answer manual on the care and feeding of children. The work combined
"simplicity, brevity and exactness with reference to matters of infant feeding
and nursery hygiene."[55] The role of the expert was more secure, and many
women now had a more reliable source of knowledge about child rearing.
Holt's identification of this work as a catechism emphasized his recognition
of the authoritarian basis of and importance of his work. Expert advice was
replacing maternal instinct as the basis of child care.

Unsuccessful breast feeding, or the death of a new mother without an
available wet nurse, caused infant malnutrition and was generally followed
by death. While traveling in 1852, a Tennessee woman encountered a baby
whose mother had died and who was "too weak to nurse. It could not suck
and I gave it some breast milk in a spoon."[56] Such efforts were rarely successful in the long term, and as was the case for this child, death soon followed. Alternative means of "dry feeding" rarely succeeded before the late
nineteenth century. In spite of such dire predictions, nearly every family and
adviser offered replacement formulas designed for the restoration of infant
health. Formulas based on water, cow's milk, goat's milk, chicken broth,
pablum, even the sweet potato were reported. When directions were carefully followed these preparations "strongly resemble[d] human milk in color,
taste and consistence."[57] Unfortunately, with an incomplete understanding of
the nutritional content of milk or other foods, it was only at the start of the
twentieth century that nutritionally adequate replacements for human milk
became available. Improper feeding caused "incalculable mischief." One
physician concluded that nothing destroyed "more young lives than improper food."[58]

Infant feeding was also difficult because sanitary facilities and methods
were not readily available. Glass baby bottles and feeding spoons were available in the early nineteenth century, but it was nearly mid-century before
rubber nipples were employed. Even with these improved means of infant
feeding, without the knowledge that bacteria soured milk and in turn caused
gastrointestinal illnesses, artificial feeding was at best difficult and rarely successful. Only with the understanding of the germ theory, the subsequent
refrigeration and pasteurization of milk, and the regular sterilization of feeding implements did artificial feeding become routinely successful.

A nutritional diet and the maintenance of general health were advised
for nursing women, and they were also offered dietary supplements, medicines, and a variety of other aids that enhanced their ability to successfully
nurse their offspring. Commercially available compounds, like Ridge's Food
for Nursing Mothers and Imperial Granum, reportedly enhanced maternal
health and increased the mother's milk supply. They were advertised to both

women and physicians. Satisfied users detailed their successes with glowing testimonials of successful lactation under adverse circumstances. Topical agents, like liniments and ointments, when applied to the breast were also reportedly helpful. One such preparation not only benefited "sore breasts," but also improved "the Piles, Rheumatism, strains, all kinds of Pains, Ring-worm, carbuncles, sunburns, freckles and chapping of the skin."[59] While such benefits were often highly exaggerated, the fact that women applied these often noxious preparations, or ingested large quantities of dietary sup-plements, was an indication of their recognition and willingness to sacrifice to fulfill their role as mothers. It was also an indication that women accepted the advice of experts about their mothering abilities and the health of their children.

While most women relied upon instinct, experience, friendly advice, and even folklore for their knowledge about infant feeding and other child-rearing problems, some nineteenth-century women, including Elizabeth Cady Stanton, recognized that the "laws governing" child-rearing practices were not merely "instinctively understood."[60] Stanton, among others, accepted not only the advice of experienced women about the health care of children, but increasingly the wisdom and recommendations of physi-cians. Throughout the nineteenth century and well into the twentieth centu-ry, the advice of physicians became the predominant source of knowledge about children's health.

Antebellum Medical Thought and Practice

As the nineteenth century advanced, physicians increasingly offered an authoritarian voice about the health of America's children. On the subject of children's health, strong words from physicians were necessary according to a London physician with 30 years experience, and whose text was available in early nineteenth-century America, because "no part of medicine . . . has been so little cultivated." He went further and concluded: "In all the work of all the best writers, from the age of Hippocrates to the present inclusive, scarcely any practical information is to be found upon this subject, unless a few scattered and detached observations may be so considered." Nineteenth-century physicians recognized the importance of children's health, in part, because of the high frequency of infant death and because they viewed the advice literature of the day as "generally of the most ignorant description,"[61] but perhaps most importantly because the nature of medical practice and the understanding of disease were undergoing a radical change. Increasingly, dis-ease was defined as localized in nature with its cause situated within specific organs, such as the liver, heart, or kidney. No longer was a generalized dis-turbance of bodily humors a reasonable explanation for death and disease.

As the definition of childhood diseases became more accurate, physicians enumerated more precisely the frequency of such health problems.

Infant death remained common in the early nineteenth century. At least one-fourth of all live-born children died before two years of age, and nearly as many more before ten years of age. In Boston during the 1820s, 1,010 infants less than one year of age died. This was 11.7 percent of the total deaths in the city in that decade. If deaths before age five were considered, nearly three times as many deaths—2,984—were counted. During the 1850s, nearly 40,000 Bostonians died, and infants and children less than five years of age accounted for 18,550, or 46.5 percent, of these deaths. Equally chilling statistics were reported throughout the nation.[62]

Physicians, politicians, and social observers not only recorded the frequency of the deaths of children, but also recognized that children's health was an important basis for the health of society. One physician noted that the "destruction of infants is eventually the destruction of adults, of populations, wealth and everything that can prove useful to society or add to the grandeur of a kingdom."[63] Clearly, infant death was a concern for the individual family and the larger society as well. These problems were important not only for an established European society, but even more so for a new nation, like America, expanding its population, horizons, and borders.

Since the death of children was frequent, American children regularly experienced the deaths of siblings and friends. Children commonly participated in funeral marches and burials. Books and stories for children reflected this phenomenon as well, with the inclusion of death scenes in nearly every work. One especially popular work, *Agnes and the Key to Her Little Coffin,* was penned by a New England clergyman, who reported the death of an 18-month-old baby and the "solemn thoughts" that accompanied her parents' recognition that she was a "maid of honor" in Heaven.[64] Hymns and paintings of the day also reflected similar scenes. They also added to a growing recognition by physicians and society at large that infants and children died too frequently. By mid-century, if personal experience and professional advice were not sufficient, authors in popular periodicals of the day, like *The Atlantic* and *Godey's Ladies Book,* emphasized this problem for lay readers.

Whether in New York, Boston, Richmond, or Cincinnati, infant death in the early nineteenth century was caused most frequently by gastrointestinal illnesses and feeding problems. A Virginia mother noted that in her area "as many as six [infants] died in the course of this week, with bowel complaints." A Charleston, South Carolina, mother lost four of her children to the same "bowel complaint." These problems—cholera infantum, summer complaint, and infant diarrhea, which Benjamin Rush described during the Revolutionary War[65]—were more severe in the warmer southern climate. The warmer climate enabled bacteria to reproduce faster and provided an environment where sick children suffered from the ill effects of dehydration more quickly than in the cooler north. Affected infants became feverish and dehydrated from vomiting and diarrhea. Mothers, families, friends, and physicians, in William Alcott's words, often tried "a thousand things" without success. Alcott (1798–1859) reported success by giving milk, a liquid that many of the day thought inadvisable because it was "heating and dangerous" and thus only increased fever. "So I took a teaspoonful of this fluid, warm from the animal, and gave it to her, only requiring her to swallow it very slowly. She not only obeyed me, but appeared to relish it. Nor was there any nausea afterward, nor any evidence of evil effects or evil tendencies."[66] Alcott was successful because the milk was taken directly from the cow before bacterial contamination occurred and because he supplied nourishing liquid to a poorly fed, dehydrated child. Few of Alcott's fellow citizens or physicians accepted his advice.

Rather than employ the technique Alcott proposed, most physicians of the era only hastened the death of sick children with heroic therapy—puking, purging, blistering, and bleeding. One physician reported a two-year-old child who died not from the dysentery but the calomel (purgative) therapy she received. The doctor wondered, "Isn't It murder? . . . Oh, When shall these things cease to be? When will parents learn that poison is not medicine? When will physicians act consistently, and give innocent remedies, or none—assisting nature when necessary, or do nothing?"[67] The expansion of the physician's role as the adviser to American mothers about children's health required a more complete understanding of nature and the recognition that sick children had needs different from those of adults.

Some physicians recognized a need for greater attention to child health. Often these physicians were professors of midwifery. The first American text on the diseases of children, published in 1826 by the Philadelphia professor of midwifery William Dewees (1768–1841), began with the need for parental care and with the "earliest formation of the embryo." He recognized the important contribution that mothers made to the "stamina" of their children and addressed a "few directions" to women. Dewees "endeavored to condense most of the important points, which reason has dictated, or experience has sanctioned, within as narrow a compass as appeared consistent with perspicuity." "European publications," not only medical texts, but the reason of Rousseau and the empiric observation of Locke formed the basis of Dewees's text.[68] While noting a debt to European thinkers for his understanding of children's health, Dewees, like most American physicians of the day, recognized that disease in America had a "peculiarity of character, an intensity of force, and a rapidity of march"[69] that required a different approach, lest "too often [we] have the mortification to see our patients hurried to an untimely tomb."[70] Without a more specific understanding about disease causation, many practitioners believed that diseases behaved differently in different places. Since they considered geography and climate to have important effects on disease, they recognized the same fevers and agues as different medical problems that often required alternative treatments, not only in the Old World compared with the colonies, but also within different regions of the New World. In effect, Dewees applied reason to his observations about childhood illnesses and ultimately offered an understanding of children's health based on the results of empiric success.

Dewees demonstrated the practical benefits of his advice by providing instruction about the care and feeding, the dress and shelter, in short the "physical treatment of children."[71] Not surprisingly Dewees favored breast feeding, as did nearly all advisers, and discussed methods to help mothers implement it. Without careful attention to the seemingly natural details, he warned, "your child for the first, and perhaps last time, receives a sufficient supply."[72] Clearly, in Dewees' eyes successful breast feeding required the cooperation of women and their physicians. The physician's reasoned guidance enabled women to complete their natural duty as mothers. Dewees's observations also led him to the conclusion that teething was "no disease."[73] He concluded that teeth were essential for childhood growth and development, but their eruption did not cause ill health.

The same skills, observations, and analysis that made Dewees a wise adviser for the nation's mothers also made him a good physician. He based the diagnosis of childhood disease in "well disciplined bed-side observation, and a correct habit of thinking."[74] Reason and empiric observation were the tools of the skillful physician that rendered the "management [of childhood illness] more easy."[75] Later in the century other physicians reported that "the most careless and inexperienced observer" easily recognized the acutely ill child because "the features become contracted, furrows and wrinkles appear about the forehead, the nostrils are dilated, or pinched and thin, and the mouth becomes drawn and rigid."[76] But other problems of child health, such as rickets, growth delays, or other chronic illnesses, were not easily identified. Some physicians soon recognized the unique features of childhood illness as well as the significance of accurate diagnosis and treatment. In fact, the second half of the nineteenth century was marked by the rise of the medical specialty of pediatrics.

The recognition of the uniqueness of childhood illness was important for children, but mothers also significantly benefited from the new medical knowledge and the relationship that they developed with physicians. This knowledge "in its practical details, and in the character of its scientific basis" had "intimate relations with the every day duties of women."[77] Elizabeth Blackwell (1821–1910), the first female graduate of a regular American medical school, noted a "link between the science of the medical profession and the every-day life of women."[78] The application of medical knowledge within the family, or domestic medicine, for Blackwell and others provided not only a new use of medical knowledge, but also new opportunities for mothers to enhance the health of their children. New medical knowledge occupied an essential place beside the domestic science of homemaking that the Beecher sisters espoused. Educated women, like Mary Wollstonecraft and Blackwell, hoped that women would transmit to each other "by virtue of their common womanhood" the best methods of child care, so that these new views on child health would become "the property of all women."[79] Mothers with the increasing aid of their physicians undertook new endeavors, like improved sanitary practices, that reduced death and disease for their children.

Childhood Death and Disease in Antebellum America

From New England to the western frontier and beyond, few families did not experience the death of a child.[80] Many, like Francis and Rebecca Hardy of Boston, suffered the loss of more than one child. Tombstones at Copp's Burying Ground near the Old North Church report that their son Francis died at two months of age in October 1807, John in August 1808 at two days of age, and Margaret at six weeks of age the following September.[81] For the Hardys and other American families, infant death shaped the family's and, notably, the mother's view of the world. A year following the death of her "dear little ones," one mother noted her heart "still bled. . . . As time rolls away, we feel our loss more instead of less."[82] Parental attitudes about their children were clouded by the possibility of the loss of the child. Mothers wrote other relatives with the hope that grandparents would visit their grandchildren before death paid a visit. One midwestern woman advised her parents in the east, "I do wish you could all see the darling, and if she lives and all is well, I intend you shall see her next spring." Fathers less frequently admitted their doubts about their children's future. John Prince advised his father-in-law: "Often I think when doting upon her, how uncertain is her continuance."[83] Women advised their husbands of the uncertain future of their children. Anna Colton Clayton concluded to her husband, "Don't forget—she is not wholly ours."[84] By agreeing not to take a child's continuing existence for granted, these mid-nineteenth-century parents recognized the reality of childhood death and shielded their emotions against its occurrence.

The effects of the death of a child were dramatically recorded in September 1848 by Henry Wadsworth Longfellow and his wife, Fanny, when their young daughter died. Some days before her death Fanny noted her daughter's "poor pale face and hollow eyes—such a contrast to her usual exuberant life." A week later Fanny experienced "a day of agony unutterable" when the doctor was "evidently shocked at baby's state," and, as a result, Fanny noted hope almost died. The following day the child was "sinking, sinking away from us, Felt a terrible desire to seize her in my arms and warm her to life again at my breast. Oh for one look of love, one word or smile! . . . Painlessly, in a deep trance, she breathed. Held her hand and heard the breathing shorten, then cease, without a flutter. A most holy, beautiful thing she lay." She was buried with an unopened rose in her hand, "that little hand which always grasp them so lovingly." On the way to her burial, she was carried "from her nursery, down the front stairs, through my study and into the library, . . . and thence after the prayer through the long halls to her coffin and her grave." The hours of "desolation" caused a "terrible hunger of the heart to hold her." Throughout the house, "every object recalls her." The following day Longfellow himself despaired "of the other children, and thinking how they will look when dead. Their gleeful voices agonize me."[85] No record of the reaction of the other Longfellow children to their sister's death has survived; however, a child of the era recorded his experiences at the death of a friend. "I touched his cheek, and it was cold as ice. I took hold of his little hand, but it was stiff. . . . He could not see, nor hear, nor move."[86] Clearly, all members of the family experienced grief and responded with strong emotions to the tragic event.

The death of a child was not easily accepted. Fanny Longfellow, a month following her daughter's death, was "very weary and wretched. I seem to have lost interest in the future and can enjoy my children only from hour to hour. I feel as if my lost darling were drawing me to her—as I controlled her before birth so does she me now."[87] Henry Longfellow also noted an "unappeasable longing to see her . . . which I can hardly control."[88]

Mothers experienced a double loss with the death of a child. They experienced the emotional loss and emptiness that Fanny Longfellow expressed; but, without other children in the home, they also lost the status and domestic function that motherhood bestowed. In 1852 Elizabeth Prentiss, the wife of a New England clergyman, experienced the second loss of a child: "Here I sit with empty hands. I have had the little coffin in my arms, but my baby's face could not be seen, so rudely had death marred it. Empty hands, empty hands, a worn-out exhausted body, and unutterable longings to flee from a world that has had for me so many sharp experiences. God help me, my baby, my baby! God help me, my little lost Eddy!"[89]

Antebellum southern women and their families experienced the same losses and bereavements as their New England counterparts. Although the health of wealthy plantation owners and their families may have been better than that of poor white or slave families, at least one-quarter of the children born into plantation families died before age five.[90] Presumably wealthier families experienced better living conditions, enhanced nutrition, and, in turn, better health for their children. Nonetheless, even for more affluent families, infant death was a fact of daily life, for "the tenure of life at such an age is extremely feeble and our brightest hope may at any moment be nipped in the bud."[91] Mary Henderson, a North Carolina planter's wife, worried about her surviving children as did Longfellow: "I feel so unhappy about the two remaining ones[,] thinking it may be God's good pleasure to recall them and shuddering at the bare idea."[92] When a mother had "a promising child at that interesting age where it is just beginning to discover the first gleam of intelligence"[93] taken by "God's good pleasure,"[94] it was a loss "almost insupportable" and one trial that no parent should experience. Clearly, the death of a child, endeared "by a thousand infantile ties known to no one but a parent," was, as one mother concluded, "the greatest trial I ever met with."[95]

Infant death was more common for black families than for whites. Reconstructed infant death rates from the 1840s and 1850s suggest that below the age of five more than twice as many black children died compared with their white counterparts.[96] According to the mortality statistics of the Seventh Census of the United States (1854), 123 of every 1,000 white children less than 10 years of age died, and twice as many black children died.[97] Nearly one-quarter of the deaths of black children were reportedly caused by teething, worms, tetanus, and suffocation. These problems were four times as frequent among black as white children. Three-fourths (72 percent) of the 1,820 deaths from whooping cough reported for seven southern states in 1849 through 1850 were of black children.[98] Poor nutrition, especially a diet often limited to salt pork and corn meal, compounded the generally sparse living conditions of slave households, and the resulting nutritional imbalance often encouraged the spread of infectious diseases. Whooping cough, scarlet fever, diphtheria, measles, and smallpox, but most frequently infantile and childhood diarrheas—the summer complaint—caused the death of southern black children. An important contributing factor to the spread of these conditions, reported by the Richmond, Virginia, Board of Health, was poor sanitation. "The city was unsupplied with sewers." Waste water "stagnated" and "became offensive to sight and smell," and more important collected refuse matter and garbage and spread infectious disease.[99] Yellow fever, a mosquito-borne tropical viral infection, provided an exception to the pattern of ill health that confronted black children. From Charleston to New Orleans to Savannah, dramatically lower death rates were reported for black children from yellow fever. Presumably, this occurred because blacks had an innate resistance, either genetic or resulting from frequent contact.[100]

Some blacks killed their children to spare them the harsh realities of the life of a slave. One black woman, whose older children were sold by the owner, decided this would not happen again for her youngest. She gave "it something out of a bottle and [pretty] soon it was dead." Other women did not actively commit infanticide, but nonetheless hoped infant death might occur. Many slave women continued field work during pregnancy and while tending infants and small children. They were often given only short breaks to tend and breast-feed their infants. One young woman recalled her mother's response to this dilemma. "She knowed she could not go home and suckle dat child and git back in 15 minutes so she would go somewhere an' sit down an' pray de child would die."[101] These episodes were not isolated events, and their occurrence certainly accounted for the deaths of more than a few slave children. Similar deaths occurred in white families of both the North and the South,[102] but the strong motivation of enforced servitude was not always present.

Some southern planters recognized that their slaves, including children, were an economic investment that required tending just like the remainder of the plantation. In 1840 Ander Flinn in his diary noted in his "instructions to the Overseers" that "the children must be particularly attended to for rearing them is not only a duty, but also the most profitable part of plantation business."[103] In 1850 one owner, Moorhead Wright, recalling several deaths over the past year noted, "I have a very goodly number of negro children coming and have paid a great deal of attention to that part of business[.] My rule is first a plenty of corn and wheat to be raised[,] negro children taken care of and cotton afterwards."[104] Unfortunately, this seeming concern for slave children did not extend to better living conditions, improved sanitation, or more nutritious food. Planters had an economic interest in promoting the health of slave children, but there is little evidence that they did so. Consequently, on many plantations many more slave children than white children died.

Children's Health on the Frontier

On the western frontier successful childbearing also had an important economic function. Childbearing and child rearing were the most important, as well as physically taxing, duties for frontier women.[105] Matilda Paul of Iowa did all her work with her infant son in hand. She wrapped him in her apron while getting water at the well so that he was not "trampled on by the thirsty cattle." While tilling the field, he was placed "in a large box where he could play." In their sod hut, she did her washing by hand, "rubbing every garment, and often [standing] on one foot while rubbing and rocking the baby's cradle with the other foot."[106] The constant and ordinary task of keeping the baby clean and dry was a major challenge for frontier women. Clothes were often in short supply; consequently, flour sacks, discarded sheets, hand-me-downs, and sometimes merely nudity were the only clothing options frontier mothers had for their children. Limited water supplies also meant that clean clothing, especially diapers, was often not available. In their place, some pioneer women used grasses or mosses as soft absorbent diapers, as did Native

American mothers. "But most evidently resorted to the common, although frequently criticized, practice of simply drying, scraping, and airing" the cloth diapers they had and then reusing them.[107] On occasion eastern women may have employed these sanitary measures as well, but the more limited resources on the western frontier made such practices more frequent.

Infant death on the frontier may have been no more frequent than in New England, but neither was it less frequent.[108] Nearly all frontier families experienced the death of at least one child. In many cases multiple deaths occurred, often in association with the journey west. In 1852 one traveller wrote back to his family in Arkansas:

> James Hanen and wife and child are dead. Craig and wife and child are dead. James Crawford's babe is dead. David's child is dead, and Samuel Hanen has been at the point of death but was on the mend. . . . Nelson's crippled girl got shot by pulling or moving a gun as she went to get in the wagon. She lived about an hour. L—— B—— lost another girl. Even Hanen's child died. Stephen C——'s child died. Nancy Graham and William Ingram's children are both dead. Eloy Hanen is delirious and is an object to look at. Jacob Rushe's widow and little girl are dead.[109]

Few women who participated in the westward migration of the mid-nineteenth century did not record the experience of an infant or family death in their letters, journals, and diaries.[110] On Christmas Day 1863, Gabriella Foster of Macon County, Illinois, advised her husband Robert, who was off fighting the Civil War:

> I seat myself this afternoon to write you a few lines, but sad sad news I have to tell you, Willie breathed his last today. [?] minutes after eleven o'clock, oh what a hard stroke it is on me, and I know it will be a severe trial to you when you hear it. Rob I feel almost heart broken to think I am severed from all my earthly ties, but by the grace of God I will try and meet our dead children [this was their second death for 1863] in a better world, where neither death nor war can sever us again.[111]

For Gabriella and many other women far from home and often without the support of family or husband, acceptance of a child's death was especially difficult. In such circumstances women called upon God to see them through to a better day.

Death did end the pain and suffering of many children, including a 12-year-old boy on the trail to California. His epitaph, "Rest in Peace, Sweet Boy, Thy Troubles are Over,"[112] was poignant and true. Travelling west, the New Englander Endicott Peabody summed up the situation when he reported the death of a young boy in Tombstone, Arizona: "I pitied the poor mother and father very much indeed. It really does not matter where one's body rests when the spirit has left it—but I should like to be where there is something green—where nature is beautiful—or else in the deep—but to be left in a perfectly sterile soil, without only rocks and lime over one seems to me incomparably dreary.[113]

Not surprisingly childhood disease on the frontier was not dramatically different from disease in New England or the South. Fevers, ague, smallpox, diphtheria, scarlet fever, whooping cough, summer complaint—in short infectious diseases—were the major causes of death. In Tucson in 1870, 70 of the 83 child deaths were caused by smallpox.[114] Few frontier citizens and especially few children on the trans-Mississippi or far western frontier were routinely vaccinated, but rather vaccination was more frequently practiced during the recurring eruptions of the disease. Neither parents nor physicians recognized the public health benefits of populationwide, pre-epidemic protection.

Other infectious diseases that, unlike smallpox, were unpreventable, such as diphtheria and scarlet fever, remained deadly. Often all the children of a household were attacked when these common contagious diseases struck one child in the family. An Arizona mother reported the domestic turmoil created by diphtheria. "Merrill was burning with fever, Trying to climb out of the window. He surely was Sick. Samuel one morning jumped from his bed, running around with Dyphthear. Croup, could not breathe. Lilly lay propped up in bed with pillows, picking big white chunks from her throat and handing them to her father."[115] In such cases, mothers, even fathers, were nearly completely occupied with nursing the sick. Unfortunately, no effective treatment was available for seriously ill children. Parents and professionals both recognized that when a child had had "not a mouthful of anything" in her "stumache" for three days death could be expected. Few were surprised when the following day she was buried with flowers pressed to her chest, "dressed to look as natural as possible" and with her doll at her side.[116]

Accidents and Birth Defects

Nineteenth-century children also were injured and killed by accidents, burns, scaldings, poisonings, and other similar injuries. Fanny Longfellow's 11-year-old son maimed his left thumb when his "gun burst, either from being over-wadded or from being worthless." This "sore trial" required painful dressing changes and for days the constant need of parental attendance. Despite Fanny's "sleepless nights and anxious days," this devoted mother was grateful "it was not his face, nor his right hand, that suffered."[117] Another child was burned "so black" from a powder flash that her mother "hardly knew her." This mother gave her child "thirty drops of laudanum and put sweet oil on her and then fanned her all night." A doctor was called from 30 miles away but never came. "All kinds of medicine" were applied, an Indian doctor called, and "her burns healed all right." She finally opened her eyes on the

30th day when her mother teased her that a snake was about. "She clapped her little hands and laughed out. I was so overjoyed I had to cry, to think she could see again."[118] These children suffered physically and emotionally, while their mothers endured the emotional pain of caring for their seriously injured children without effective treatment to reduce their pain and suffering or prevent death.

Mothers experienced similar worries about their children with common birth defects. Cleft lips, for example, not only caused emotional turmoil for children and their parents but, without routinely available means of artificial feeding, resulted frequently in death because feeding problems and infections were common for infants affected with clefts. If they could not effectively cure their children, mothers hoped and prayed for their emotional and physical health. As one mother concluded: "I cannot help wishing my children to be beautiful, for it seems to me that it is likely to have a bad effect upon the character of a child to feel a sense of inferiority to others in outward attractions."[119] Mothers, then and now, desired the best for their children, and worked to smooth the rough edges of their lives.

By the end of the nineteenth century, the south had rejoined the burgeoning industrial north in the Union, and the western frontier was closing. A new century was dawning with the United States holding a position of increasing importance internationally; but American society continued to hold that mothers should remain in charge of home and family. The importance of motherhood, as President Theodore Roosevelt told the National Congress of Mothers in March 1905, was "the first and greatest duty of womanhood." The duty of mothers was "to bring up as they should be brought up, healthy children, sound in body, mind, and character, and numerous enough so that the race shall increase and not decrease."[120] Mothers tended their children's bodies and souls, but increasingly over the course of the nineteenth century, maternal instinct was tempered with the enlightened advice of experts, which was becoming increasingly more easily available to America's mothers. Successful mothers employed these measures in the care of their children. "Ideal motherhood you see," the readers of *Ladies' Home Journal* were advised at the turn of the century, is "the work not of instinct, but of enlightened knowledge conscientiously acquired and carefully digested."[121] At the 1899 national meeting of the Mother's Union, mothers were asked to assimilate, "to put forth every effort," to acquire this new knowledge so that their children might develop into "healthy and vigorous manhood or womanhood."[122] Mothers had new sources of knowledge and new professional advisers, but, in the end, the application of that knowledge and the day-to-day acts of maintaining and promoting children's health remained, as they had been in the new republic, in the hands of mothers who healed their sick children and comforted the dying.

In the mid-nineteenth century, attention was increasingly drawn to the conditions in which poor urban children lived—and frequently died.

Photograph "Minding the Baby" by Jacob A. Riis. Reprinted by permission of the Jacob A. Riis Collection, Museum of the City of New York.

3

Child Saving

On a chill April day in 1874 Jacob Riis spotted "a little animal who happened to have a soul" in a New York courtroom.[1] Mary Ellen, as the unfortunate nine-year-old waif was known, was wrapped in a horse blanket against the cold and the stares of the curious. The plight and bruises of the Hell's Kitchen orphan were announced by an ailing neighbor, who could not "die in peace while the miserable little girl" was abused and beaten by her stepmother. The still courtroom scene was punctuated by sorrowful tears from the gallery. The judge "turned his face away." An advocate for the child voiced his plea for her protection "in the name of the homeless cur on the streets." Riis and the other members of the court's gallery witnessed the writing of "the first chapter" of the protection of children's rights "under the moral mandate of animal protection" sponsored by the Society for the Prevention of Cruelty to Animals.[2]

Before the mid-nineteenth century, the citizens of New York had overlooked the pain, suffering, and all-too-frequent death of the city's children. Mary Ellen's frightful life was not an isolated event. In fact, during one week in July of 1876, more than 100 infants died each day, leading the editor of the *New York Times* to conclude that there was "no more depressing feature" of urban life than child abuse.[3] Such problems provided an impetus for child protection programs. Initially these efforts began with nineteenth-century animal rights advocates. But, as the aims of the Wisconsin Humane Society emphatically stated, the prevention of cruelty to animals remained their central goal. The protection of children was of lower priority, but more important than the needs of criminals and defectives.[4] Nonetheless, nationwide child-saving efforts were sparked, and in little more than a quarter of a century, more than 100,000 dependent children resided in 1,151 child care institutions.[5]

The New York Society for the Prevention of Cruelty to Children, founded in 1875, was not the first institution started for the benefit of American
children,[6] but its organization in the nation's largest city was significant. The
aim of the Society was "to aid suffering childhood, through the law, by the
law, and under the law."[7] These efforts were necessary because too many
children resided in "degrading conditions," and without outside efforts they
and their families were headed for "inevitable shipwreck." The "bad social
conditions of the community" required the attention of society and experts
for their prevention.[8] While the society was founded by laypersons, increasingly physicians assumed the role of scientific experts and moral spokesmen
about child health and child protection.

Childhood Death and Disease
in the Mid-Nineteenth Century

In nineteenth-century America, dramatic social changes, particularly growing
urbanization, compounded the health problems of America's children. Urban
growth, which resulted in a population in New York City of more than
500,000 by 1850, was fostered by immigration. Because of overcrowded
housing and poor sanitation, many immigrants suffered the ill effects of
urban growth more readily than did native-born citizens. Children, as the
least powerful members of their families and the weakest voices in the community, suffered acutely the harsh effects of crowded housing, poor sanitation, enforced labor, and poverty. Not surprisingly, this unhealthful urban
environment caused needless death and disease.

The problems of overcrowding and poor sanitation "spread over
Manhattan Island like a scab."[9] By 1850 one observer recorded that annually
1 of every 33 New Yorkers died, while the proportion of deaths was only 1
in 67 in the rural areas of the state. More than 8,000 deaths occurred for
children under 10 years of age. Two years later during seven weeks of the
summer of 1852, 2,480 children under 10 died in the city. The bills of mortality reflected what many physicians, mothers, and social activists were well
aware of: that children reared amid the stale air of filth and overcrowding
lacked the "vital energy" necessary "to resist the invasion of disease."
Physicians recognized part of the problem, but they lacked successful means
of therapeutic intervention. "To direct any kind of medicine to be given to
them is positively absurd; it is disheartening to visit such a place [a crowded
tenement], and to be required to relieve physical suffering when the first and
indispensable pabulum of life is wanting."[10] In short, children's health was
more dependent upon adequate food and shelter than the pharmaceutical

tools of the nation's physicians. At the same time few physicians concerned themselves with the provision of adequate food and shelter for their sick patients, and thus attention to the important social aspects of healing often fell to social activists, the clergy, and women.

The problems of urban growth were not limited to New York City. The *Daily Democrat,* a Chicago newspaper, reported in June 1849 that "in walking through the city the stenches that are met with and pollute the olfactories are both numerous and powerful." As a result an east wind brought such "disgusting odors" to areas of the north side that some were unable to eat.[11] Problems were only compounded during the "bread riots" and virtual depression of the 1870s. Michael Schwab, a former bookbinder and labor organizer, described the living conditions for many of Chicago's laborers: "[They live] in rooms without sufficient protection from the weather, without proper ventilation, in which never a stream of sunlight flows. There are hovels where two, three and four families live in one room. How these conditions influence the health and the morals of these unfortunate sufferers, it is needless to say. And how do they live? From the ash barrels they gather half rotten vegetables, in the butcher shops they buy for a few cents offal of meat, and these precious morsels they carry home to prepare from them their meals."[12]

Comparable problems also existed in the growing cities of the trans-Mississippi frontier. Sanitary facilities and sewers were incompletely developed, and consequently unpaved city streets often became the avenues for sewage disposal. Dead animals were left where they died, and when removed they were frequently dumped with garbage, ashes, and other sewage into a nearby river that generally doubled as the local water supply.[13] Even though regulations for privy construction and cleaning were frequently enacted, overuse of limited facilities was a problem. In 1865 the Cincinnati Board of Health reported 102 inhabitants of a two-story tenement with but a single privy.[14] This house dramatically demonstrated the two central problems that Dr. Howard Damon of the Boston Dispensary concluded contributed to ill health—"overcrowding and imperfect drainage."[15] The impact of these problems was "even more pernicious upon the children" who regularly suffered from diarrhea and other intestinal disorders, as well as bronchitis and pneumonia. A greater emphasis on health and sanitation led to fewer deaths in some western settlements, like Mormon-settled Utah, where from 1850 to 1870 infant mortality ranged from 52 to 71 deaths per 1,000. In the nation as a whole the death rate was more than 50 percent higher.[16] In another rural settlement, the Oneida Community of upstate New York, only five neonatal deaths occurred during the 1870s, and not a single case of diphtheria, cholera infantum, or croup had occurred during the previous 15 years. Improved "sanitary conditions" were responsible for fewer deaths and less pain and suffering for some frontier children.[17]

The health problems of urban life were compounded by the waves of immigrants that arrived on America's shores in the second half of the nineteenth century. Whether Poles from Warsaw, Italians from Milan, Germans from Bavaria, or Norwegians from the Scandinavian north, all experienced the difficulties of settling in a foreign land. Even the Irish, which Henry Cabot Lodge told the 60th Congress "presented no difficulties of assimilation" because of their common language and heritage, experienced ill health in their new homeland.[18] In Boston during the 1850s, one-quarter of the reported deaths were infants less than one year of age, and nearly one-half (46.5 percent) were children under five years of age. Many of these deaths involved poor immigrant Irish families,[19] who lived with their children in overcrowded, poorly ventilated, and unsanitary tenements.

Other eastern cities from New York to Philadelphia reported similar problems. A physician from Providence, Rhode Island, where large numbers of Italian and Portuguese immigrants settled, reported that it was "well known that the foreign population" was under "entirely different sanitary influences from the American population." Immigrants lived in a "miserable class of tenement houses, with all the want of conveniences, and positively injurious influences of such houses; their social habits are not calculated to preserve health; and a knowledge of the laws of hygiene is entirely wanting among them. Of course, the children of foreign parents are subject to the same injurious influences upon health, and suffer from them more than the parents themselves."[20] The root of the problem was not ethnicity, as this physician concluded, but rather poverty. Many, in fact most, immigrants were poor and simply had to make do with limited diets and overcrowded tenements. Unfortunately, although these poor sanitary conditions affected the whole family, children paid a disproportionate price with their pain and suffering, and all too often with their lives.

The conditions under which immigrants lived were hardly better in Chicago or other Midwestern cities. One Chicago establishment, which served both as a residence and a bakery, flooded whenever the sewer system backed up. Bakers wore rubber boots, as they carried freshly baked bread from the oven to customers. The work area remained "dirty and foul smelling" until a hole was knocked in the building's floor allowing the filth and offal to drain to other premises. Bakers, family members, and their children, all looked "sickly."[21] In Milwaukee "swill children" or "little garbage gatherers" collected the choicest kitchen garbage for their family's tables. They left the city's backyards and alleys "reeking with filth, smelling to heaven" and spread disease to family and friends.[22]

Ill health in America's cities was apparent to many immigrants to America. A Norwegian, who arrived in Chicago from the eastern seaboard, noted that "there were sick people wherever we went." He found deaths from cholera five times higher among Norwegians than the population of the city as a whole. The problem, as one doctor reported, was that the immigrants were "backward" about cleanliness and sanitation. Bathing was reportedly a "rare operation and many women under ordinary circumstances will not wash their face or hands for days."[23] Poor sanitation was not simply the result of ignorance, but rather primarily the result of the poverty and overcrowding of urban life. A Chicago newspaper, the *Free West,* reported that when the Angel of Death had "stretched out his hand over our city," killing poor immigrants and their children, the wealthy enjoyed a "short sojourn in the country."[24] Physicians, social commentators, and citizens increasingly recognized that the social conditions of American life determined the health of its citizens.

The plight of orphans and unwanted infants was especially dire. They died from accidents and diseases and, not infrequently, infanticide. A New York City mother, charged with the death of her child, concluded that "she thought it would be happier out of the world than in it."[25] Family and friends helped as best they could, but the number of orphaned children was simply too great to be solved by individual families. By mid-century a more "formalized infanticide" had developed whereby babies were placed in foster homes and then simply neglected until they died of starvation, dehydration, exposure, or infection. The proprietors of these so-called baby farms had no interest in the survival of their charges. This fact was tragically confirmed by news reports about neglected children. A 21-month-old child, who was "wasted to skin and bones," died from being fed only condensed milk (one teaspoon in a pint of water).[26] A postmortem examination of another child showed that the stomach was "empty and not a trace of food" was found.[27] During several months in 1890, Boston authorities recovered the bodies of 30 babies within blocks of a suspected baby farm labeled as a private nursery.[28] After examining the extent of the problem, New York City officials estimated that 90 percent of infants placed into "baby farms" died before their first birthday.[29]

Some children survived the malnutrition, filth, and disease of the early years of institutional life; but many of these youngsters suffered emotional and psychologic aftereffects. Too often, the emotional toll of institutions drained "all the joy" from their lives.[30] The evidence of this was reflected in the faces of the nearly 60 inmates of the Westchester County Poor House. As one observer noted in 1873, "saddest of all is to see the stolid look gradually stealing over the faces of these little ones."[31] Those children who survived their ordeal had emotional scars that time did not easily heal, and for which physicians and society had no immediate remedies.

The conditions found on baby farms were only symptomatic of the larger health problems faced by children in nineteenth-century America. Poor living conditions and inadequate sanitation promoted the spread of infectious diseases like diarrhea, smallpox, measles, and tuberculosis. As one tired and obviously experienced physician of the day noted, drugs were of "utter uselessness" when "there is no possibility of nourishing and warming the patient."[32] As this contemporary observer correctly concluded, child health was dependent not only on formal medical care, but even more importantly on the family and social setting in which children lived. The promotion of children's health required the solution of socioeconomic problems like poverty, overcrowded housing, and limited sanitation. Without these fundamental tenets of health, neither society nor physicians had the means to reduce death and suffering.

Institutions for Children

While society at large, and physicians in particular, failed to develop solutions to the problems of children's health, women, as mothers and the guardians of children's health and child rearing, emerged as the vanguard of the nineteenth-century child-saving movement. From Mary Dubois to Lillian Wald, women originated, sponsored, promoted, defended, and worked for a myriad of child-saving organizations. From orphanages and foundling homes to child protection agencies, programs were established that aided and protected children. Efforts that promoted children's health, reduced death and disease, and saved children from "the wrongs of adults" were fostered.[33] In the process children were rescued from the streets, from cruelty, from disease, and, ultimately, from death.

At the heart of the benevolent efforts to protect and save children were middle-class women, who formed the backbone of American morality and motherhood. Their domestic beliefs and moral tenets based on traditional Christian virtues that fostered the home and family, were expanded to envelop the social space of the streets and the city.[34] These efforts were necessary, in the words of one observer of the day, because the "multitude of half-naked, dirty, and leering children signified an absence of parental love, a neglect of proper child-rearing."[35] In short, children suffered because the middle-class moral values associated with republican motherhood, which nurtured children within individual families, required a broader base of social support from financiers, industrialists, and the general public to deal with the larger social problems of the nation's children. Importantly, these middle-class values transcended the interests of political parties, women reformers, and civic groups.[36] Thus, broad-based support prompted financial contributions from many segments of the population, including wealthy industrialists. These new social programs were facilitated by the philosophical and intellectual support of new scientific organizations, like the American Social Science Association. These professional groups not only provided scientific credence to the child-saving movement but also supported the same middle-class moral values proposed by the sponsoring women.[37] Mothers equipped with the financial support of the nation's industry, the moral backing of its churches, and the ideas of its scientists fostered new institutions that promoted children's health.

Initially, child-saving programs were directed at individual children. But these efforts had broader "social interests," according to Roscoe Pound (1870–1964), the founder of American social jurisprudence, to promote the "rearing and training of sound and well-bred citizens for the future."[38] In essence, women, society, and government became partners in the business of child saving. Increasingly, successful programs that corrected the moral and social wrongs experienced by nineteenth-century children combined public and private efforts. These projects succeeded because, as the child advocate Homer Folks (1867–1963) noted, government provided a "more intelligent, resourceful, impartial and effective administrative unit."[39] Governmental action and funding, as well as public support, were necessary for the establishment of child care institutions, but their success was dictated as much by the individual actions of founders as by the municipal funds expended. Governmental participation made possible broader "public remedies" to larger social problems and the provision of more services to those deemed morally deserving of intervention and relief.[40] Public efforts included the restoration of slums, the construction of parks, control of delinquent children, and the promotion of children's health. Only later in the century were children's hospitals founded in response to these same needs.

The first institutions in North America specifically designed for children were founded during the eighteenth century. These were generally orphanages operated by private religious groups. In 1728, following an Indian attack at nearby Natchez that left large numbers of homeless children, the Ursuline nuns of New Orleans opened the first American orphanage. For the next century Protestants and Catholics alike founded similar institutions, often, as occurred in New Orleans, in response to major events and epidemics that left large numbers of needy children without families to provide for them.[41]

In 1740 the English evangelist George Whitefield founded the Bethesda Orphan House in Savannah, Georgia. This home, as was typical throughout the nineteenth century, not only housed and cared for orphans, but taught "the little ones" a trade, in this case carding and spinning.[42] Acquisition of a trade by orphans was essential because it provided evidence of the moral reconstitution and acceptability of saved children. Child savers believed they must not only preserve and heal the body but also heal the soul, carrying on the tradition of colonial era healers. In 1886 the founders of the New York Salvation Army Home opened their doors to all "who desire[d] and are earnestly seeking the salvation of their bodies and souls."[43] Such efforts provided moral reform for individuals and, according to the first director of

New York's Association for Improving the Condition of the Poor, prevented "a massive threat to social stability."[44] Sound bodies contributed to the physical growth of the nation, and saved souls promoted the accepted tenets of middle-class morality.

By 1850 more than 100 institutions for children were in operation throughout the nation. They included New England special care facilities, like the American Asylum at Hartford for the Education and Instruction of the Deaf and Dumb and facilities for the blind and the "feeble-minded" in New York and Massachusetts. Nationwide, there were an estimated 25,000 institutionalized dependent children. These facilities had benevolent goals. According to the manager of the Protestant Orphan Association of St. Louis, their efforts succeeded "by taking the children away from these contaminating scenes of depravity" and placing "these tender plants to a more genial soil, where they may acquire strength to bloom forever."[45] As early as 1800 the rules for children at the New York City Almshouse codified the position of dependent children within society: "The children of the house should be made the government of capable matrons. . . . [T]hey should be uniformed, housed, and lodged in separate departments, according to their different sexes; they should be kept as much as possible from the other paupers, habituated to decency, cleanliness, and order, and carefully instructed in reading, writing, and arithmetic."[46] Accepted children were placed on a par with children raised within their own families, directed by authoritarian fathers, and nurtured by republican mothers. In this setting dependent children were "considered in every respect as the children of the public" under the care of the institution's superintendent.[47]

In many ways the idealistic goal of the advocates of child saving, to rescue all children, was not achieved. Diets were limited, facilities were overcrowded, and death and disease were common. During 1881, nearly four times as many infants died within the walls of foundling homes as died in homes out of the city.[48]

The most successful child-saving organization in New York City was founded in 1853 by Charles Loring Brace (1826–1890). In establishing the Children's Aid Society, Brace concluded that "if an hour or two a week in a disciplined and hierarchical environment could improve character, then surely the benefits would be multiplied if the impressionable childhood years were spent full-time under such a regimen!"[49] Brace, whose plan was strongly influenced by the European facilities he visited in 1850 and 1851, emphasized work and education rather than alms as the basis of his program. The Hamburg Rough House in Germany that was "so benevolent, so practical and so truly Christian" became the model for Brace's programs in New York City.[50]

Even within the protected homelike environment of the asylum, children became sick and died. Alfred Stille (1813–1900), a physician at the Blockley

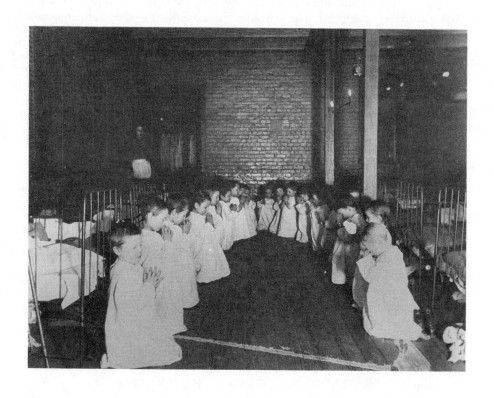

"Prayer time in Five Points Nursery." Orphanages emphasized moral salvation of the children under their care.

Photograph ca. 1889 by Jacob A. Riis. Reprinted by permission of the Jacob A. Riis Collection, Museum of the City of New York.

Asylum in Philadelphia, reported that ophthalmia [an eye infection], "that curse of children's asylums, made of them a sore-eyed, puny group most pitiable to see."[51] The doctor, reporting before germ theory was understood, concluded that improper cleanliness, poor ventilation, limited exercise, and insufficient food created a less than idyllic environment that caused child-hood disease. In fact, infectious diseases were endemic at such facilities, and while Stille and his colleagues recognized the important contributors to childhood death and disease, they lacked effective means of prevention or treatment.

Since the health of institutionalized dependent children was problematic, some sought solutions outside of institutions. An essential and distinctive fea-ture of Brace's New York program was the placing of children in rural homes. Brace concluded that if the city was both physically and morally filthy, then when children were "taken to good homes in the country,"[52] some health problems and much moral decay would be avoided. Two hun-dred and twelve children were placed during the first year, and by 1893, 91,536 children had been placed in homes in upstate New York and other rural areas.[53] Although the reduction in urban crime and the moral salvation of the child were primary concerns, the improved physical environment pro-moted children's health. A Wisconsin mother advised the Society in 1868 that a formerly sick child's "health has been good since he has been with us."[54] Placing out was not always easy. One boy, placed in Nebraska, later recalled that his foster mother worked for two weeks to get him clean. Another boy, sent to Georgia, hoped that "whoever picked me would have plenty to eat."[55] Not unexpectedly, some placements did not result in restored health. An Indiana mother had "the melancholy duty" to inform Brace that the black boy they received had died: "I don't know what his dis-ease was, [but] he had all the care and attention it was in our power to give him."[56] Not all placed children survived, but probably many more than would have survived in the urban environment.

The physical health of New York's children became increasingly impor-tant to the Society, and by late in the century they sponsored the Sick Children's Mission. By 1894 the program employed 15 physicians and pro-vided free medical care to poor children. The physicians prescribed medica-tions, visited tenement homes, provided information cards, and ordered ice distributed to cool urban milk supplies in the city.[57] The Brooklyn Children's Aid Society provided similar services and, in addition, sponsored the Sea Side Home for Children on Coney Island to help poor mothers and their sick children. "Not only was the sick one benefitted, but the worn-out mother was relieved of all care, except that of her child, thus enabling her to attend the sick one more assiduously, more like her more fortunate, richer sister." In short, "no trouble or exertion was too great, if some little life but be made more bearable."[58]

In contrast to the successful child saving reported by Brace and others during the 1860s, the New York City Foundling Homes on the East River's Blackwell and Randall Islands regularly reported that 80 to 90 percent of their charges died. As late as 1896 and 1897, only 12 of 366 infants at the homes survived.[59] Poor sanitation with leaking and improper sewage disposal and inadequate infant feeding methods, including an insufficient supply of wet nurses, contributed to this high death rate. In part because of Brace's successful programs and in part because of the high death rate, these municipal facilities also began to place infants out of "the filthy conditions of New York City."[60] During 1881, nearly four times as many infants died within the walls of the Foundling Home as died in homes out of the city. By 1887 the death rate for babies placed outside the city was only 5 percent. The problems of child care in municipal facilities led Abraham Jacobi, the patriarch of American children's health and founder of the medical specialty of pediatrics, to the conclusion that "the accumulation of many infants under one roof . . . is conducive to ill health and unavoidable mortality."[61] Physicians and social activists both recognized the basis of children's health problems, but neither offered satisfactory solutions for the poverty that faced many dependent children.

In other cities beyond New York, child savers struggled with similar problems. Orphanages and homes for destitute children were founded by religious leaders and social activists. Women like Kate Gannett Wells (1838–1911), who founded the Massachusetts Society for the Prevention of Cruelty to Children, were often the leaders of efforts that "fed the lambs."[62] Poor children and those with special problems—blindness, feeble-mindedness, and crippling physical conditions—were given special consideration. Samuel G. Howe recommended to the Massachusetts Legislature in 1848 that "measures be at once taken to rescue this most unfortunate class from the dreadful degradation in which they now grovel."[63] Fund raisers for these institutions promoted their causes with before-and-after photographs of needy children. Potential contributors saw not only the physical reconstitution of saved children, but the dress, the demeanor, and the aura of moral salvation as well.[64]

More essential for the ultimate success of these endeavors was direct knowledge of the conditions in which poor children lived. To educate benefactors and promote contributions, Louise Bowen (1859–1953), a prominent member of the Chicago Women's Club and supporter of Hull House, the Chicago settlement house founded by Jane Addams, urged her sisters on various "charity boards" to become "conversant with the daily lives of the poor."[65] In the process they encountered a six-year-old boy whose "back was one mass of bruised flesh, while on the left shoulder were deep red scars, evidently inflicted with some pointed instrument, although the frightened little fellow, when questioned said, 'the cat did it.'" Bowen was convinced that such encounters "would be a great asset" for the child-saving movement.[66] She brought the sights, sounds, and smells of the poor to the attention of potential contributors and in the process saved American children.

While the moral salvation of the nation's children was clearly important, the physical health of dependent children was often more easily demonstrated. In 1852 the Boston Children's Friend Society reported no deaths at the facility, and "such general [good] health has prevailed, that only in two instances has it been necessary to call a physician; and, at the present date, we believe no sickness whatever exists."[67] Mothers who cared for infants that had been "placed out" were instructed to call the medical officer of the society "at the first appearance of real illness." Attention to such health problems was facilitated because the doctors were "never off duty" and they were to make monthly "preventive visits."[68] Some facilities, like the Boston Children's Friend Society, did have fewer deaths and less disease than others. Some private facilities achieved this result by maintaining more spacious, cleaner facilities, practicing better sanitation, providing a better diet, and thus promoting a healthier atmosphere. At the same time, some facilities achieved better results because they only admitted healthy children.

While regular physicians were called "in cases requiring the attention of an educated physician," the matron of the home often treated her sick children. Ideally the matron, as was said of the head nurse at a Cincinnati facility, combined the "skill of a physician with the tender motherlike ways of a gentle woman."[69] The matron of the Boston Children's Aid Society provided pellets of aconite and belladonna "according to the instruction of the book and [her] judgement." Often she made use of the "real Home Materia Medica, consisting of hamamelis, court plaster, tincture of rhubarb, and fir balsam."[70] Although these remedies had limited, if any, therapeutic effect, their use demonstrated the concern of nineteenth-century child savers for the health of their charges and the vital daily role that women played in this process, employing what were recognized as the best therapies of the day, as well as taking on the role of mother.

As the physical health of children received more attention, many institutions emphasized their institutional health rules. The rules and procedures at Chicago's Chapin Hall Home were typical of other late nineteenth-century facilities. Only healthy children were admitted. Children with signs of contagious diseases were at the least quarantined, often for several weeks, and more often excluded from admission. If not previously vaccinated against smallpox, they were vaccinated. Following admission children were bathed and dressed in clean clothing. "Scalp disease," especially lice and ringworm, was prevented by shaving the head. Girls often regrew their hair before leaving the home; boys, however, were not routinely allowed this luxury. Attendants and care givers believed that this new attention to cleanliness and hygiene was physical proof of the moral order that had been restored to the souls of the newly saved. The efforts at teaching order and hygiene at Chapin Hall were at least partially successful as demonstrated by the report of a Sanitary Commission inspection: "All the beds in the building were examined . . . and were found clean and in good condition and almost free of insects." The health of many dependent children was improved by such efforts; however, epidemics of diseases like scarlet fever and measles still occurred, and as a result children in institutions and their own homes died.[71] Nonetheless, by the end of the nineteenth century, many American institutions for the care of dependent children had taken significant steps to improve the physical health of the children under their care.

Children's Hospitals

At the start of the final third of the nineteenth century, one group of dependent children remained largely forgotten. Sick and dying children without family support were not accepted by most child care facilities. The establishment of children's hospitals filled this void, and in the process they became the most important legacy of the child-saving movement. The same factors—benevolence and the desire for moral control, social betterment, and regimentation—that promoted the growth of American general hospitals enabled the formation of specialty hospitals, including facilities for the care of children. The establishment of children's hospitals was especially important, not only because facilities for dependent children were needed, but also because most general hospitals of the day provided no medical care for sick children. Changes in medical practice, including the rise of new medical specialties—particularly the surgical specialties, like orthopedics—the development of hospital-based technical facilities, and the training of skilled nursing personnel, enabled hospitals to provide care for sick children that was not previously available. Children's hospitals promoted the professionalization of children's health care and provided facilities for studying and teaching about children's health. More knowledgeable physicians employing stethoscopes and microscopes, among other new ideas and technology, more accurately diagnosed and treated sick children than did their predecessors earlier in the century. In the hospital, medical personnel controlled new medical procedures, such as "antifebrile and antiseptic" treatment; only within this environment were they "most successfully applied and tested," and as Abraham Jacobi noted, these "opportunities for observation and instruction" enabled professionals to teach not only other professionals about children's health but mothers as well.[72] As a result, physicians gained an important means of promoting their own professional position and, even more important, a new role alongside mothers within the moral structure and discourse of the day, as the nation's advisers about children's health.

Further, hospitals provided physicians with new authority and control over their sick patients. Physicians not only had control over the dispensing of drugs but, through the hospital, had social and personal control of patients as well. The manager of the Boston Children's Hospital summed up these functions in the institution's Third Annual Report in 1871:

> It is known to all medical men that poor food, want of pure air, and uncleanliness are fruitful sources of disease. The condition of ignorance which marks the lower classes of the community is constantly acting to debase the tone of society; it allows the lowest wages for labor, and it leads to the squandering and improvidence for successive generations of that which might afford considerable support. Agencies such as these are constantly at work to lower the vital force of the poorer classes of society, and to render the children an easy prey to the attacks of disease. The aim of all judicious medical treatment is directed not alone to relieve immediate disease, but by a thorough change of life and circumstance, by supplying a rational course of diet and regimen, by substituting for ignorance and thoughtlessness, and the thousand indiscretions which they suggest, judicious and gentle nursing, warmth, nourishment, light and air, to lay the best foundation for relief from disease.[73]

By controlling diet, education, and sanitation, not to mention healing methods and practices, physicians promoted the health of body and soul, and the hospital provided facilities for healing where the physician's voice alone spoke with authority.

In 1854 Nursery and Child's Hospital in New York City became the nation's first children's hospital. Children's Hospital of Philadelphia opened the following year, and facilities in Chicago and Boston the following decade. By 1880 more than a dozen children's hospitals had opened their doors, and within another half century, more than 70 children's hospitals with a total of 6,597 beds received and cared for sick children.[74] These new health care institutions for children were needed because the death rate of children was not only excessive but rising, as Dr. James Stewart, a graduate of the College of Physicians and Surgeons, concluded in considering New York City death rates. Problems for dependent children were greatest in cities, where "the peculiar conditions in which people live" resulted in overcrowding and poverty. As a result a "deterioration of the air that they breathe[d]" occurred, and children became sick and died. Stewart concluded that when such "urgent wants" were at hand, "surely no one can hesitate to do what is in his power to assist in the establishment and support of a children's hospital."[75] While the spread of infectious bacteria and poor nutrition, not foul air, were the causes of childhood illness, Stewart correctly identified a need for hospitals for the medical care of sick children.

When the Nursery and Child's Hospital opened, no other hospital in New York City received children as patients. Within seven days of opening, the facility was filled to capacity. Before the decade ended, children hospitalized at the facility experienced epidemics of scarlet fever, measles, whooping cough, chickenpox, erysipelas, ophthalmia, and cholera infantum. In fact, epidemic diseases frequently plagued hospitalized children. In spite of these dangers mothers begged "as a favor to enter their children, preferring the risk of contagion to leaving them in the usual boarding places, where they are subjected to want and neglect." In 1858 the hospital managers reported that only 54 children died among 238 admissions, and 41 of those children "gave evidence on admission" of the "fatal character" of their disease.[76] Children's hospitals may not have solved all the problems of children's health, but physicians, hospital managers, and parents all noted the benefits of these new facilities for the care of sick children.

Within four years "long experience" had "fully taught" the lay managers of the New York facility "what rules are necessary for the health, comfort, and cleanliness of the neglected little ones and these rules [were] rigidly enforced." These health rules were virtually identical to those adopted at Chicago's Chapin Hall Home and many other contemporary child care institutions with the obvious exception that sick children were admitted for care and necessary medical attention at the hospitals. In addition, schooling was permitted four hours per day, while all able children attended the nearby Mission Church, where "very many have received prizes from the Sunday School Teachers." As the tissues of the body healed, this "nurture of heart and soul" helped form the future moral fabric of the nation.[77]

At the Nursery and Child's Hospital and other similar facilities, lay women and wet nurses were responsible for the care, cleanliness, and feeding of the facility's children. These women individually cared for as many as a dozen ailing children. Wet nurses, who were "of good character," married (as documented by a marriage certificate), and approved by a physician's examination, fed their own children and one other from the hospital nursery. Since good methods of artificial feeding were not available, the dedicated efforts of these women saved many babies that would have otherwise died of disease and malnutrition. The hospital's matron had implicit authority over these women. In turn for their "good conduct," the wet nurses of the facility secured the "assistance and recommendation of the ladies of the Institution" in obtaining future employment in a "desirable setting."[78] Within the walls of the Nursery and Child's Hospital, just as within the nineteenth-century home, women, not physicians, were responsible for the daily health care of children,[79] and women maintained the moral tone of the facility by promoting Christian virtues, just as they did within the private homes of the nation.

Other professionals, including the clergy, helped establish other New York children's hospitals. In 1865 the Reverend Richmond aided the campaign of the New York Infant Asylum to reform poor and unfortunate women. Not surprisingly, the aim of the facility was "to thwart and prevent suicide, infanticide and murder, those demons that follow hard upon the track of the unfortunate, and to shield, save and restore them as well as to protect their innocent offspring."[80] Apparently, needy families and New York society accepted the Asylum's services and its managers' philosophy, for 45 babies were placed in the facility within the first month of operation, and 1,498 within the first year.[81] As the president of the Toledo Humane Society concluded in an address to the American Humane Association near the end of the century, not only in New York City but throughout the nation there was a need "to secure the life, the care and the welfare of this army of discarded and unwanted children."[82]

Following an 1870 European tour, Abraham Jacobi returned to New York and rapidly issued a report on the success of foundling homes in Berlin, Munich, Prague, and London. Jacobi concluded that comparable physician-directed facilities were needed in New York City. Without new facilities and a new role for physicians, he concluded, newborns and infants could not enjoy their "right" to the "security of life and health."[83] In Jacobi's view the New York Infant Asylum did not meet this goal since less than half the accepted infants survived. He proposed that safeguarding the life and health of children was "both economically and morally of paramount importance to society and to the commonwealth."[84] Among Jacobi's proposed goals was the construction of a children's hospital that was staffed with more nurses and equipped with complete physical facilities for the care of sick children. These expanded programs were necessary because children, especially sick infants, required more nursing attention, including care by wet nurses, than adults. Sick children also required more hospital floor space, better ventilation, and facilities for the isolation of infectious cases. All of these efforts were needed, according to Jacobi, if children were to realize their right to life and health.[85] Children could realize these goals because they were now tended in hospitals where physicians had the authority and control that provided the necessary environment for the promotion of children's health.

Jacobi's ideas were similar to those of Francis H. Brown (1835–1917), a Harvard medical student and later superintendent of the Boston Children's Hospital. Brown concluded in his medical school senior thesis (1861) that "abundance of air; abundance of sunlight; [and] simplicity of construction [were] the essentials without which no hospital can exist."[86] Brown and Jacobi echoed Florence Nightingale's call for cleanliness and ventilation as the means for reducing the excessive infant mortality. Jacobi's efforts in New York and Brown's proposals in Boston determined the essential features of the Boston Children's Hospital, built eight years later, following years of work by Brown and others and with the support of what *The Boston Evening Telegraph* called the "blue blood of Beacon Hill."[87]

As was the case with many other cities, the wealthy and philanthro-pic supported Boston's hospitals from a sense of benevolence and because such efforts provided public evidence of their "title to social position." Contributions from the public at large, and even children, were encouraged at neighborhood fairs and entertainments. These projects not only raised money, but also provided moral satisfaction and instruction to the participants. "What better instruction can be given the children of the city than that which teaches them, in their earliest years, to take their share in the care of the poor."[88] The moral basis and tone with which advocates raised funds for construction of nineteenth-century hospitals were sustained within these new institutions. As a result, America and its children enjoyed better physical and moral health.

Like New York City, Boston had a high infant mortality rate. In 1865, for example, 276 of every 1,000 live-born infants died before they reached one year of age. By five years of age, 1 of every 10 surviving children died. The magnitude of this problem led the publisher and statistician, Lemuel Shattuck, to the conclusion that in some Boston neighborhoods "children seemed literally born to die."[89] But the need for a children's hospital in Boston was based on more than the medical needs of the community's children. Brown also recognized that the social problems of the city and the moral duty of the community and its citizens necessitated a hospital for sick children: "Children of the poorer classes from their insufficient and poor food, the want of care for their cleanliness, and protection from the weather, their unsanitary abodes, the want of air and sunshine, and, perhaps, equally the want of healthy moral tone in the family, of kindness and affection, develop a condition of depressed vitality which renders them easily the prey of disease. To this consideration is to be added the thought of every farseeing philanthropist, that their children are the future members of society, and that the sound mind of the coming citizen depends largely on a sound body." Brown articulated the needs of Boston and the nation. He promoted, as did other managers of child care institutions, the proper moral tone based in "order, purity and kindness." These ends resulted from "intelligent and tender nursing, by attractive books, pictures and toys, and by the visits and attention of the kind and cultivated."[90] These efforts were facilitated by women, like the sisters of St. Margaret, who provided nursing care for the first 45 years the hospital was in operation and later by the members of the institution's Ladies Aid Society.

By the end of December 1870, 99 patients had been treated at Children's Hospital with only five deaths. Many factors were responsible for the initial broad success of the facility's programs. At least in part this success was due to the refusal to admit infectious cases. This policy was in contrast to the more open admission policy of New York facilities, where many children sick or dying of infectious diseases received admission. The larger nursing staff of the Boston facility, which by 1890 included 10 nurses and by 1900 more than 35, may have also provided more individual care and attention. Since some of Boston's sick children were admitted to other hospitals (approximately 10 percent of admissions to Massachusetts General Hospital and the Boston City Hospital in this era were children), it was likely that their number included children with potentially fatal conditions. Brown's strong leadership as hospital administrator and his emphasis on the principles of the hospital's founding, especially the construction of clean, well-ventilated facilities, also promoted the institution's early success. But, perhaps most influential in the hospital's initial success, was the fact that the institution served essentially as a hospital for sick children, and not just as a foundling home or repository for dying children.

Boston Children's Hospital also provided outpatient services. A dispensary was an early component of the institution. By 1890 more than 7,000 patients had received care. This number tripled to 21,436 visits in 1900.[91] In 1874 a country sanitarium was established in Weston, Massachusetts. This addition made available the "pleasant sights and sounds of the country" to the recuperating children of "the narrow and gloomy courts and alleys of the city."[92] Children stayed an average of three weeks following hospital discharge. They recovered in an atmosphere that clearly provided superintendent Brown's essentials for a successful hospital. Boston Children's Hospital provided both the physical and the spiritual atmosphere essential for the healing of sick children.

In Chicago in 1859 a group of "tender hearted" women came to the aid of a neighborhood friend who was widowed with six young children by forming the Chicago Nursery and Half Orphan Asylum. This facility, as well as the previously noted Chapin Hall Home for children and the later Maurice Porter Memorial Hospital for Children, was "dedicated to the free care of sick children."[93] Particularly at the Memorial Hospital, the medical and surgical treatment of sick and injured children was emphasized. The facility "intended to reach those cases which require such attention on the part of surgeon, physician and trained nurse as cannot be obtained at home." This emphasis on specialty hospital care continued in Chicago with the founding of the Home for Destitute and Crippled Children in 1892. The medical staff of this new facility were "all men of special training and skill in the treatment of cripples, and all men of ripe experience."[94] In addition to the emphasis on the care of the body, the staff of the Home encouraged and fostered "all healthful diversions for mind and body." This included not only abundant and palatable food, "sweet and clean" accommodations, and hygienic surroundings, but also "love" and "sweet peace" with "heavenly visitant[s] brooding over all."[95] Cincinnati's Episcopal Bishop Jappar's conclusion about the Hospital of the Protestant Episcopal Church for Children applied as well to Chicago's Home for Destitute and Crippled Children: "a

Christian home with heart in it, where not only the best medical and surgical treatment, but also the tenderest care, await, without charge, every little sufferer."[96] Not only were the physical ails of these children remedied, but, as the managers of the St Louis Children's Hospital reported in 1886, "Christian principles were instilled and fostered" as well.[97]

By the end of the nineteenth century children's hospitals were firmly established as major institutions that provided health care to America's children. Increasingly, new and more specialized medical procedures were available, and larger better-equipped facilities were created to provide such care. No longer were hospitals supported only by neighborhood fairs and fund raisers. State and local governments, as well as national philanthropies, like the Commonwealth Fund, and major industrialists, like Hiram Walker in Detroit and William Proctor in Cincinnati, provided new financial support for the health care of the nation's children. Few argued with this newfound emphasis on child care; after all "every child [was] worthy of kindness and care."[98] But, while many hospitalized sick children may have received tender care and consideration, at least some did not. In 1893, at Chicago's Cook County Hospital, one-third of the estimated 75 children at the hospital were scorned by the staff and society. According to child advocate Julia Lathrop (1858–1932), these children were "unattractive" or "scarred" creating a "melancholy company" that "haunt[ed] the memory of whoever has seen it."[99]

Following more than a century of growth, the limitations of American child care institutions were illustrated during the fall of 1918 when the United States was in the midst of a worldwide epidemic of Spanish influenza. Before the disease abated the following year, as many as 400,000 Americans lay dead. Nearly 30 percent of those who died were children less than five years old. Death was most frequent in boarding schools, tenements, and immigrant households, where overcrowding and poor living conditions promoted the spread of the disease.[100] The plight of one Boston immigrant family dramatically demonstrated the limitations of the available child care. A recovering 14-year-old boy awaited discharge from the Boston City Hospital. To ensure the boy's further recovery at home, a social worker visited his home and discovered that the father and two other siblings were stricken with the disease. Two other children were already dead. "The youngest to die, a baby, had remained on the kitchen table for three days before the Board of Health was notified. There was no money because the father was too sick to work." Hospital treatment of sick children was increasingly successful, but such efforts were all for naught when the child was returned "to the same conditions that produced the disease."[101]

The death in 1918 of more than 125,000 American children from influenza, and the rising rate of infant mortality in general, provided dramatic evidence that new child-saving efforts were needed. Nearly all Americans must have agreed with the child advocate Felix Adler (1851–1933) that the life of a child was sacred,[102] and many had also come to agree with Edward T. Devine, secretary of the New York Charity Organizations Society, who told the National Conference of Charities and Correction in 1906 that the root of children's health problems lay within "the essential vices and weaknesses" of parents and that children were often the "victims of needless accidents, preventable disease or industrial exploitation."[103] Nearly a century later, however, the basic social problem of poverty continues to frustrate both physicians and child advocates, and all too often poor health remains tied to preventable childhood conditions.

Chapter 4

The Rise of the Pediatrist

Traditionally, American children have suffered illness and disease within the confines of their homes, attended by their mother, family, and friends. The adolescent daughter of an Iowa farmer and Methodist minister, Hannah Hawke, remembered "full well the day, 28th August, 1858 when I experienced the first ague chill." Soon other members of the family were ill, and they "were unable to give each other a drink of water when we were parched with thirst during the fever which succeeded the chills." Her parents, particularly her father, "escaped more lightly than any of us" and prepared some food and tended the family as best they could. Neighbors brought "a dish of jelly or a luxury of some kind," when the demands of their own invalids permitted. One neighbor boy performed the essential, but arduous, task of carrying "a pail of water for nearly half a mile." A physician was not called. The disease ran its course, but not before "the screaming of the panthers and catamounts in the woods nearby" made "night hideous" for a family in such a "weak state."[1]

Nineteenth-century American children experienced the common illnesses of childhood—measles, mumps and chicken pox—and less frequently potentially fatal conditions, like diphtheria, scarlatina, and smallpox. At 14, William Alcott, later a physician, was put to bed with the measles. His mother "applied a bottle of hot water" to his feet and gave him "hot drinks most liberally, and among the best some 'hot toddy.' Her object was to sweat away a supposed attack of fever."[2] This mother's tender attention was the most essential ingredient for the healing process. Medicines and physicians were of limited value. According to the Boston physician and author Oliver Wendell Holmes (1809–1894) "if the whole materia medica, as now used, could be sunk to the bottom of the sea, it would be all the better for mankind—and all the worse for the fishes."[3] Not only was medication therapeutically limited, but it was difficult to get children to take it, as it is today. The popular adviser, John Abbott, concluded that the basic problem was that "after a long and wearisome conflict, the mother is compelled either to throw the medicine away, or to resort to compulsion, and force down the unpalatable drug."[4] Such conflicts were often not worth the battle when the drugs employed offered little benefit beyond the refreshing hydration of water, soup, or broth. In short, parents cured their sick children with tender loving care and not infrequently with the word of God. They prepared herbal preparations, dosed their children with the potions their neighbors suggested, and, less often, employed the elixirs that physicians recommended, but rarely did these remedies provide specific treatment for ailing children.

Physicians occupied the end of this list of therapeutic options because for nineteenth-century American parents physicians were not the primary source of medical care for their sick children. By the end of the century, however, physicians who specialized in the medical care of infants and children, *pediatrists,* became recognized medical specialists. Increasingly, physicians assumed a larger role in the health care of children. Several factors were responsible for the expansion of professional medical attention for sick children. First, physicians, and parents for that matter, recognized that childhood illnesses were different from adult diseases; but, perhaps more important, they recognized that something could be done to ameliorate the pain, suffering, and death that too many children experienced. Second, during the nineteenth century American medical practice changed. While early in the century heroic medical therapy that often created more pain and suffering than it relieved was widely practiced, by the end of the century physicians more effectively treated childhood illness and disease. The understanding of the germ theory, successful artificial infant feeding, the use of anesthesia, and the application of the principles of immunization to childhood illnesses were a few of the important changes in medical practice that benefited American children. Third, increasing codification and professionalization of the field of medicine promoted educational and practical opportunities for physicians concerned about the health of the nation's children.

Childhood Death in the Late Nineteenth Century

In April 1859, a Kansas toddler was "very sick with inflammation of the Bronchial Tubes." She was ill for more than two weeks and at one point was "so sick that [her family] did not know as she would live." She survived through "the grace of God," and soon "walk[ed] alone," although without her illness "she would no doubt have walked before this time."[5] At times parents wanted and sought professional attention for their sick children, but the results were often no better, and frequently worse than when they tended their children alone. A Milwaukee family, whose older child died in the city isolation hospital, was supported by an armed crowd of 3,000 when they refused to remove another child to the facility. The child's mother concluded that she provided "better care and nourishment" than that given at the city hospital.[6] Although the outcome for the child was not recorded, this woman's worried reaction was typical in an era when physicians and hospitals offered few services that parents did not employ in the home and clearly understandable when past professional intervention offered the family only a dead sibling.

In spite of the careful and tender attention of mothers, infant death remained frequent in nineteenth-century America. When children died their families found comfort and solace in the word of God and the assistance of family and friends. Nonetheless, it remained a taxing and emotionally trying experience for parents. Emotional losses loomed larger when the child was first born, and adjustment was especially difficult for families far from supporting relatives and friends. A frontier mother graphically recorded these events as she and her husband buried their firstborn son amid the struggle to establish a homestead on the central plains: "I held him in my arms till the last agony was over. Then I dressed the beautiful little body for the grave. Clyde [her husband] is a carpenter; so I wanted him to make the little coffin. He did it every bit, and I lined and padded it, trimmed and covered it. Not that we couldn't afford to buy one or that our neighbors were not all that was kind and willing, but because it was a sad pleasure to do everything for our little first-born ourselves.[7] No physician attended this child during his final hours, and no clergyman comforted the family during their days of need.

Throughout the nineteenth century, but less commonly near its end, American families often buried their dead children without consulting a physician. Many frontier families lacked ready access to practitioners, and many others simply questioned the value of available medical care. This uncertainty was greater for questions of children's health because both families and professionals often doubted the benefit of treating sick children. Mothers, advisers, and physicians often concluded that childhood illness was either trivial or so abrupt and fatal that professional attention was useless. On the one hand, all children experienced teething and feeding problems, while on the other, diphtheria and whooping cough were often fatal within hours of their onset. By the middle third of the nineteenth century, William Dewees, Philadelphia midwifery professor and the author of professional tomes on childhood illness, concluded: "The belief that the diseases of children almost constantly present nothing but perplexing obscurity or embarrassing uncertainty, has much retarded the progress of inquiry, by engendering doubts of their susceptibility of successful investigation, lucid explanation, or useful arrangement, and of course, that every prescribed remedy has but an uncertain aim, and consequently, a contingent or doubtful effect."[8] If physicians were to assume a significant place at the bedside of sick children, they needed both a new understanding of the nature of childhood illness and effective means of medical treatment.

The Medical Care of Children

After 1850, the growing emphasis on children's health among physicians was reflected in an expanded professional literature. From the *Boston Medical and Surgical Journal* to the *Leavenworth (Kansas) Medical Herald,* physicians increasingly advised their colleagues about children's health. In fact, the lead article in the first issue of the *Herald* was "The Proper Constitution of the Food of Infants."[9] The same issue of the journal reported the introduction at a meeting of the local medical society of the clinical thermometer, a device reportedly of "great importance in the diagnosis of disease."[10] These articles provided evidence of the increasingly important role that children's health played in the daily practice of America's physicians, and the rapidly expanding volume of new information about the children's health care.

Notwithstanding the limitations of their physicians' abilities, Victorian American parents more frequently consulted medical practitioners about the health problems of their children. Physicians attended children with pleurisy, measles, summer complaint, teething—in short all the common, rare, or fatal conditions of the youthful years. They attended births and deaths and comforted parents and child during the "uneasy moments" between life and death. One physician visited a child with pleurisy on seven separate occasions in a single day. The boy recovered.[11] Another physician reported using the stethoscope on his patients, and with one he "hear[d] a rattling noise showing the Bronchial tubes were secreting too much mucus."[12] By attending to these sick children and utilizing the best available medical technology and theory, these physicians demonstrated a new role for themselves in the health care of American children. And while these practitioners may not have provided specific therapy, the mere presence of a physician even without the "performance of any manual operation whatever" reassured parents with a "balmy hope" that survival was possible.[13] If physicians did not deserve credit for the "unspeakable amazement" when a child "roused up, nursed and then fell into a sweet sleep" of recovery, they were increasingly in attendance as the nineteenth century advanced when such miraculous events occurred.[14] Not surprisingly, physicians accepted credit for their professional actions even though their therapeutic efforts were not responsible for the outcome. As a result, more parents gave physicians credit for their medical skills, and more often parents called upon physicians for assistance when their children were sick.

Physicians increasingly recognized "those external agents to whose influence the child is subjected from the time of birth, and which, while they are essential to its existence, become by mismanagement, the cause of nearly all its losses."[15] In other words, some physicians recognized that knowledge of children's health extended to an understanding of the care and development of normal children. When carefully analyzed these "external agents" included the benefit of fresh air, cleanliness, proper clothing, adequate sleep, and regular exercise. The health care of children was situated within a broad field of knowledge, which, one professor concluded near the end of the century, required that the pediatrist "know everything."[16] Yet, at the same time, this physician and others noted a lack of professional literature about fundamental aspects of child care and development. The doctor reported no professional discourse about the selection of infant clothing, a subject he concluded was essential knowledge for a children's doctor. From feeding to children's shoes and proper bathing instructions, other physicians reported their needs for accurate information about the care of normal children. By the 1890s more and better information was available. This was reflected in a growing number of textbooks on the diseases of children that included information about the care of well children. The New York pediatrician L. Emmett Holt devoted more than 30 pages of his 1897 text to concerns about hygiene and "external agents" that affected children's health.[17]

By understanding normal children, physicians had a better grasp of the ill effects of disease. In addressing the American Medical Association, one physician concluded there was "no way better [to] employ the time allotted to me than in calling attention to the importance of securing statistics in regard to the physique of growing children."[18] This physician not only recognized the need for accurate information about normal children and their care, but also the importance of its systematic and scientific analysis. Essential information included growth rates and physical measurements and, importantly, an understanding of normal physiological changes ranging from teething to pubertal development. Unfortunately, as Abraham Jacobi noted, these normal processes were not always easy to define. Teething, for example, was a "normal physiological development, taking place at an age which for many reasons is subject to a large number of diseases, [and] has a strong hold on the imagination of frightened maternal minds."[19] Consequently, teething and many other aspects of child development were defined by parents and some physicians as diseases when in fact such definitions were based on traditional lore rather than thorough study and analysis. If physicians were to be recognized as authorities on children's health, then an understanding of the normal growth and development of the child was necessary to "afford valuable indications for the guidance of the family physician" and parents.[20] Pediatrists were recognized as experts on children's health and disease only when they had a broad base of knowledge about both normal and diseased children.

By the end of the nineteenth century, physicians employed normal standards of growth as a measurement of health: "Anthropometry infallibly discovers the child that is below the mean of his age. It separates every school into two classes—those physically competent and those physically incompetent for a clearly defined degree of mental work. When great numbers are considered, this system is practically absolute in its infallibility. Those children below the mean should be under almost paternal solicitude. Those below the twenty-five percentile grade should certainly be under the supervision of a properly experienced physician."[21] The experience of the physician was important in determining normal growth, but as this St. Louis physician concluded, statistical analysis was nearly infallible. Physicians used statistics to define normalcy and gave medical attention when problems were identified. Increasingly, physicians encouraged medical attention for childhood problems not previously considered the responsibility of medical practitioners.

As they gained a better understanding of normal child development, child advisers noted its importance for parents: "One of the great facts of our time is the raising of the physical standard for the entire generation by the prevention and cure of disease. We no longer regard poor digestion and weak nerves as disciplinary arrangements of Providence, to be accepted uncomplainingly, but if we find ourselves handicapped by them we discover their cause and correct it. Better than this, we so start our children in life that they may avoid these and other evils and have sound nerves, strong digestion, and vigorous brains as a matter of course."[22] Parents and physicians who understood the process of digestion and the development of the nervous system promoted the health of America's children by recognizing and preventing, among other problems, malnutrition and "weak nerves." The collection of new information about childhood growth and development and physiological functions placed physicians in late nineteenth-century society as authorities on the health and rearing of America's children. As a result physicians advised parents about the care of normal children and assumed public, professional, and political roles that furthered the health of the nation's children. At the same time, more parents listened to the professional counsel of physicians, and many sought advice about the daily care and rearing of their offspring.

Dietary and nutritional knowledge was important. A professional emphasis on infant feeding was not unfounded, for mothers regularly requested advice about infant feeding, weaning, food supplements, and remedies for the colic and other digestive disorders of early life. The summer complaint and other gastrointestinal illnesses were also the leading causes of death for children. Physicians, as Jacobi concluded, also recognized the importance of accurate information about nutrition: "Proper feeding and nursing of the infant prevents the numerous gastric and intestinal diseases of the earliest period, which either destroy life at once or lay the foundation of continued ill health. For that reason a rather large part of my literary labors has been dedicated to the question of diet and hygiene."[23] Other pediatricians of the day, including Jacobi's successor at Columbia University College of Physicians and Surgeons, L. Emmett Holt, also emphasized the importance of feeding practices. Thomas Morgan Rotch, the first professor of pediatrics at Harvard, did more than offer advice about infant feeding. During the late 1880s, he established a laboratory for the chemical analysis of milk, so that the "science of infant feeding might be based on the chemical composition of milk." In short, medical experts, armed with new scientific insights about infant feeding, the chemical composition of milk, and the growth and multiplication of bacteria, now answered the "vexatious questions" that many mothers posed to physicians. In the process the health of the nation's children was maintained, and physicians assumed a larger role as authorities.[24]

One of the most frequently lethal results of improper infant feeding was gastrointestinal illness, especially summer complaint or cholera infantum. In retrospect, a number of different medical problems were responsible for the medical complications that infants with the summer complaint experienced. Many of these infants had bacterial or viral infections, others had food intolerances or allergies, and some had simple dehydration or malnutrition from insufficient or improper feedings. The repeated episodes of diarrhea and vomiting that attacked these infants left them with the "same sober, melancholy expression or countenance; the same pale, thin lips, sunken eyes, and blanched skin; the same small, weak pulse and general emaciation."[25]

Infectious diseases—generally gastroenteritis—sometimes caused summer complaint. Before the 1870s microorganisms, such as bacteria, yeasts, and viruses, were unknown. Physicians attributed such problems to ill defined miasmas, improper feeding methods, and diets that contained an improper quality or quantity of nourishments.[26] Since problems were most severe during the summer months, mothers were advised not to wean their children during that time of the year. The problem not only prevailed "universally in the different portions of the United States" but often was fatal "to the dearest interests of society."[27] Physicians treated these conditions by dietary manipulation and by dosing with purgatives, cathartics, opiates, and anodynes. Most of these agents were ineffective, while purgatives and cathartics often exacerbated the problem and increased the death rate. A pragmatic late nineteenth-century midwife concluded that "if the vomiting and purging can be rested, the outlook is hopeful," otherwise the "majority of the acute cases result unfavorably."[28]

The laboratory study of microorganisms by Louis Pasteur (1822–1895) in France and Robert Koch (1843–1910) in Germany, along with the clinical studies of Joseph Lister (1827–1912) in England, provided American physicians with evidence that germs caused infectious human disease. The germ theory was not accepted immediately, but by the final decade of the century many physicians recognized that hand washing, sterilization, and the rapid consumption of fresh milk, all steps that reduce bacterial growth, promoted children's health by reducing the spread of common infectious conditions like summer complaint. As more successful results were reported, more physicians and parents accepted germ theory and took corresponding precautions.

Only after knowledge of the germ theory was understood and accepted did the death rate from summer complaint significantly decrease. More effective therapy was not available until intravenous fluids and antibiotics were developed in the twentieth century, but the prevention of infant gastrointestinal disease was possible once the transmission of infectious diseases by contaminated milk supplies and unsanitary feeding practices was stopped. Improved feeding practices, better nutritional status, safer water supplies, better sanitation, and a clean pasteurized milk supply all combined to reduce the mortality from these conditions (see discussion of infant feeding in chapter 5).[29]

Treating Diphtheria

In 1873 more than 175,000 Americans died of infectious diseases. More than one-half of these deaths were caused by tuberculosis and gastrointestinal illnesses, such as cholera infantum. The majority of these deaths were of children who died of common childhood diseases like whooping cough, measles, diphtheria, and scarlatina.[30] In Chicago three years later, there were 1,243 fatal cases of scarlatina among a population of slightly more than 400,000. More than 90 percent of these deaths were of children. Charles W. Earle, a Chicago health officer, made the important observation that deaths were four times greater among the poor.[31] These unfortunates, as a New York pediatrician reported, often lived in "damp and dark alleys and in crowded and filthy tenement-houses, breathing night and day an atmosphere loaded with noxious gases" and, as observers began to understand, microbes.[32] This physician, as was true of many of his colleagues of the day, had not yet accepted the germ theory. Rather, he concluded that "noxious gases" and other vapors, smells, odors, and miasmas caused disease. While physicians may not have recognized that bacteria caused disease, recognition that poverty and unsanitary living conditions were important factors was essential for improving the health of American children.

Diphtheria, the throat distemper that killed hundreds of children in colonial New England, remained an important cause of death for nineteenth-century American children. The disease caused inflammation, edema, and swelling of the trachea. Severe infections impeded breathing, and when the process was severe, children died. Cleansing the throat and removing the membranes that obstructed respiration was generally unsuccessful. *Intubation*, the placement of a breathing tube in the trachea, or *tracheostomy*, a surgical opening in the trachea or windpipe, was helpful for some infants. Nearly three-quarters of its victims were children, most less than two years of age.[33] One Kansas physician concluded that the diphtheria germs were "so tenacious, that when once present they may remain latent for years."[34] Everyone recognized the danger of the disease, but before public and professional acceptance of germ theory, the question remained whether the disease was "contagious." Throughout the 1870s, this "old, vexed question" of the nature of diphtheria remained, and a New York physician concluded it was "likely to be definitely settled about the same time, as that of cholera, yellow fever, scarlatina, typhoid fever, . . . for it belongs in this relation to the same class, is developed and spreads with the same erratic manifestations."[35] The doctor rightfully concluded that diphtheria, cholera, and yellow fever were all communicable. But neither this physician nor his colleagues knew that diphtheria was caused by the bacteria *Cornebacterium diphtheria* and that the coughing and sneezing of droplets from the throats of infected children directly spread the disease to bystanders.

By 1880 Pasteur, Koch, and others, employing bacteriological culture methods, demonstrated that diphtheria and cholera, among other conditions, were in fact contagious diseases transmitted by microbes. This knowledge provided new opportunities for an understanding and the prevention of "putrid sore throat." In this country, Charles Chapin of Providence, Rhode Island, established the first Health Department bacteriology laboratory in 1888.[36] Once the bacterial cause for diphtheria was known, precise diagnosis with bacterial cultures and the demonstration that sick children with negative cultures no longer spread the disease to others was possible. By the mid 1890s Chapin's laboratory routinely required a negative diphtheria culture as a criterion for releasing children from quarantine. This new basis for disease control offered professionals an accurate method of diagnosis and facilitated the enumeration of affected individuals and the likelihood of their infecting others. Chapin demonstrated, and others soon agreed, that the broad application of general public health and sanitary measures reduced the spread of diphtheria. Quarantine was rigidly enforced, and hygienic rules for the Providence schools enacted and enforced. Children were directed not to spit, pick their noses, put their fingers in their mouths, cough or sneeze on one another, or share food, whistles, or bean blowers with other children.[37] Cleanliness was mandated and regular hand washing encouraged. A Chicago health officer concluded that Chapin's results and interpretations would "irritate, anger, inflame the legislatures into properly providing for the protection of the people."[38] Despite Chapin's understanding of the nature of the spread of diphtheria and its acceptance by some physicians, many lay persons and politicians were reluctant to accept the tenets of the germ theory or the sanitary measures it dictated. Consequently, families often avoided or disregarded quarantine rules when possible, and many adults and children were slow to cease public spitting and coughing. Both public and professional acceptance of the germ theory were initially slow, but before the end of the century, public health problems and their control were the most important children's health topics in the nation. Since infectious diseases were a common source of childhood death, public health measures based on the new understanding of germ theory, such as better sanitation and the practice of quarantining infected patients, were able to prevent many cases of death and disease (see the discussion of infectious disease in chapter 5).

A better understanding of diphtheria was hampered by physicians' and hospital officials' concern about public perception of their successes and failures. At Boston Children's Hospital in 1888 the official hospital mortality rate excluded cases of the disease in order to depict a better state of health. Concerns about reputation were not unfounded, for 176 diphtheria patients died that year at the facility, as did 239 the following year. In fact, from 1876 to 1894 at Boston Children's Hospital 46 percent of the children admitted with the disease died.[39] The death rate, as high as 90 percent, was worse when intubation or tracheostomy was performed. The burden was not eased by the recognition that these hospitalized children were presumably more seriously ill and therefore more likely to die from the disease. The high frequency of death and the fear that nearly any child might develop the disease worried physicians, parents, and the public.

Evidence from the application of the principles of bacteriology led to the most efficacious therapy. Laboratory studies demonstrated that the diphtheria bacillus produced a toxin that caused "heart failure, paralysis and other symptoms of the disease when injected into animals." By isolating this toxin, bacteriologists then produced a serum, the diphtheria antitoxin, that neutralized the action of the bacterial toxin. According to one physician, when given within 48 hours of disease onset "every case of pure diphtheria" was cured.[40] The discovery of effective therapy for diphtheria provided an early example of how a basic understanding of germ theory and disease causation enabled physicians to control and eventually prevent an important childhood disease. Successful control of diphtheria would encourage the application of similar methods to other childhood illnesses.

Individual physicians reported the successful treatment of diphtheria with antitoxin administration, but much more impressive results demonstrating the general efficacy of this treatment were reported by hospitals and citywide campaigns. Fewer deaths were reported in New York, Milwaukee, and Kansas City. In Milwaukee, the health department established free diphtheria stations in 1894. At these facilities antitoxin was provided to children at no cost. Within the first year the number of cases of diphtheria decreased by nearly 40 percent, with further declines the following two years.[41] The same year Boston Children's Hospital began the routine administration of antitoxin to all new hospital admissions. Within two years the mortality rate dropped to less than 15 percent and by 1900 to less than 10 percent. The citywide diphtheria mortality in Boston decreased from 18 per 10,000 in 1894 to 3 per 10,000 in 1898. Over the same time period the incidence of the disease decreased six-fold.[42] Holt reported similar successful results from New York City, and he concluded that antitoxin therapy was of "inestimable value."[43]

Initially, not all physicians accepted the value of antitoxin therapy. Dr. Joseph Winter of Cornell University told the American Pediatric Society in 1895 that he was violently opposed to antitoxin therapy. At a meeting of the New York Academy of Medicine the same year, Winter filibustered for more than three hours against a resolution that favored the therapy. Holt described this episode as an "imposition." "It was an awful outrage" that only delayed successful treatment of sick children.[44] In spite of such incidents, both the Academy and the Pediatric Society concluded that the initial results justified "further and extensive trials." The following year members of the same society heard reports of 5,794 cases of diphtheria treated with antitoxin, more than 80 percent with positive bacterial cultures for diphtheria, and an overall mortality "less than one half as great as has ever been reported by any other method of treatment."[45] Antitoxin therapy successfully cured many sick children, but the production of serum was not always easy. In St. Louis, where the city bacteriologist produced diphtheria antitoxin, a batch of serum was contaminated with *Clostridia tetanii,* the bacteria that causes tetanus. Several children died from the injection of this deadly bacteria. In response to this and other comparable episodes, Congress passed the Biologics Control Act of 1902, so that a safe national supply of antitoxin was soon available.[46]

The development of successful therapy against diphtheria was of inestimable value to American children and provided important evidence of the medical expertise of pediatrists. Physicians had successfully applied the scientific method and the concepts of the germ theory to the treatment of an important childhood disease. In the process the health of American children was dramatically improved, and the position of the physician as an authority about children's health was widely enhanced. Physicians not only offered advice, but now dramatically reduced morbidity and mortality from an often fatal childhood disease. While not as successful with many other common infectious diseases, physicians had taken an important initial step in improving the health of American children.

Childbirth and Newborn Care

During the second half of the nineteenth century, childbirth and the care of the newborn received new attention. From New England to the western frontier, physicians increasingly assisted birthing women by providing anesthesia and operative deliveries.[47] In addition to identifying new methods of feeding, bathing, and dressing, physicians emphasized the resuscitation of the asphyxiated newborn. These efforts, based on a new physiological understanding of birthing and infant respiration, were "intended to produce alternative contraction and expansion of the chest walls,"[48] that is, to substitute for the natural process of spontaneous breathing. Physicians offered specific methods, including some that succeeded.[49] According to a Kansas physician, more important than the specific method employed was "perseverance and yet very gentle handling . . . so that we may not still more exhaust the condition of the child."[50] Persistent gentle measures were not always successful, and some physicians remained uncertain of their ability to help the newborn. After two hours of effort, undertaken "with not the remotest idea of accomplishing anything so valuable as the saving of a life," a frontier physician "set about artificial respiration, by holding the nose of the babe, adjusting my lips to its mouth, inflating the lungs, and then by gently compressing the chest, again forcing from them, in imitation of expiration. The facility with which I could accomplish this, induced me to keep it up for a considerable time, out of mere idle curiosity." He ultimately resuscitated the newborn. The "true physician" not only learned from others but also possessed the requisite "native intellect," today called clinical judgment. Because he saved a child who would have died without medical assistance, the doctor was "worthy to occupy a place in the exalted profession of medicine."[51] As Abraham Jacobi concluded, the treatment of sick children was based on "advancing years and experience during a period of increasing exactness in medical methods."[52] Medical science provided the knowledge of the pediatrist, but the successful children's doctor tempered this knowledge with experience.

If intervention at birth benefited the newborn, some physicians reasoned that "a strict observance of the laws of health, and an avoidance of all exciting or perturbating influences during the time when the foetus is being developed" would reduce the frequency of miscarriages, stillbirths, and the "large number of ill-formed and puny infants born to a precarious and short existence."[53] Physicians promoted the successful completion of pregnancy by offering women advice about diet, exercise, sleep, and general behavior during gestation. By the early twentieth century such advice provided the basis for prenatal care. Mothers were also advised about the dangerous effects of "vivid mental impressions" on the fetus. In 1890 J. Lewis Smith (1827–1897), professor of the diseases of children at New York's Bellevue Hospital, reported a female Irish infant born without fingers or thumb on one hand. During the first month of the child's fetal development, the child's mother, a woman of "strong emotions and superstitions," was "accosted by a beggar, who raised her hand, destitute of thumb and fingers, and in God's name asked for alms." The mother later concluded she had committed "a great sin" by not aiding the beggar. According to the doctor, the woman's "wretched" emotional state caused the child's problem.[54] While physicians applied science to many health problems, on some occasions, such as this, their knowledge was no more accurate than superstition and harkened back to Governor Winthrop's explanation for the anomalies that afflicted infant Dyer 200 years before. The development of pediatricians included some progressive steps, such as the use of diphtheria antitoxin, and some side steps, but the maturation of professional expertise required both successes and failures in the development of mature clinical judgment.

Birth of the Pediatrist

As knowledge about childhood diseases expanded and therapeutic intervention became more successful, nineteenth-century physicians and parents became more concerned about the special problems of children's health. This narrower focus contrasts with practice in the eighteenth century and the early decades of the nineteenth century, when special study of children's health was generally undertaken by physicians who concentrated on midwifery. By the final quarter of the century a small, but increasing, number of physicians identified themselves as specialists in childhood diseases and demonstrated a new relationship between physicians and American children. The birth of the specialist in children's diseases, the *pediatrician,* or to use the nineteenth-century term, the *pediatrist,* was under way.

In the early nineteenth century American medical students received information about the diseases of children in courses about the theory and practice of medicine, and advice about their treatment in lectures on materia medica, the use of drug therapy. These discussions generally presented limited material. One Harvard student noted in 1871, when the school catalog first listed children's diseases, that the available studies were limited to "a few lectures on the eruptive fevers."[55] Benjamin Rush gave lectures for more than 20 years on the "Diseases Peculiar to Children" at the University of Pennsylvania. But neither Rush nor the professor of midwifery at Pennsylvania, William Dewees, offered an entire separate course on the diseases of children. They both wrote papers and chapters in textbooks on children's health, however. These works, as well as Benjamin Waterhouse's "Cautions to Young Persons Concerning Health" (1805),[56] were written for physicians rather than lay readers. In contrast to the child advice texts of the day, which were written for both lay and professional readers, this new professional discourse by physicians was written so that doctors could more effectively treat sick children, making use of the improved knowledge about childhood disease. The increasing amount of scientific information available in the nineteenth century furthered the growth of the medical school curriculum on children's health.

The first dedicated and systematic course in childhood diseases was offered at Yale Medical School by Dr. Eli Ives (1778–1861), the first American professor of the diseases of children. Ives taught courses in materia medica, botany, the theory and practice of medicine, and the diseases of children for nearly 40 years (1813–52).[57] He emphasized, as had John Locke, the empiric nature of his knowledge about children's health. Ives learned "from older Physicians or from experience." As he accumulated information about children, their behavior, and diseases, he noted that it was more difficult to acquire information about the diseases of children than adults because "the seat of diseases in infants arises from their inability to communicate their sensations by language." While the study of sick children was more difficult, Ives considered the symptoms of disease "more uniform and more certain in their indications than those of adults."[58] As a Yale student recorded in his lecture notes for 1826, these differences and the unique nature of the diseases of children required the attention of a physician, not merely the efforts of interested parents. As "men of science," physicians were uniquely prepared for "a part of practice in which [the] community is deeply interested."[59] The skilled pediatrist offered a new understanding of children's health and, as the century progressed, new means to aid sick children.

Ives was interested in the symptoms, diagnosis, and treatment of children's diseases. His lectures covered common gastrointestinal problems like cholera infantum; colic and teething; fits and convulsions; pneumonia and croup; and infectious diseases from consumption and catarrh to earaches. Interestingly, "whooping cough" was one of the few childhood diseases that Ives recognized as contagious. He correctly noted that the disease rarely affected the same person twice.[60] On other subjects, Ives was less accurate. He spent "much time in investigating the origin" of worms, but concluded he was "much in the dark on the subject."[61] His only conclusion was that their "rudiments" were contained in "certain kinds of foods [such] as apples, pears, cider, water and fruits not boiled." Treatment with tonics and flavored emetic syrups or decoctions of garlic was indicated because worms obstructed the bowels and consumed "too much of the food."[62] By modern standards, Ives's understanding of disease was incomplete, but his application of observation and reason to a new field of medical study demonstrated the best medical practice of the day.

In June 1815, while examining a 5-year-old with a cough, Ives demonstrated the scientific tools of an early nineteenth-century physician. He found the pulse "very frequent," palpitations of the heart, the circulation "much increased," and the face swollen and livid. "All of the symptoms aggravated to an alarming degree during the paroxysms of cough."[63] He palpated the child, but he did not listen to the heart or lungs, measure the temperature, or perform laboratory procedures because these diagnostic methods were not yet known. The doctor concluded that the child would die; but nonetheless prescribed the best therapy of the day—ipecac, blood root, cathartics, clysters, and tonics. Despite the doctor's efforts, the child and his family "became disgusted with [the] medicine, and it was suspended." The boy recovered on a diet of baked pears, melons, and sweet cake and later became a Yale student. The boy's family did what many nineteenth-century American families did when faced with the noxious remedies of the era's physicians: they abandoned the therapy. Ives, however, recognized that "heroic" therapy was often too strong, especially for children.[64] Few physicians of the day understood that children in a medical sense were not simply miniature men and women and that the successful restoration of health required medical therapy specifically adapted for them.

But, gradually, other physicians recognized that "admissible" remedies for adults were often inappropriate for children. Charles Meigs (1792–1869), a professor of midwifery and popular author, considered mercury, a common component of cathartics, "a most desirable thing for the young child to avoid," since its effects were "too dangerous and powerful."[65]

"The ignorance of parents" was also responsible for the unnecessary deaths of children. According to a University of Baltimore medical student, parents resorted to "dear old Grandmother somebody, whose life has been passed in retailing out to her neighbors, and their children, some herbs and roots, the nature and medicinal virtue of which, she knows no more of, than we do of the philosopher's stone." In this situation, according to the future physician, if the disease was not enough, the "old woman's tea" completed the work of destruction, and the "unfortunate little sufferer [sunk] calmly in the arms of death."[66]

The "fearful picture" painted by the bills of mortality of the day was "humiliating" to the doctor's science[67] because the physician's doses of calomel were as ineffective as "grandma's tea" for sick children. While the "safest and most successful" physician applied his "hygienical ordinances in the best exposition of nature's laws,"[68] heroic medical therapy generally did not follow nature's law, and, consequently, few children or adults actually benefited from its use. Nonetheless, some physicians recognized that infant death was not a "necessity" but that "various causes" that were "measurably at least, within control" were responsible for frequent death among American children.[69] In the hands of the pediatrist, medical science was becoming the means by which the diseases of children would be controlled.

European physicians, especially practitioners in France, England, and Germany, also emphasized the study of childhood diseases. Textbooks were published, and in 1834 a medical journal devoted solely to the diseases of children was started. By the middle of the nineteenth century, more physicians limited their activities to the care of sick children, and more medical school professors were appointed in the new discipline. Beginning in the 1840s, the English physician Charles West, who had practiced for 26 years and witnessed more than 400 autopsies, noted that children's diseases deserved special study. In essence, he concluded that children's diseases were different from adult diseases, and sick children behaved differently from sick adults. West, like Ives earlier in the century, was charting new medical domains, and he proposed science as the compass with which to map the new area of children's health care:

> Your old means of investigating disease will here, to a great degree, fail you, and you will feel almost as if you had to learn your alphabet again, or as if, entering a country whose inhabitants you expected to find speaking the same language and having the same manners as the people in the land you had lately left, you were to hear around you everywhere the sounds of a foreign tongue, and to observe manners and customs such as you had never seen before. You cannot question your patient; or, if old enough to speak, still, through fear, or from comprehending you imperfectly, he will probably give you an incorrect reply. You try to gather information from the expression of his countenance, but the child is fretful, and will not bear to be looked at; you endeavor to feel his pulse, he struggles in alarm; you try to auscultate the chest, and he breaks out into a violent fit of crying.[70]

Sick children speak a unique language that some physicians were increasingly able to translate with reasoned evaluation and analysis into measures that improved children's health.

When physicians listened to and examined sick children, and then pondered their observations in relation to the growing body of medical information about children's health collected by Ives, Meigs, and their European and American colleagues, they were further codifying and expanding the scientific basis of their medical knowledge. The physical diagnosis of childhood disease was more accurate, more easily completed, and, importantly, confirmed by frequent anatomical dissections of dead children. Wheezes, rales, and rhonchi (abnormal breathing sounds often accompanying bronchitis and pneumonia) heard through the stethoscope, and the dullness of the chest to percussion that was characteristic of pneumonia, were confirmed by postmortem dissections. With such methods, more physicians, like Edward Henoch of the University of Berlin, accumulated "personal experience" based upon "carefully observed material" that was essential for an understanding of the diseases of children.[71] American physicians led by the German-born Abraham Jacobi emphasized these principles as the basis for the rising science of pediatrics.[72]

Pediatrists, like many other American physicians of the nineteenth century, received much of their early training at the bedside of sick children in European hospitals and clinics. In fact, most important American physicians of the last decades of the nineteenth century studied in Europe.[73] While Jacobi's scientific ideas and new philosophy about the medical care of children were rooted in his extensive studies in Europe, there were striking similarities between these ideas and Charles Ives's recognition of the unique nature of childhood diseases half a century earlier.

Professionalization of Pediatrics

By the end of the nineteenth century physicians regularly investigated and analyzed the diseases of children. The establishment of this knowledge base about children's health provided the tools with which pediatrists established themselves as members of a growing list of medical specialists. Improved medical education combined with the scientific analysis of the problems of children's health provided the professional backbone for the care of the nation's children. These efforts were promoted by and in turn spawned the foundation of new professional publications and the formation of new medical societies. These organizations enhanced the professional knowledge of physicians and, in turn, expanded the professional power and position of pediatrists.

In 1860 Abraham Jacobi established what he called "the first systematic course, in our country, of clinical instruction in the diseases of children."[74] Jacobi overlooked Ives's educational efforts four decades before, but, nonetheless, the New York physician did set up a comprehensive series of lectures, supplemented by bedside teaching about children's health and disease. Jacobi became the central figure in the establishment of pediatrics as the "science of the young."[75] He was professor of the diseases of children at New York's College of Physicians and Surgeons for 40 years. Within two decades of his appointment, 10 medical schools in the nation, including Yale, Harvard, and Johns Hopkins, had similar full-time positions for pediatrists, and an additional 700 physicians designated themselves as children's doctors. By 1966, 12,558 pediatricians practiced medicine in America.[76]

Jacobi recognized "pediatric science" as a new medical specialty that was no longer "a simple attachment to obstetrics and the diseases of women."[77] It was a unique specialty that required special means for the diagnosis, treatment, and management of sick children. While Jacobi considered pediatrics a medical specialty, the medical care of children also remained a significant part of general medical practice. Jacobi recognized the value of medical specialization, but he also concluded that such changes were so far advanced that the human body was no longer seen as an organism "but a conglomerate of organs which have no connection with each other."[78] Instead Jacobi proposed the study of the child as an entire organism, from before "he is born, while he is being born, and after." From infancy to "the dangerous period of puberty" and from the home to the school, the "watchful care" of the pediatrician was needed for the adequate provision of children's health.[79]

Medical specialization required special educational opportunities. The leadership of men like Jacobi, Holt, Smith, and Rotch, with their unique visions of the future of children's health, was equally as important as the availability of sick children in the home, in dispensaries, and in the beds of children's hospitals. Dedication and hard work were the requisite skills with which medical students and young doctors heard "lectures on that subject, read books and monographs, search[ed] journals for information, [and] studied the anatomy and physiology of the young."[80] When physicians followed in the footsteps of Jacobi, intensive study, methodical analysis, and personal experience were necessary for the creation of an expert medical specialist.

As more physicians became interested in the diseases of children and studied in a systematic manner, medical knowledge about childhood diseases, especially infectious diseases, rapidly progressed. Common childhood diseases were more accurately described, and when germ theory was applied, (as occurred with diphtheria), a better understanding of their pathogenesis was possible. Measles (rubeola), for example, was first distinguished from German measles (rubella) during this era.[81] Systematic study of the rash that accompanied these conditions, particularly its duration and extent, and the identification of other accompanying findings, like the size of lymph nodes and the presence of Koplik spots on the lining of the mouth, allowed the careful observer to distinguish these two similar conditions. Physicians offered families a better prognosis when the less severe rubella affected their children. The cause (a virus) for both conditions was not known, nor was therapeutic advance made, but careful description of each disease gave pediatricians specialized knowledge beyond that of most other physicians. Jacobi and his colleagues had established a "branch of medicine, science, art, and practice that is of the greatest importance to the general practitioner in both city and country."[82]

While pediatricians increasingly described and understood the diseases of childhood by Locke's method of empiric observation, doctors also recognized that the growing field of pediatrics was more than merely the description of disease. Some practitioners reported both successes and "reverses," and nearly all observers "preferred not to speak of those subjects on which [they] could not base very practical opinions."[83] Jacobi concluded at the founding session of the Section of the Diseases of Children at the 1880 American Medical Association Annual Meeting that "[t]he pathology and therapeutics of infancy and childhood do not mean the very same things in adults[;] they mean more than merely reduced ages and doses."[84] Jacobi and his colleagues were beginning to understand that knowledge of behavior, hygiene, growth, and development—in short, the nature of the normal child—was essential for the medical care of children. Not only physicians but also mothers, nurses, educators, social workers, and a myriad of other observers "combined knowledge of each student in his own particular province of research" into the "intelligent solution" of the problems of America's children.[85] Ultimately, this new knowledge supported "the fundamental truth that everything in medical science, in order to be both scientific and humanitarian, should be conducive to the prevention or the cure of disease."[86] While pediatricians increasingly studied and practiced medicine as a science, they remained child savers at heart.

The growing knowledge base of the professional pediatrician was expressed in an increasing number of professional publications. Medical texts, pamphlets, journals, and letters reflected the growing body of professional discourse on the health of children. The *Archives of Pediatrics* founded in 1884 was the first journal devoted exclusively to the consideration of the diseases of children. Two more specialty journals appeared before 1900, and the *American Journal of the Diseases of Children* began publication in 1911. General medical journals, such as the *Journal of the American Medical Association* and the *Boston Medical and Surgical Journal* (later *New England Journal of Medicine*) also regularly reported upon the health and disease of American children. The regular issue of these medical journals provided medical students, general practitioners, and specialists with an increasing volume of knowledge about normal and sick children.

By the 1890s pediatric textbooks for medical students and practitioners were widely available and voluminous in their coverage of the diseases of children. John Keating's *Cyclopaedia of the Diseases of Children* (1890) was reportedly the work that "opened the eyes of the profession to the fact that pediatrics was a field that was cultivated in a special way."[87] This four-volume work was dwarfed two decades later by Isaac Abt's massive eight-volume work that provided a "system of pediatrics" on nearly ten thousand pages.[88] Perhaps the most influential of all these works was L. Emmett Holt's *The Diseases of Infancy and Childhood.* This 1,100-page work appeared in 1897 for "the use of students and practitioners of medicine." The author of this work for both specialists and generalists justified the need for another text on the diseases of children on the "rapid advance [in pediatric knowledge] made during the past few years." The science of medicine not only promoted the health of children, but it mandated the dissemination of this new knowledge as well.

Holt's work chronicled not only the diseases of children, but also other aspects of children's health—hygiene, nutrition, growth, and development. Thirty-six pages of the text were devoted to the peculiarities of disease in children. The nearly 300 pages on the major causes of child mortality—

nutrition and gastrointestinal illness—and Holt's discussion of infectious diseases together composed nearly one-half of the volume. Holt allotted space to each subject "in some degree commensurate with its practical importance to the physician and student."[89] The educational value of the text for both the experienced practitioner and the new student was enhanced by the inclusion of 204 illustrations. Seven color plates enabled the interested reader to distinguish the subtle features of rashes and other childhood complaints. The publication of this work was evidence that pediatricians had a broad and unique knowledge base that promoted their professional position and the daily practice of medicine.

The effort to compile and systematize the knowledge of childhood diseases, even in 1890, was a monumental task. Some measure of the effort involved was recorded by Holt in a letter to his wife:

> I have been getting too selfish in my life, and in my strong desire to write a book and make a name for myself that I am doing so at the cost of something that perhaps I do not realize. I don't want to sacrifice every other interest in life to patients and medicines and my professional work. I am anxious to do my duty both to you and the children. But it does seem so hard to give all things their due place. I have resolved, however, to do better in this respect the rest of the winter than I have done so far. I want to live with the children more, and not simply board in the same house with them, and treat their colds when they have them.[90]

Although Holt's family and children suffered because of his work and dedication to this project, the children of America benefited from the successful completion of his work.

By the turn of the century pediatricians were increasingly recognized as America's authorities on children's health and child care. Diapering, dressing, feeding, even the physical layout of the nursery, were in the hands of the pediatrician.[91] Not only mothers and the public accepted this view of the pediatrician, but other physicians did as well. In 1906 John Zahorsky concluded in the *Golden Rules of Pediatrics* that "the universal conscience of the medical profession" acknowledged that pediatrics was a specialty and further that "the practical results justify the contention."[92] Zahorsky furthered this process, as the subtitle of his work indicated, by providing "Aphorisms, Observations and Precepts on the Science and Art of Pediatrics: Giving practical rules for diagnosis and prognosis, the essentials of infant feeding, and the principles of scientific treatment." While Holt's work may have been too extensive and verbose, Zahorsky's "golden rules," like "fever is the most common symptom in the diseases of infancy and childhood,"[93] enabled the busy practitioner to rapidly distill the new essence of pediatrics. Ultimately, the application of this new knowledge to the care of sick children was the essential function of the pediatrician. Diphtheria was treated with antitoxin, club feet repaired with new surgical procedures, and infants artificially fed.

Yet, as Jacobi concluded, babies "thrive or die, crow or wail without regard to the 500,000 or more books and pamphlets which have been written about them in all countries in the course of a century."[94] The duty of the physician was not only to amass and report new medical information, but, more important, to treat sick children and ease their pain and suffering from the diseases and distresses of daily life.

The new medical knowledge and technical skills that physicians possessed had dramatic effects on the medical care that American children received. One ailing South Dakota boy, who "had never been in a doctor's office," was examined by a local practitioner. "He ran his fingers over my stomach, poked around one little spot gently and suddenly stopped." The doctor diagnosed appendicitis, and following an overnight train ride, the boy arrived at a hospital that smelled of medicine and where everyone was in a hurry. The boy later dramatically recorded his memory of the appendectomy:

> Everything was white and there was a high, narrow table. Four or five nurses were in the room and they seemed to be waiting for me. I was laid on a narrow bed. One of the nurses went over me with a damp cloth; she said it was alcohol. Someone else put a pad over my face that was supposed to put me to sleep. . . . I was scared. Suppose the stuff in the pad wouldn't work on me and I didn't go to sleep. They might start taking out the appendix, or maybe I would go to sleep and never wake up. Suppose they might think I was dead and bury me and then I would wake up in the coffin. I was getting frantic and tried to get off the table and knock the pad away, but I couldn't move and a nurse held my hands. It seemed I couldn't breathe.[95]

The boy survived. His recollections of his encounter with turn-of-the-century medical care provided both a personal and a touching record of the application of surgical techniques and inhalation anesthesia. More than this, the use of these methods in rural South Dakota indicated the spread of medical knowledge about children's health across the nation. The more frequent performance of these procedures demonstrated the faith that both practitioners and the public placed in physician's knowledge. When relatives, friends, and neighbors were advised of such therapeutic successes, the professional and public position of America's physicians rapidly rose.

By the late nineteenth century the growing body of pediatric knowledge and the recognition of pediatricians as medical specialists prompted the formation of professional societies. These endeavors advanced the professionalization of medical practice in general, legitimizing it and promoting the social, economic, and political position of American doctors. Generalists and specialists spoke with a single voice that advanced the position of regular physicians at the expense of sectarian practitioners and midwives. Specialists, such as pediatricians, surgeons, obstetricians, and ophthalmologists, also expanded their professional interests and practices at the expense of general

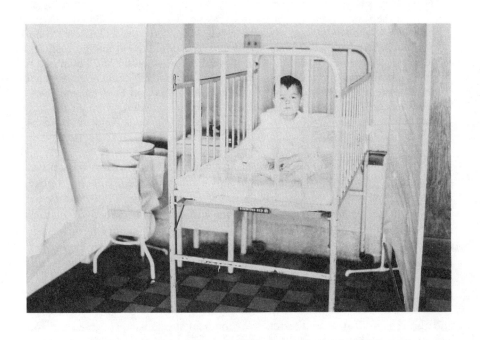

As this child poignantly demonstrates, hospitalization and medical attention can be as confusing and frightening for children as disease itself.

Hospital Archives, University of Kansas Medical Center, Kansas City, Kansas.

ists. Both generalists and pediatricians cared for sick children and advised their parents, but as the twentieth century began, pediatricians became the spokespersons for both their colleagues and the nation's children.

The founding of the Section of the Diseases of Children of the American Medical Association in June 1880 confirmed the new professional position of children's doctors. The formation of this organization of specialists was recognition that children's health care was a unique form of medical care based in a growing body of knowledge. Eight years later similar factors prompted the formation, in Baltimore, of the American Pediatric Society. The Society's object was "the advancement of the Physiology, Pathology and Therapeutics of Infancy and Childhood."[96] The scientific collection and vigorous analysis of medical knowledge formed the foundation for this society. Nearly all the founding members of the organization were members of medical school faculties. Only one of the founders was more than 50 years of age. These young practitioners had received more scientific educations than their older colleagues, and their participation in this society was an indication that scientific analysis, not merely empiric observation, was becoming an important cornerstone of specialty medical practice. By 1890 the Society had 42 members. All but seven of these practitioners lived east of Chicago, an indication of the geographical concentration of medical specialists of the day. Interestingly, however, none of these physicians totally limited their medical practices to the care of children.

In 1892 the eminent Johns Hopkins Professor of Medicine William Osler (1849–1919) became the fourth president of the Society. Osler concluded that the society's professional fellowship offered "to men who are working and teach in pediatrics an opportunity of knowing each other, of discussing subjects of common interest, and through the medium of their publications making general the more special details of value in practice."[97] This emphasis on scientific thought provided "precise and critical" methods that created "well trained" practitioners and attracted "first-class men" into the profession.[98] An emphasis on high professional standards based on the growing body of scientific knowledge was needed, as Frank Spooner Churchill, professor at Rush Medical College and head of the American Medical Association's Section of the Diseases of Children noted, because "personal ignorance" on the part of physicians, parents, and society was the major problem faced by the young specialty.[99] The successful professionalization and public recognition of pediatric practice required the continued education of colleagues, other practitioners, and the public about the abilities and skills of pediatricians. These steps were necessary, as a Louisiana physician concluded, because "if the physician to whom they naturally look, and to whom they apply for correct information is unable to give it," then the public may conclude that "the doctor does not know much more than other men, notwithstanding his collegiate education, his diploma, and his high pretensions."[100] The expanding range of skills and the growing body of medical knowledge that pediatricians possessed promoted the acceptance of their authoritative position and action. The increasing number of physicians who specialized in children's diseases (11 percent of medical students in 1920 entered the specialty) was further evidence of the rising importance of pediatrics as a medical specialty. This rate of increase was unequalled by other rapidly developing medical specialties—including surgery, obstetrics, and ophthalmology.[101]

While scientific knowledge promoted the professionalization of pediatricians, professional organization enabled physicians to address the many social issues that confounded the health care of children. In this role pediatricians helped shape American public policy as it related to children's health. Pediatricians not only treated and tended sick children but also became the spokespersons for the "weakest members of the community."[102] Voicing concern for issues related to children and for a larger social consciousness as well, pediatricians called attention to the specific social and economic issues that promoted ill health.[103] In the process they furthered public health campaigns that provided safe milk supplies, immunized children, and reduced infant mortality.

Pediatricians argued that preventive measures—immunization, nutrition, counseling—that promoted children's health were especially important "to secure a really healthy generation."[104] These issues included not only public health measures, like vaccination and sanitation, but also school health problems, the construction of playgrounds, the control of child labor practices, and a myriad of other social questions and problems that faced American children. The American Pediatric Society, speaking as a body of professional and societal experts on children's health, was in a position to "guide the progress of various reforms connected with early life . . . so that they do not go astray."[105] Pediatricians helped formulate and direct American social policy. The health care of American children increasingly included more than the day-to-day care of sick children. Pediatricians correctly understood that solutions to many of the complex problems of children's health were situated within the maze of broader social discourse. Scientific developments might occur in an isolated laboratory, but the solutions to the problems of children's health were found in the application of that knowledge in the tenements and on the playgrounds of the nation.

While a majority of pediatricians supported an emphasis on the social basis of children's health, some did not. During the first decade of the twentieth century, no less a figure than Emmett Holt opposed this broader social agenda. He argued against too "large [a] part of the work of this Society devoted to subjects of this kind which, though of sociological interest," did not emphasize "matters more strictly medical."[106] Medical science and the experience of daily medical practice formed the basis of twentieth-century pediatric practice, but increasingly Holt's reservations were replaced by an emphasis upon a biosocial model of children's health, a move that enabled pediatricians to extend their influence "to the millions of homes throughout the land."[107] In the process, as Jacobi noted, pediatricians occupied a seat on "the councils of the republic" and were "the legitimate adviser[s] to the judge and the jury."[108] Physicians in general, and pediatricians in particular, viewed children's health as both a biological science and a social science. In short, pediatricians had both medical and social functions. They advised judges and penal institutions on delinquency, they informed educators on children's health and its maintenance, they lobbied politicians for greater funding for child welfare, and they counseled parents about the growth and development of their children. Within a quarter of a century, Holt also recognized this dual role for pediatricians. "The duty of the pediatrist . . . is not only to advance knowledge in all subjects related to the growth and health of children, but to see that such knowledge is applied, for of what value is our knowledge unless it is used."[109] By helping the nation solve the problems of children's health, pediatricians reduced death and suffering for American children and defined and promoted their professional position as the experts on child care.

By the early twentieth century, pediatricians were "citizen[s] of a commonwealth, with many rights and great responsibilities."[110] Physicians faced both professional and social questions. Their efforts to aid children, treat disease, and, especially, to prevent disease with "public hygiene" were powerful tools in promoting children's health and the overall social position of children. Pediatricians not only had tools that aided children but also recognized and accepted the social responsibility that accompanied the position of children's doctor and child advocate. The skillful use of this knowledge enabled "a child to be well born, to come into the world strong and healthy, to thrive lustily without halt in infancy, to develop and grow in a normal way during childhood, to be able physically and mentally to attain a sound education, to acquire good habits of living and avoid bad ones, to avoid psychological abnormalities so that the child adjusts himself to his social environment."[111] Practitioners who promoted this broadly conceived biological and social nurture of children had attained a unique position based on their scientific knowledge, professional organization, and policy advocacy. These efforts benefited America's children and facilitated the birth of "the century of the child."

Many immigrant families lived in crowded and unhealthy tenements, such as this room on New York's Lower East Side.
Photograph "Room in a Tenement Flat" 1910 by Jessie Tarbox Beals. Reprinted by permission of the Jacob A. Riis Collection, Museum of the City of New York .

5

Cleanliness Is Next to Godliness

In an era when flies often occupied the next place at the dinner table and Americans "would believe anything, eat anything, drink anything—and with the sorriest kind of results," a frontier Kansas doctor sold the nation on a campaign to "swat the fly." In 1905 Samuel J. Crumbine, secretary of the Kansas State Board of Health and later a leader of the American Child Health Association, began his cleanliness campaign with ball park calls for a "sacrifice fly" and a "swat" from the next batter.[1] Within days and with the aid of a local school teacher, Crumbine (1862–1954) developed the fly bat into the fly swatter and launched a campaign for personal and public hygiene that placed cleanliness next to godliness in the minds of millions of Americans. This effort was accomplished by posters and flyers that described the means of constructing fly swatters. Children were urged to wage war upon the lowly fly. Chicago school children, for example, received awards for capturing the most flies. Even brick sidewalks were laid with public health messages that encouraged hygiene and promoted cleanliness baked into stone.[2] In essence, as John M. Toner told the first annual meeting of the American Public Health Association in 1873, the duties of the sanitary physician "in places . . . interlace with those of the moralist and the priest."[3]

Health concerns extended beyond "disease breeding flies" and included inadequate sanitary facilities, unclean water supplies, contaminated milk, and the general failure to check the spread of childhood disease. Flies became merely the visible symbol of the importance of cleanliness as a means of disease prevention. Too few Americans realized that the fly that "feeds at your privy and greets you with unwashed lips and unwiped feet in your parlor and at your dining table" carried the microbial agents of disease from contaminated cesspools and ailing patients to the healthy. Death and disease were the result for thousands of American children. Crumbine and other public health leaders throughout the nation realized that the battle against unsanitary living conditions would only be won when "the mothers of babies and the makers of homes" recognized that the fly and other unsanitary conditions were enemies of the public health.[4] A successful campaign against unwanted disease and unhealthy living conditions required that mothers, physicians, and health officers mount a joint effort against death and disease.

The prevention and eradication of disease became the hallmark of physicians' efforts during the burgeoning sanitary campaign. Treatment of disease remained important, but increasingly the goal was to "check or eradicate the epidemic."[5] This effort was based upon the application of the principles of "scientific medicine," especially the now more widely accepted tenets of the germ theory. Physicians, who studied the principles of bacteriology and the spread of infectious disease with the aid of the microscope and the bacterial culture, were in a unique position to identify, study, and eradicate the causes of infectious disease. In 1902 Alice Hamilton, a physician and resident of Chicago's Hull House, used these methods against a neighborhood epidemic of typhoid fever. With the aid of two other residents of the settlement house, she collected flies from "privies and filthy water closets." "We would drop the flies into tubes of broth and I would take them to the laboratory, incubate the tubes and plate them out at varying intervals. It was a triumph to find the typhoid bacillus."[6] While these measures made Hull House "an oasis in a desert of disease and monotony,"[7] larger measures than the identification of disease were needed if the infant mortality rate on Chicago's West Side, which was seven times greater than the rate in affluent Hyde Park, was to be reduced. The basic problem, as the young reporter for the *Chicago Daily News*, Carl Sandburg, concluded in 1919, was "a gaunt involuntary poverty."[8] In this context, swatting flies was truly symbolic of the much greater problems of providing sanitary sewers, ventilated housing, clean food, and pure water. The elimination of these problems required "the scrutiny of scientific investigation"[9] to find and identify the microbial causes of disease and the education of the public so that they were "in touch with the profession."[10] In other words, public, as well as professional, education was necessary. If those with consumption were not to spit on the street and diphtheria was not to threaten the child with a sore throat, then the public, and particularly mothers, had to learn that "cleanliness was next to Godliness." In so doing, the "hearty educated support of the quarantined," led by "scientific" physicians, would save thousands of lives each year.[11]

The pragmatic approach to disease prevention was based on an understanding of the germ theory and an acceptance that human not divine intervention both caused and potentially prevented infectious diseases. However, sanitary reformers equated cleanliness with godliness in order to establish a moral basis for public health measures. Cleanliness of the body was but an external manifestation of the purity of the soul, reformers claimed. As a result, there was "religion in cleanliness, in ventilation and in good food." This rhetoric was actually and symbolically manifest in the popular discourse of the day. Pear's soap advertisements concluded that soap "must be considered as a Means of Grace and a Clergyman who recommends moral things should be willing to recommend soap."[12] The maintenance of the public health was a moral duty for the mothers of the nation, it was believed, just as republican motherhood had been a century before. This chapter will consider the role that physicians, nurses, health officers, and parents played in the adoption of sanitary and public health measures that reduced childhood death and disease at the start of the twentieth century. The successes and failures of these efforts were illustrated in national campaigns to reduce infant mortality and to provide a pure milk supply.

The Nature of Cleanliness

Germ theory provided a new understanding of disease that offered the public and physicians specific means of disease prevention like hand washing and the drainage of public sewers. By 1900 few physicians and health officers still believed that infectious diseases were spread by vague miasmas, spirits, and unknown plasmas. They had replaced the ideas of the English sanitary reformer Edwin Chadwick (1800–1890) that "all smell" was disease[13] with the knowledge that microbes—small but physically identifiable agents—transmitted common diseases like tuberculosis, diphtheria, scarlatina, and whooping cough. The identification and recognition of these agents documented the transmissible and communicable nature of infectious diseases. The work of European investigators, particularly Pasteur in France, Koch in Germany, and Lister in England, provided physicians with the bacteriological principles of disease prevention.

As physicians came to understand the germ theory, they did not immediately alter their clinical treatment of infectious diseases. In fact, such measures did not develop until the middle third of the twentieth century when antimicrobial agents like the sulfa drugs and penicillin were developed. While the therapy of infectious diseases did not dramatically change, methods of disease prevention were possible. The same methods that Pasteur utilized to prevent disease in his studies of silkworms formed the basis for the prevention of human disease. Pasteur's experiments in the isolation and quarantine of silkworms, fermenting wine, or infected animals became the foundation upon which disease transmission in humans was prevented. Germs that spoiled wine and soured milk were bred in dirt and filth. By swatting the fly and scrubbing the privy, physicians, public health workers, mothers, and the public eliminated the common sources of dirt, filth, and disease. In turn,

their efforts promoted a healthful world, one that sparkled from the eradication of disease and the prevention of infant death. Nowhere were these
facets of medical progress more clearly recognized than for childhood infectious diseases; and nowhere were results more successful than in the efforts
that provided a pure milk supply for America's children.

The first step toward the prevention of infectious diseases was an understanding of the extent of the problem. Compilation of such information was
difficult, since before the 1870s few cities or states maintained vital statistic
records. New York in 1866 was the first major city to establish a board of
health, and three years later Massachusetts became the first state to establish
the systematic collection and analysis of vital statistics.[14] The state agency
that collected and analyzed statistics was an outgrowth of the "Report of
the Massachusetts Sanitary Commission," the first major American docu-
ment on public health. This work was written by a layman, Lemuel Shattuck
(1793–1859) and emphasized the need for the accurate collection of vital statistics under the direction of a health officer with the enforcement of sanitary
measures performed by health inspectors. Disease was no longer merely "a private misfortune," but rather the failure of prevention was "an offense to public
order."[15] Physicians, mothers, and the American public had a moral and a
political mandate for disease prevention.

The problems that faced the proponents of sanitary reform were not
new. "This slaughter of innocents," as the president of the Milwaukee Board
of Health concluded in 1872, was "found chiefly, in crowded parts of the
city, where families are massed together, in filthy, dark, ill ventilated tenements, surrounded by dirty yards and alleys, foul privies, and imperfect
drainage."[16] Jacob Riis (1849–1914), described by Theodore Roosevelt as
"the most useful citizen of New York," reported similar problems among the
filth and squalor of the nation's largest city.[17] Immigrants and the poor experienced the most significant problems. One-third of Italian immigrants in
Buffalo, New York, died from "unsanitary conditions."[18] Similar problems
befell the Irish in Boston, the Germans in Chicago and Milwaukee, and the
Portuguese in Providence. In 1895, in the first systematic investigation of an
American immigrant community, Florence Kelley of Hull House recognized
that ignorance, poverty, and unsanitary living conditions "insure[d] the max-
imum probability of disease."[19] The poor died more frequently than the rich,
from which the secretary of the New York Charity Organization Society concluded that "ill health is perhaps the most constant of the attendants of
poverty." Measles, which trod "ever so lightly on the avenues," killed "right
and left" in the tenements.[20] Riis reported three blocks of New York's
Elizabeth street where such an epidemic "had spent its fury." "The death-
maps in the Bureau of Vital Statistics looked as if a black hand had been laid
across those blocks." The disease track through the "teeming barracks" of
the street was as "clearly defined as the track of a tornado through a forest

district." When families sought to care for their sick children, their poverty and the "wretched home conditions" made their efforts futile.[21] Because the eradication of death and disease was beyond the control of individual families, broader public efforts were required if the health of the nation's children was to improve.

Children's health was not necessarily better in smaller cities. The 1890 United States Census called Newark, New Jersey, (population of 180,000) "the nation's unhealthiest city." Considering Newark's size, compared with nearby New York City, more than one thousand extra deaths proportionally occurred each year in Newark.[22] Perhaps these problems were not surprising in a city where seven cents per capita was spent by the board of health and where two-thirds of the population relied upon privies and cesspools without sewer drainage. Consequently, the populace employed "garbage strewn streets" for the disposal of "kitchen slops," wash water, and other sewage.[23]

This public sanitary disarray was evident to local observers as well as national officials. The *Newark Daily Advertiser* reported in June 1883 that "[o]ur weekly mortality reports show the outbreak from time to time of preventable diseases in certain quarters, easily traceable to direct violations of the rules of health, and the ratio of deaths is generally above average of our sister cities. If further evidence was needed we have only to use our eyes and noses to discover abounding causes.[24]

When sewage was not deposited on the streets of Newark, the Passaic River was employed as an open sewer. This stream was so heavily filth-laden that in May 1890 *The Sunday Call* concluded that the "lives of more people are menaced by the sewage-laden water, than by any other agency." The paper reported that 500,000 persons downstream were "directly or indirectly, exposed to the disease-breeding effluvium and noxious odors of the river."[25]

Poor sanitary disposal facilities were not limited to the urban east. In 1896 eight cities along the Mississippi River reportedly "deposited 152,675 tons of garbage, manure and offal, 108,250 tons of night soil, and 3,765 dead animals into the waters of the nation's largest river.[26] At nearly the same time the Chicago Board of Health reported that a "rise in the water pollution line" in the city was "followed with almost mathematic accuracy by a rise in the death line of acute intestinal disease and of typhoid fever."[27] Alice Hamilton confirmed this circumstance when she surveyed 2,002 Hull House neighborhood homes for typhoid fever. The problem was "greatest in those streets where removal of sewage [was] most imperfect."[28] These efforts across the nation provided documentation of the ill health of many children and adults in America's cities and towns.

This chaotic state of health among late-nineteenth-century Americans was ameliorated by application of the new knowledge of the germ theory, particularly by improving public sanitation. In spite of the fact that many authorities, including physicians, believed that those most affected by the problem, the poor and the foreign born, were uneducable on such matters, the late nineteenth and the early twentieth centuries saw major changes in the promotion of public health. Some measure of the success of these efforts was found in the changing causes of death for Americans. From the mid-nineteenth century until 1915, the crude death rate decreased by one-third, and the average male life expectancy increased by 12 years. Most of this change occurred in the decades between 1880 and 1920. The most significant factor in this change was the decrease in the frequency of infectious diseases and their replacement by cardiac diseases as the leading cause of death for Americans.[29] Clearly, physicians and the public alike had succeeded in efforts to swat the fly, build sewers, and clean privies. In the process the health of America's children had dramatically benefited.

The large-scale public health and sanitary measures necessary to eliminate infectious disease were based in the home. Admittedly public efforts including clean water and safe milk were important, but when houses were properly constructed, adequately ventilated, and drained by sanitary sewers then pure air and cleanliness filled the home. Within the nursery special attention to hygiene prevented the spread of disease.[30] These steps toward domestic hygiene were perhaps more easily achieved on an individual scale than on a national, even citywide, scale. As Joseph Edwards concluded in *How We Ought to Live* (1882), "you cannot look into the sewer and see whether it is clean or not. But, into all the arrangements of your own individual house you can peer at all times, and can plainly see whether they are right or not."[31] On this personal level, women, who were seen as protectors of the moral order of the home and the nation, through mass education became the leaders of the day-to-day campaign for disease prevention.[32] Mothers became more than mere observers as they were inspired with the aim of saving their children "from needless illness." Consequently, Mrs. Max West, a popular adviser of mothers, in her publications emphasized cleanliness and sunshine as the formulas for feeding and rearing healthy children.[33]

Increasingly, both mothers and their pediatric advisers recognized the harmful nature of germs—those "microscopic plants of very simple structure"—which were spread by persons suffering from infectious diseases and were transferred by flies, sewage, dirty hands, and other communal instruments to milk, food, water, and healthy people.[34] Health officers counted their successes in flies killed, sewers installed, or privies drained, and tabulated the number of houses quarantined and children vaccinated. These activities all provided evidence of successful public health measures and the direct application of an understanding of the principles of the germ theory. As a result, fewer American children died from recognized infectious diseases, like diphtheria, smallpox, and typhoid fever.

The Medical Application of Sanitary Measures

Tuberculosis was not recognized as an infectious disease until the German Robert Koch isolated the tubercle bacillus in 1882. Because the disease spread insidiously, it was initially less easily controlled than many other communicable diseases. Public health measures for the eradication of this condition became important, although hard to implement. Control measures were essential. As Dr. Henry S. Baker, secretary of the Michigan State Board of Health, advised an 1890 meeting of the state sanitary commission, the "communicable diseases," of which consumption (tuberculosis) was "one of the most dangerous," "can be restricted."[35] He concluded prevention was crucial because 200 of every 100,000 Americans died of the disease.[36] While not dramatic in onset like smallpox nor rapidly fatal like diphtheria, tuberculosis, or the white plague, was easily spread by the congestion, overcrowding, and inadequate ventilation of urban centers like the "lung block" on New York's East Side reported by Ernest Poole. Poole counted nearly 4,000 human inhabitants, including 400 babies, but by his own account did not count dogs, cats, parrots, and at least one "weakened old monkey."[37] Living in this environment, where others of her family had died, one young girl "took the Plague" in "the winter, when cool had gone up, when the sleepless nights grew freezing cold." She had that "pitiful, hunted look which young eyes must have when suddenly meeting death," and she knew what the cough meant when it shook "her thin hollow chest."[38] Turn-of-the-century physicians offered young consumptives few remedies, other than anodynes and cough syrups, which were not effective.

While the treatment of tuberculosis was ineffective, the disease was preventable by the application of the principles of public health.[39] Campaigns began in New York City and soon were implemented in other urban and rural areas around the nation. Public health officials directed efforts that mandated the reporting of infected individuals, their accurate diagnosis with bacterial cultures, and official supervision of their isolation. Other measures that promoted cleanliness and disinfected the tenements and homes also reduced spread of the disease. The provision of visiting nurses and neighborhood dispensaries provided the public with easier access to professional care. The success of all these efforts, however, required public education about the disease and especially the fundamental means of disease prevention. Pamphlets, circulars, and notices were printed and posted, and lectures scheduled and given around the city.[40] Too often, as Samuel J. Crumbine concluded after attending the 1908 International Congress on Tuberculosis, "we suffer from disease through ignorance." The solution was education, which provided an "escape through knowledge" from death and disease.[41] One measure of the extent of this campaign was the more than 50-fold increase in the number of antituberculosis organizations, from 24 in 1905 to

1,285 by 1923.[42] These efforts were accompanied by reams of publications and fewer deaths from the disease, but tuberculosis remained an important health problem among poor families. Native American, black, and immigrant children more frequently contracted the disease, and as a result their coughing spread the tubercle bacillus to their peers more often than to children with better living conditions. Public education and preventive practices alone, without attention to the problems of the overcrowded housing and poor sanitation that accompanied poverty, limited effective control of tuberculosis and many other infectious diseases.

At least as troublesome as tuberculosis were viral conditions like infantile paralysis (poliomyelitis). In 1916 there were record numbers of cases—more than 27,000 cases with 6,000 deaths occurred in 26 states. One federal official concluded that this disease was a "menace for the future." The problem was especially perplexing because the disease was apparently transmitted and spread like an infectious disease, yet no microbial cause was found. Indeed, in the absence of isolation of the virus now known to cause the disease, proposed causes included moldy flour, poisonous caterpillars, foul sewage odors, Swedish gooseberries, and, as one San Francisco man concluded, electric radio waves that caused "pressure on brain substance and madness."[43] Physicians and the public were frustrated by an apparent infectious disease for which no bacterial cause was found. At the same time, the condition was terrifying not only because it caused death and paralysis but because before 1900 the largest known epidemic of the disease had been the 132 cases reported from Vermont in 1894. Disinfection, isolation, and other public health measures reduced the spread of infantile paralysis, but complete eradication awaited the development of an effective vaccine during the 1950s.

In 1918 the pandemic of Spanish influenza also caused many Americans to question the reliability of the principles of the germ theory. In the first week of October 1918, 159 citizens of Providence, Rhode Island, died, including at least 98 with Spanish influenza or pneumonia.[44] In Chicago, where on 17 October 1918, 2,395 new cases of influenza and 381 deaths from the disease were reported, and where more than 47,000 cases with 6,905 deaths were tabulated by year's end, preventive measures were undertaken.[45] There was no cure for the condition, and the sacks of garlic that children in Butte, Montana, wore about the neck did not "ward off some of that influenza."[46] In short, as the poet and physician William Carlos Williams concluded, "we hadn't a thing that was effective in checking that potent poison that was sweeping the world."[47] Officials promoted public education about preventive measures, including the quarantine of infected cases, the prohibition of open coughing, spitting, sneezing, and the elimination of public assemblies, including funerals. The Chicago Health Commissioner concluded that "the sooner everybody joins in fighting the epidemic the quicker it will disappear."[48] But the disease toll did not immediately decline, and before it did hundreds of thousands of deaths were recorded worldwide.

If viral diseases, like poliomyelitis and influenza, challenged the possible validity of the germ theory, a century of success with vaccination against smallpox confirmed that disease prevention was possible. When vaccination was routinely performed, the inference, as one health officer concluded, was that "small-pox can be utterly eradicated."[49] Presumably, the safety and efficacy of smallpox vaccination was so great that homeopathic physicians, who favored minute quantities of therapeutic agents in the belief that the least quantity of a drug was the most therapeutic, often favored vaccination. One homeopath concluded that "through vaccination the triumphs of homeopathy have been shown to the world by innumerable blessings, in arresting such a loathsome disease as small-pox."[50] Physicians were convinced, based on their success with smallpox, that the scientific principles of the germ theory prevented needless deaths from infectious diseases.

Physicians were readily convinced of the efficacy of vaccination, but the public was not always certain of the efficacy or safety of the procedure. Some deaths occurred following vaccination, and some of those vaccinated had fever, pustules, and even abscesses from the procedure. One Michigan woman, who was vaccinated more than four weeks before, "had a very sore arm and it discharges yet. I think I was as sick with it as most of them have been with the smallpox." This woman tolerated the ill effects of vaccination because there was a "terrible scare" in the community with death and quarantine throughout the city. One "little babe only five weeks old" was so severely afflicted that the doctor "had to lance it in different places several times."[51] While some feared the morbidity and mortality associated with smallpox vaccination, others, especially immigrants, were reportedly ignorant of the potential benefits of the procedure. Many physicians agreed with a Milwaukee practitioner who concluded that these opponents were "cranks" and "blockheads, who will not be convinced, and I think it will be quite useless to attempt to educate them."[52] A Kansas physician concurred with his Wisconsin colleague and concluded that "only by compulsory law" can adequate vaccination be completed.[53] Other health officers noted that inadequate facilities, time, finances, or supplies of vaccine were available to complete the task of vaccination. All of these problems resulted in Americans not being vaccinated against smallpox, and often those who were not—children, the poor, and immigrants—were the very populations at greatest risk of infection. They lived in the most crowded housing, had the most limited sanitary facilities, and often incompletely understood the reasons and methods for disease prevention.

When large numbers of the population were unvaccinated, the spread of smallpox even to epidemic proportions was common. Consequently, cities actively campaigned to prevent such problems. For example, in 1894 the Newark Board of Health expended 70 percent of its $24,500 budget for the quarantine, therapy, and vaccination of smallpox patients.[54] These efforts prevented many cases of smallpox, but by the early twentieth century, many cities, like Boston, New York, Philadelphia, and Cleveland, each still reported more than one thousand cases of the disease with a mortality rate of 20 percent.[55] Most of these cases were preventable, but both incomplete vaccination and failed quarantine procedures allowed the disease to spread to unprotected children and adults. In crowded New York tenements, "it has happened more than once that a child recovering from smallpox, and in the most contagious stage of the disease, has been found crawling among heaps of half-finished clothing that the next day would be offered for sale on the counter of a Broadway store."[56] Unfortunately, the unsuspecting customer purchased the garment impregnated with enough smallpox virus to infect an entire neighborhood. When Florence Kelley investigated the sweat shops of Chicago in 1894, she found cases of the disease among garment workers and their families, as well as evidence that only 5 percent of the workers were vaccinated against smallpox.[57] The continuation of these problems over the following two decades led Dr. Charles Chapin (1856–1941) of Providence to describe the United States as "the least vaccinated of any civilized country."[58]

Incomplete vaccination against smallpox, combined with overcrowded, unsanitary living conditions, caused epidemics of the disease. These factors and the crowds at the Chicago World's Fair caused an epidemic in the city in 1893 and 1894. More than 3,500 cases were treated at the Chicago Smallpox Hospital. There were 1,033 deaths, and, reportedly, 1,084,500 doses of smallpox vaccine were administered.[59] Father George D. Heldmann, the facility's chaplain, recorded the terror and fear of afflicted families: "In that awful season I saw more babes and children deserted by mothers who feared infection than I had ever believed possible. I saw fathers and sisters and brothers innumerable who begged and pleaded and fought to be allowed to stay with little ones who had the disease, when in so many cases the mothers had fled at the first warning. In one case that I recall the whole family had fled with all its belongings, leaving two little ones frightfully ill in the deserted house."[60] As the World's Fair ended, Florence Kelley (1859–1932) discovered similar problems among the immigrants of Chicago's West Side, where she found parents who often feared the disease whether received by vaccination or natural infection: "Many infants and little children we found concealed on closet shelves, wrapped in bundles, sometimes to keep them from being vaccinated, sometimes to keep them— with the disease so fully developed that concealment was unthinkable—

from being sent to the sorely dreaded hospital."[61] These scenes were especially pathetic because, as both Heldmann and Kelley recognized, vaccination prevented the disease.

The success of preventive methods, like vaccination and improved sanitation, encouraged pediatricians to emphasize disease prevention for infectious diseases, rather than disease treatment (which was generally unavailable or ineffective in the pre-antibiotic era) as the cornerstone of the care of America's children.[62] Ultimately, this preventive philosophy led pediatricians beyond the bedside and the hospital. As Abraham Jacobi predicted, pediatricians entered the schoolhouse, the health department, and the state legislature, where they were "legitimate adviser[s] to the judge and the jury" and "councils of the republic."[63] If the problems that contributed to the poor health of the nation's children were to be solved, then pediatricians and politicians needed not only medical solutions but social and political ones as well.

As physicians entered the council chambers of the nation's governments, stronger public health programs were initiated. Many of these measures, including the codification of health statutes and their regular enforcement, were proposed nearly a century before by the founder of the modern public health movement, the German Johann Peter Franck (1745–1821).[64] His six-volume work on the subject was based on the enlightenment principles of "erudition and rich practical experience" tempered with humanitarianism extended from the "womb to the tomb."[65] Franck's counsel was perhaps more useful to politicians than physicians, but, nonetheless, a comprehensive codified system that provided provisions for enforcement became the model for American public health programs. As a result, physicians, health officials, and citizens all received a mandate for political and moral reform that prevented disease.

By the early twentieth century, a political framework for American public health programs was developed and instituted. As the results with polio, smallpox, and tuberculosis illustrate, both successes and failures were reported. These initial endeavors were limited, and early advocates of the process recognized that expanded efforts were needed if preventable diseases were to become less frequent. Charles Chapin advised the American Public Health Association that there was "so much to be done and so little to do it with. There are so many technical problems to be solved, and there are so many difficulties outside of the health department, in the way of efficient administration, that one fears it will be a long time before the dreams of the enthusiasts come true."[66] The early twentieth-century public health campaigns that reduced infant mortality and ensured a safe milk supply illustrated these circumstances. The health care of America's children was interwoven with the social fabric of society as a whole. Solutions to significant health problems required medical, social, and political action.

The Identification of a
Public Health Problem: Infant Mortality

The study of infant mortality was, and is, an especially "sensitive indicator" of community health. It "reflects the positive or negative influences exerted by various social factors" upon children's health. It is "particularly sensitive to environmental conditions, such as housing, sanitation, and pure food and water."[67] In other words, infant mortality is an indicator of the very factors that form the basis of and promote public health. Thus, as Josephine Baker, the first director of the New York City Bureau of Child Hygiene, concluded, "everything that affects the health of the child, from the beginning of the prenatal period to the end of adolescence"[68] forms the basis for children's health in general; and infant mortality is an especially sensitive indicator of the good or bad influence of these factors.

According to most observers, too many American babies died. In 1880, 288 of every 1,000 live-born infants in New York City died.[69] During the following decade in Milwaukee, 10 percent of all deaths were infant deaths, and during the first half of this decade the number of infants dying with gastrointestinal illnesses more than doubled.[70] As late as 1912, more than 1 in 10 New York children died during infancy, while the *Newark Evening News* reported a Russell Sage Foundation study that found that in 1910 more than 1,300 infants under one year of age had died in Newark.[71] These profound tragedies affected some segments of the population more than others. Most frequently, immigrant and minority infants died. For example, twice as many black as white infants died. The biggest difference between the death rates for black and white infants was seen in the rural South, where more than twice as many black babies died. Two-thirds of the deaths of black infants occurred in the first three months of life.[72]

Many factors, including poverty, poor housing, limited nutrition, and inadequate medical care, were responsible for these deaths. Infant deaths increased as the number of family members per room increased, as the family income decreased, and when mothers worked outside the home.[73] In addition, the president of the New Orleans Board of Health was of the opinion that southern black families (other officials included other immigrant and minority groups) were "as savage almost in their ideas of hygiene as their ancestors in Africa."[74] While this statement was clearly prejudicial in word and intent, it underscores the importance of education about the scientific ideas of health and hygiene for black and white, native and immigrant Americans for the reduction of infant mortality. The education of mothers about children's health was, according to the 1912 Annual Report of the American Association for the Study and Prevention of Infant Mortality (AASPIM), "the strongest weapon for fighting infant mortality."[75] By calling mothers to a moral campaign to save their children, physicians and health officers hoped that their educational programs would provide mothers with the tools to reduce infant deaths.

The ill effects of poverty were well known to turn-of-the-century observers. Jacob Riis recorded a child in a "dreadfully stifling room," stretched across two chairs with a "death sentence on her wan and pinched face." "The whole family, father, mother and four ragged children, sat around looking on with the strong resignation of helpless despair that had long given up the fight against fate as useless."[76] Poverty was so extreme for some families that they saved funeral expenses by the abandonment of their dead or dying children in the streets. As a result municipal authorities often provided for burials in "squads of a dozen." On at least one occasion, a police officer investigating an apparently abandoned corpse found "an inhuman wretch trying to bury" a live baby in a small pine coffin.[77] Such scenes were all too common, and according to one authority, the "most surprising" part of the story was that the mortality was the "greatest in the most enlightened centers."[78] Infants died more often in New York, Chicago, and other metropolitan areas than this early twentieth-century authority thought should. He reasoned this should not be the case since such localities were more affluent and had better medical and public services than other areas of the nation.

Institutionalized infants and children fared no better than, and often worse than, other poor or abandoned children. In 1909 Riis counted nearly 340 deaths among the 508 babies received at New York's Randall Island Hospital. He concluded that, given the conditions under which the infants lived, it was a "wonder" that any of them survived.[79] At the more prestigious Babies Hospital, infant death was also frequent. Emmett Holt, director of the facility, justified the apparent high death rate to the public and the profession by concluding that the increasing death rate in 1900 was "more apparent than real":

> We have received absolutely every child who has come to us without regard to its condition. There are institutions in this city where patients are not allowed to die on the premises if it can be avoided. To accomplish this requires a great deal of chicanery. . . . It is not pleasant of course to have a dozen babies sent to us, as happened last summer, who died within 24 hours, but our reward may be to save the thirteenth. If we have a high mortality rate it is certainly to our credit that we take greater chances. Our usefulness cannot be gauged by our death rate. I am positive myself that the results for this year have been relatively much better than before.[80]

Significant reductions in the frequency of infant death required not only good professional practices but also broad social programs. By the early twentieth century, physicians, health officers, advisers, and laywomen promoted programs that reduced infant mortality. New efforts that emphasized prenatal care and provided special attention to women during pregnancy were started. From Elizabeth Lowell Putnam in Boston to Samuel Crumbine in Kansas, these authorities offered evidence that prenatal care reduced infant mortality. Putnam showed that maternal deaths, premature births, stillbirths, and neonatal deaths were less than half as frequent among Boston women who received prenatal care than those who did not.[81] Crumbine agreed and suggested that diet, exercise, rest, sunshine, fresh air, and cleanliness during pregnancy, among other factors, all reduced infant mortality.[82] The Baltimore obstetrician and leading American authority on pregnancy care, J. Whitridge Williams (1866–1931), concluded that "no other prophylactic measure" than prenatal care provided the means "by which the lives of so many children can be saved."[83]

If prenatal care helped reduce infant mortality, not surprisingly, improved obstetrical care did also. American birthing practices dramatically changed during the early twentieth century. Physicians replaced midwives as birth attendants, operative births replaced spontaneous unassisted births, hospital birthing became standard, anesthesia was utilized, and women increasingly accepted the physician's voice in the birthing chamber.[84] In the middle third of the twentieth century, a more consistent application of sterile technique with childbirth, newly available blood transfusions, safer anesthetic methods, and more skilled operative obstetrical interventions made childbirth safer; but in the first decades of the century, little change in infant mortality accompanied the new birthing practices. In fact, during the first three decades of the twentieth century, maternal and infant deaths were more frequent with physician-assisted births than with those attended by midwives.[85] Rather than addressing the implications of this observation most physicians argued that midwives, not physicians, were responsible for these needless deaths and that the solution to the high frequency of infant deaths was the elimination of midwives. Since physicians were unwilling to accept responsibility for maternal deaths, they also did not alter their obstetrical practices and procedures at the patient's bedside. The result was that while physicians criticized midwives for the problem, through their own failure to adequately wash their hands and avoid needless obstetrical intervention, some mothers and infants died when they should not have.[86]

Although the larger issue of who should attend births remained problematic, simpler measures like eye washes for the newborn to prevent eye infections were available for use by both midwives and physicians. One authority estimated that neonatal infections were responsible for the blindness of 7,000 Americans.[87] The bacterial infections that caused ophthalmia neonatorum were easily prevented with routine instillation of a silver nitrate solution into the baby's eyes. The standardization of birthing practices, including routine eye prophylaxis, as exemplified by the inclusion and specification of these procedures in the publications of the federal Children's Bureau, was evidence not only of growing professional, public, and governmental interest in children's health but also of the expanding authority of governmental officials and programs in promoting the health of the nation's children.

Infant mortality, according to Emmett Holt in a 1913 address to the fourth annual meeting of the AASPIM, was the "great social and economic problem" of the day. It demanded a solution. The problem was not the loss of the "unfit" but rather the death of the "unfortunate."[88] In other words, many children died, not because they were biologically defective, but because society was sociologically defective. Adequate solutions were needed not only because unnecessary infant death caused needless economic losses for society but simply because the moral order and the humanitarian spirit required its correction. The social problems of poverty, inadequate housing, incomplete diets, and generally unsanitary living conditions, which were the basis for the medical problems of infectious diseases and improper or inadequate infant feeding, were initially addressed by expanding programs for parental advice, constructing new medical facilities, improving medical education, developing more advanced medical technology, and encouraging the public to utilize all of these efforts to reduce infant deaths. As with the prevention of neonatal blindness, the majority of infant deaths were preventable. Such efforts, as William Henry Welch (1850–1934), dean of the Johns Hopkins University Medical School and an authority on infectious diseases, told the inaugural meeting of the AASPIM, were part of "one of the most important campaigns in preventive medicine in this country."[89] Successful solutions required not only an attack on the medical bases of the problem by physicians and health officials but also the creation of broad-based social programs. Solutions were not immediately available, and, consequently, infant mortality did not immediately decline. In fact, near the end of the "century of the child," infant mortality in America remains excessive, and many deaths are preventable with attention to the social problems that plagued American families in 1915.

The Solution of a Public Health Problem: Pure Milk

While in the early part of the twentieth century infant mortality remained high, by 1930 the rate was declining because general living conditions were enhanced, disease was prevented by vaccination, nutrition was improved, prenatal and maternal health were advanced, and, perhaps most important, a system of pure milk supply and distribution had been established. While twentieth-century physicians and advisers recommended breast feeding, methods of artificial feeding became more readily available and successful; and more American women employed these alternatives. Successful artificial feeding required the application of the principles of the germ theory, like sterilization of bottles and the provision of pure milk, and nutritional knowledge about the composition of infant formulas. Interest in cow's milk as a nutritional source for infants and children was not new, but attention to measures that ensured its safe supply and healthful composition for infant feeding were. Before 1880 only 13 scientific articles were published about milk and infant health, an indication of the lack of interest by physicians about this topic. Over the next four decades more than 1,200 articles appeared, most after 1890. This newfound knowledge enabled the development of methods for safe and successful artificial feeding. Holt concluded not only that this task was "the most important branch of pediatrics" but also that "at no other time in life does prophylaxis give such results as in the conditions of infancy."[90] Infant feeding was not problematic because it was innately unhealthy, but the methods employed by most turn-of-the-century mothers were improper, inadequate, unsanitary, and often nutritionally incomplete. Consequently, as knowledge about artificial feeding became available from the chemical analysis of milk, the development of better feeding techniques, and the supply of bacteria-free milk, infant feeding became more successful.

Because of its widespread availability and similar composition to human milk, cow's milk became the standard replacement for infant feeding. Pediatricians, led by Thomas Morgan Rotch (1849–1914) in Boston and Emmett Holt in New York, established milk laboratories for the analysis and compounding of infant formulas based on cow's milk.[91] These often complex formulas, as a former student of Rotch recalled, were compounded "with a chemical composition, including fat, sugar, protein and acidity, that chemically equalled human milk."[92] Because each component was included on a precise percentage basis, this method was termed *percentage feeding*. Not all physicians accepted the percentage feeding methodology. Jacobi, for example, opposed it, and others, including a Boston physician, objected "to doing an algebraic or even considerable arithmetic sum at the bedside."[93] Despite problems with the daily use of percentage feeding, the development of this method not only provided an understanding of the nutritional composition of milk but also promoted the acceptance of milk as a basis for infant feeding. In the process pediatricians advanced their professional stature by becoming the recognized authorities on infant feeding. The complexity of this methodology and the initiative by physicians to gain its acceptance sent American mothers the message that infant feeding was "to be used only under the direction of a physician."[94] By recommending complex formulas that were compounded with difficulty and periodically altered for each baby, pediatricians placed themselves in an indispensable position as advisers about infant feeding.

By the 1890s physicians increasingly accepted the nutritional value of cow's milk, and most agreed that 90 percent of infants could be successfully artificially fed.[95] If large numbers of babies were to be artificially fed, simpler methods of feeding and widely available pure milk supplies were needed. Popular advice authors provided simplified recommendations for child feeding. In 1901 a Chicago woman based her work on "years of practical experience" and wrote her text so plainly that "anyone can understand it."[96] The work was apparently so useful that Henry T. Byford, an important Chicago obstetrician of the day, recommended that the work "be in the hands of every young mother."[97] From the mother's perspective feeding problems began with the purchase of milk and concluded with the washing of used baby bottles. In between, bottles and nipples required sterilization, and successful infant feeding necessitated a defined feeding schedule. Physicians also expanded "in detail" their knowledge about infant feeding.[98] While advice on feeding for mothers was being simplified, many pediatricians spent the next quarter of a century disputing the specific composition of infant formulas and the best methods of their preparation. The complexity of this discourse and the individual preferences that many physicians espoused complicated the daily tasks of infant feeding for many mothers.

At least as important for successful infant feeding as an understanding of the chemical composition of milk was the supply of pure milk. As early as 1881 bacteriological evidence was presented that milk-borne infections resulted from the bacterial contamination of fresh milk.[99] These early microbial studies of fresh milk soon were combined with the nutritional analysis of milk and provided pediatricians and health officers with accurate information about pure milk as the nutritional basis for infant feeding. The protein and fat content, the bacterial count, and even color and taste were analyzed. Health authorities and scientists established official criteria for and recommendations about infant feeding, and a precise definition of nutritious, high-quality milk. Nonetheless, the problem remained that commercially produced milk often contained "hairs from the cow, particles of excrement and all kinds of dust and dirt from a filthy barn, rusty cowpail, and dirty milkers."[100]

Physicians, health officials, crusaders for children's health, and mothers soon recognized that a pure milk supply was essential for safe infant feeding. A safe milk supply was necessary because "the world has come to realize," reported the *Brooklyn Daily Eagle,* that "disease may lurk in the innocent appearing fluid so necessary to infants."[101] The problem as Boston's Elizabeth Lowell Putnam told the Massachusetts Legislative Committee on Public Health in March 1912 was that milk was "one of the best foods for bacteria as well as for human beings, and under favorable conditions, one germ multiplied a million times within a very few hours."[102] Once contaminated, milk readily spread typhoid fever, scarlet fever, even diphtheria and tuberculosis. In 1900 more than 200 Harvard students contracted a streptococcal infection from milk that "showed pus and abundant streptococci" upon laboratory examination.[103] When properly and widely applied, the bacteriological analysis of milk provided the means to prevent the spread of infectious diseases to artificially fed infants.

Initial efforts to supply safe milk to urban children were based on European examples of farm and bottling inspection programs, particularly those employed in Hamburg (1889) and Paris (1892). Services were provided at milk stations where mothers received both fresh milk for their infant and health information for their family. In short, these were educational centers—"consultation des nourrissons."[104] Beginning in 1889 at New York's Good Samaritan Hospital, Dr. Henry Koplik established, on the European model, the city's first milk station and regularly dispensed milk and professional advice to attending mothers.[105] Nearly a decade later Rochester, New York, established the first citywide program of municipal milk stations. During the first two months of summer operation, 40,000 bottles of milk were dispensed at the four stations spaced throughout the city. The nurses (not physicians) that attended each station provided advice about children's health and dispensed pamphlets like "How to take Care of Babies During Hot Weather."[106] Importantly, these educational materials were printed in English, German, Italian, and Yiddish, so that both immigrant and native-born Americans benefited from the latest medical advice about infant feeding. Although initially designed to aid the poor, the facilities were patronized by mothers of all social classes. Participating mothers received the benefits of a safe milk supply for only a few cents each day, and the infant death rate in Rochester was reduced by 50 percent. During the eight years before the milk stations were established, 1,744 children under five years of age had died during July and August, while only 864 did so in the first eight years after the stations were started. This success was achieved with the expenditure of less than 10 dollars for each life saved. As one mother reported: "May God bless you. I have lost three children with summer complaint, and I think the milk and the book kept my fourth baby."[107] Mothers, physicians, nurses, and health officials jointly achieved this dramatic improvement in the health of children.

Milk is a natural culture medium for bacteria. It was easily contaminated with microbes during collection and storage. Refrigerated storage and rapid delivery of fresh milk were generally absent in turn-of-the-century America. Thus, milk stations alone did not ensure a safe milk supply. In addition to dispensing milk under sanitary conditions, the filthy conditions of its production on the nation's farms needed improvement.[108] Lay observers and state health inspectors reported cows that were tied in the dairy barn during the fall and not released from the "reeking filth" until spring. They observed "cows by the score, with tails rotting off by the disgusting nastiness in which they drag on their lives."[109] Not surprisingly, when notified of these dirty conditions, parents whose children consumed milk raised a public outcry for a safer milk supply. While some dairymen opposed efforts to produce pure milk by correcting dirty conditions, others cooperated fully in providing safer conditions for milk production. In 1910 a Waltham, Massachusetts, dairyman advised Putnam that the milk from Cedarcrest Farm was "produced under absolutely clean and sanitary conditions according to the most modern and approved methods." Interested parties were invited to visit the farm, "so that you can know under what conditions your milk is produced" for only 12 cents a quart.[110] Admittedly, some farms produced milk under clean conditions, but an adequate milk supply for an entire city required that hundreds, if not thousands, of farms also meet sanitary standards.

To encourage the cooperation of more dairy farmers, legal criteria for pure milk were established. During the first decade of the twentieth century, pure milk that met these legal criteria was termed certified. It was clean, pure, and natural just as it came from the cow and, most important, largely free of bacteria. Certified milk was not completely sterile, but rather contained relatively few bacteria, while milk produced under less acceptable conditions contained millions of bacteria.[111] Certified milk was safer for consumption because fewer bacteria were less likely to cause disease than were larger numbers of organisms. Fewer bacteria also meant that stored milk kept for longer intervals before it soured. Unfortunately, as the editor of the *American Dairyman* reported in 1905, less than 1 percent of all milk sold in America was certified.[112]

In addition to consumer demand for pure milk, an important factor in promoting more sanitary milk production was the formation of medical milk committees. The first was founded in 1893 by Henry L. Coit (1854–1917) in Essex County, New Jersey. Coit, a physician and the son of a Methodist minister, wrote his sister that same year that his intentions were "to revolutionize the entire milk business."[113] Other commissions were soon formed from New England to California. Within a decade, more than two dozen programs were active across the nation. Coit aided organizers from Ohio to Kansas as they established local programs. In June 1907, 125 physicians from 22 cities formed the American Association of Medical Milk Commissions. They worked for uniform national standards for the inspection and control of certified milk production. More certified milk was produced as more physicians, health officers, and private citizens encouraged the production of pure milk.

By 1916 an estimated daily production of 25,000 gallons of milk met the criteria for certification.[114] This represented less than 1 percent of the nation's total milk supply. The magnitude of the problem of producing pure milk was staggering. Each day New York City alone received milk from more than 30,000 dairies and farms. Dr. P. H. Mullowney, the Boston milk inspector, noted in his February 1912 report that 6,700 dairies, some more than 250 miles away, supplied the city of Boston.[115] At the same time, some authorities, including Coit, advised the Borden Condensed Milk Company

BORDEN'S

PURE MILK AND CREAM

Is produced under rigid rules and regulations governing the care of the cows and dairy buildings, the Milking, Bottling, Transportation and Delivery, which are substantially the same as when Gail Borden initiated the first system for the production of Pure Milk in the early '50s. This exacting system, combined with the most modern and scientific construction of Dairy Buildings, Utensils, etc., give you a safer milk supply than you can obtain elsewhere.

BORDEN'S GUARANTY IS SOME-THING YOU CAN DEPEND UPON

Borden's Condensed Milk Company

"LEADERS OF QUALITY"

Established 1857   NEW YORK

At the turn of the century, the assurance of a pure and safe milk supply was of concern to mothers, physicians, and city health officials.
Courtesy of Borden, Inc.

that the medical milk committees were not designed "to make possible a supply of milk for general consumption, but rather under strict medical control at close range, to obtain a grade of milk designed especially for medical purposes in the sickroom, in the hospital and for the feeding of delicate infants."[116] Coit and his medical colleague experts limited their supervisory role to the feeding of sick children; therefore, other methods were needed if all American children were to have a safe milk supply.

While some physicians, health officers, and health crusaders championed the production of certified milk, other authorities on children's health, including Abraham Jacobi, favored the pasteurization of milk—the intentional heating of milk without changing its chemical composition in order to destroy the bacteria and other microbes it contained. The process was named for the French bacteriologist Louis Pasteur, who demonstrated in 1857 that bacteria caused milk to sour. As early as 1873, Jacobi, in a paper read before the Public Health Association of New York, concluded that "cow's milk ought to be cooked at once in order to keep it as long as possible from turning sour. It ought to be preserved in a cool place if not in the ice box."[117] (Access to ice boxes was problematic for most Americans; as late as the 1920s, only about one-third of American homes had facilities for keeping milk on ice.) During the 1890s, studies that first established that pasteurization effectively killed bacteria and provided a safer milk were completed. For more than 15 years, physicians, health officers, and food scientists debated the timing, temperature, equipment, and detailed methodology of pasteurization. By 1906 the holding method of pasteurization, whereby milk was heated and held at approximately 160° for 20 to 30 minutes, was established as the accepted methodology.[118]

The regular use of pasteurization dramatically reduced the transmission of infectious diseases. In New York bovine tuberculosis in children and adults was reduced 60 percent. More dramatically, in Massachusetts more than 90 percent of the cases of the disease were eliminated by routine pasteurization.[119] In 1908 Chicago became the first city in the world to require pasteurization of the city's milk supply. Over the next decade the Chicago Department of Health reported that no epidemics of milk-borne infectious diseases had occurred. According to a spokesman for the city health department, this finding was "fully explained by the fact that ninety-eight percent" of the city's milk supply was pasteurized.[120] Other cities around the nation soon mandated this safe and effective means of promoting children's health.

Not all physicians supported pasteurization. Newark's Henry Coit opposed the process. In 1909 Joseph Winters, a New York pediatrician for 30 years, told the *New York Herald* that "pasteurization does not render dirty milk clean, stale milk fresh, nor germs harmless. Pasteurization is a recourse to palm upon a credulous public milk unfit for food."[121] Two days later the paper reported in a large headline that "the makeshift" process was a "humbug."[122] This interpretation of the value of pasteurization was supported by William Northrup, chief of Children's Diseases at New York's Bellevue Hospital. These physicians, some dairymen, and many members of the public opposed the pasteurization process because in their view it was not effective and the heating process destroyed the nutritional quality of the milk.

While physicians debated the merits of pasteurization, American mothers noted less illness in their children fed pasteurized milk. They received circulars and read newspaper and magazine accounts of the benefits of the process. In the September 1910 issue of *Good Housekeeping*, women were advised that mothers of the day could "do more to banish disease than [their] predecessor[s] who wielded broom and scrubbing brush in the pursuit of the virtue of cleanliness."[123] Home pasteurization units that reportedly had no effect on the taste or nutrition of treated milk were advertised for popular sale. Mothers not only had access to the latest popular information about infant feeding but now could employ these methods in their own homes.

In addition to supplying pure or pasteurized milk, many city health authorities, including those in Boston, New York, and Chicago, educated mothers. In Boston the Milk and Baby Hygiene Association had 10 milk stations that employed more than a dozen nurses. In addition to ensuring a safe milk supply, authorities conducted classes, gave lectures to high school students, ran prenatal care programs, and examined babies. Typically, one infant was examined with several mothers in attendance. Thus, all the mothers heard the advice given to other mothers, and each benefited from the instruction given the other women. "In this way mistakes made by one mother are pointed out to her in a kindly way and made to do duty as texts for the education of other mothers." Thorough education of mothers was needed, "not only to teach them how to care for their baby's milk, but also to convince them of the necessity of cleanliness."[124] The benefits for the nation's children rapidly multiplied, and fewer infants died from poor nutrition or the bacterial contamination of infant formulas.

Whether in Boston, New York, New Haven, or a dozen other cities, infant feeding programs decreased the frequency of infant death. Safer milk supplies provided at widely available milk stations to wiser mothers improved the health of the nation's children. During 1914, in New York City alone, municipal milk stations enabled the survival of 12 more infants for every 1,000 fed than in the general population. While a clean milk supply benefited all infants, poor families most frequently utilized the services of milk stations. Consequently, the benefits of milk stations were most dramatically seen among the poor. For example, among infants in the borough of Manhattan fed at supervised milk stations, 1,850 deaths were prevented. In Boston the infant death rate was twice as high in the city as a whole as it was for infants fed at milk stations. While these results were impressive, they indicated that wider application of successful programs would further reduce infant mortality. More complete solutions for the problems of infant feeding rested on more financial and political support. The officials of Boston's Milk Fund, for example, concluded that "the scope of the work is limited only by the amount of the contribution."[125] The expansion of children's health services on both a local and a national scale demanded governmental and public support. Medical solutions for the problems of infant feeding were at hand, but the larger social problem of poverty awaited attention.

Physicians based their medical practices and the care of the nation's children upon the technological tools that controlled infectious diseases. In 1925 the popular author Sinclair Lewis in his novel *Arrowsmith* placed his main character of the same name in a bacteriology laboratory beneath the signed icon of Robert Koch.[126] Life reflected art in the medical practice of the New York physician John Sedgwick Billings, who "worked four hours a day in a Tammany bacteriology laboratory."[127] On a July morning in 1902, Billings reported 102 diphtheria cultures before noon, but this performance paled in comparison to the 587 cultures reported in a single day the following April. Like Arrowsmith, Billings was mesmerized by "a cluster of organisms delicate as a narcissus, with their purple nuclei, their light blue cells, and their lives of the flagella."[128]

Applying the principles of the germ theory, physicians, nurses, health officers, dairymen, mothers, and the public prevented disease by pasteurizing milk, sanitizing sewers, and vaccinating children. But these measures did not reduce the toll of disease for children already suffering with disease or those too poor to benefit from incomplete programs. Physicians prevented the transmission of many cases of infectious disease by emphasizing cleanliness. But at least as important were efforts by nurses and health crusaders to educate mothers about infant feeding, baby hygiene, and good nutrition. In turn, maternal efforts in scrubbing floors, boiling water, and bathing children promoted children's health. The daily activities of mothers, pediatricians, and health officers reduced pain and suffering for many children; but too many of the nation's children still suffered and died from preventable diseases that life on the edge of poverty fostered.

Welfare worker visiting New York City tenements, early 1900s.
Reprinted by permission of the Community Service Society of New York and the Community Service Society Records, Rare Book and Manuscript Library, Columbia University.

6

The Century of the Child

When President Theodore Roosevelt called the first White House Conference on the Care of Dependent Children in 1909, he was responding to the call of social activists, like Lillian Wald (1867–1940), Jane Addams (1860–1935), and Grace Abbott (1878–1939). These women spoke for America's children, and Roosevelt spoke for the government and the people of the nation. This union of social and governmental efforts for children's health was necessary, as Wald advised Roosevelt, because "the national sense of humor was aroused by the grim fact that whereas the federal government concerns itself with the conservation of hogs and lobsters and has long since established bureaus to supply information concerning them, citizens who desire instruction and guidance for the conservation and protection of children have no responsible government body to which to appeal."[1]

During the previous three centuries mothers, organized religions, physicians, scientists, child savers, public authorities, and a multitude of private and public institutions all participated in the care of American children. But, if as the Swedish feminist Ellen Key (1849–1926) hoped, the twentieth century was to become the "century of the child," then an organized nationwide effort supported by federal programs was essential.[2]

The "century of the child" offered mothers, physicians, and child advocates new opportunities to promote children's health. From sanitarians to visiting nurses and pediatricians, professionals placed a renewed interest upon the health care of children. When 25 percent of draftees for the Great War were rejected because of ill health, poor vision, flat feet, and congenital heart disease and when 300,000 infant deaths occurred each year, it was no wonder that many Americans recognized the "conservation of child life" as a vital issue to the welfare and strength of the nation. Pediatricians did not want future generations to conclude that the "pediatric men of the medical profession in the United States were derelict in their duties."[3] In fact, as Henry Coit told the First Annual Meeting of the New Jersey State Pediatric Society in 1900, "conservation of child life is a question of vastly more importance to the American people and vital to the integrity of the nation than the conservation of minerals, rivers, or forest preserves."[4] These calls for increased attention to the health of children spurred governmental action and private campaigns, which, in turn, engendered a renewed nationwide interest in the problems of children's health. An emphasis on children, as Felix Adler concluded, was the "promise of something that is to be . . . the possibility of something finer, something better, something greater on this earth than has yet been."[5] Adler concluded that a society's attitude toward its children was an index of its civilization. From this perspective children's health in America was an essential measure of American civilization, but also, as the voices of Coit, Adler, and others recorded, it was an aspect of American culture that needed much more public and private support.

The late nineteenth century was a transitional era. Industrialization was on the rise, governmental institutions were proliferating, American society was melding and maturing, and science and technology were established in the hands of experts as the basis for the understanding and control of the world.[6] In the process, areas of knowledge as diverse as journalism, social work, psychology, and health care received new emphasis and new importance and offered new ways of understanding the lives of America's children. In essence the codification of thought during the progressive era and the emphasis on the role of the social sciences in daily life created new experts in children's health. Physicians solidified their position as the nation's authorities on children's health, child labor laws were enacted, juvenile delinquency was defined, and school reforms were started. Physicians alone were not responsible for this broader social vision; moral reformers, child advocates, mothers, social activists, teachers, judges, politicians, and philanthropists all worked to create the century of the child. One measure of this growing emphasis on children was the number of participants at the White House Conferences on Children. The first conference in 1909 had 200 attendees, while the third in 1930 boasted more than 3,000 participants. In short, "the wisest friends of neglected childhood"[7] sought solutions for the major social problems that faced children in a growing urban, industrial nation.

Medicine, which the medical historian and sociologist Henry Sigerist called the most social of all the sciences,[8] was at the heart of changes in American society during the progressive era. From the construction of hospitals to hospital-based childbirth to campaigns against infant mortality and for improved public sanitation, progressives and reformers offered a new vision of American life. Science, as the English socialist William Walking concluded in 1911, was "becoming more consciously pragmatic, more consciously concerned with the service of man," and the "most able and advanced" scientists, physicians, and social reformers utilized this new practical application of technology as the basis for improved children's health.[9] According to one thinker of the day, the "union of the idealist and the efficient" provided the ideological basis for changes in American society and changes in the health care of the nation's children.[10]

Progressive social reformers offered a new agenda for social reform. From educational practice to legal recognition of children and their rights, and from child labor control to the aid of mothers with dependent children, national social efforts were started that fostered the century of the child.[11] It was recognized that disease was a "removable evil" and that the elimination of social problems, like crowded housing, poor nutrition, and limited sanitation, could improve children's health.[12] Broad-based social programs with public and private support were needed, as Felix Adler, the chairman of the National Child Labor Committee, concluded, because only a "holy war" with "its object the stability of civilization as well as the welfare of the child" would yield conditions that promoted the growth of healthy American children.[13] This moral campaign against the problems that faced American children combined the duties of individual mothers with the scientific study of children's health to create public and private, lay and professional institutions and organizations. Physicians, social workers, psychologists, child advocates, and mothers worked side by side in local and national organizations, like the Congress of Mothers, the American Academy of Political and Social Sciences, and the American Association for the Study and Prevention of Infant Mortality, to further the health of American children. As a result, from the establishment of the federal Children's Bureau in 1912 to the defeat of renewed funding for the Sheppard-Towner Act in 1929, social programs were founded and political actions initiated for the benefit of the nation's children. This chapter considers children's health in America in relation to these social and political actions in the first decades of the twentieth century.

A Renewed Maternal Role

If moral reformers and social activists provided an ideology for the promotion of children's health and physicians among others provided the technological expertise to enable social change, then mothers were the agents of such change. Mothers, and only mothers, as President Theodore Roosevelt told the First International Congress on the Welfare of the Child, were better citizens than "the soldier who fights for his country." The successful mother was one "who does her part in rearing and training aright the boys and girls who are to be the men and women of the next generation, is of greater use to the community and occupies, if she only would realize it, a more honorable, as well as a more important, position than any successful man in it."[14] In short, the ultimate success of the century of the child, like the health of individual American children, was found in the arms of caring mothers.

While politicians and society emphasized mothers' role in children's health, women themselves both accepted and expanded their maternal roles. As one woman reported, "while there lives, or dies, one rickety baby, one sickly, ill nurtured, or diseased child, the task of the world's conscious womanhood is not completed."[15] The moral duty of women became a social duty, and, in turn, motherhood became, according to one woman of the day, the "passion of the day."[16] The widespread acceptance of this renewed emphasis on motherhood was exemplified by the formation of the National Congress of Mothers in 1897. The 2,000 delegates to the third congress in 1899 heard New York pediatrician Emmett Holt speak on the "Physical Care of Children."[17] By appearing before this body and, in effect, discussing normal children's care, Holt demonstrated the growing acceptance of medical science, including the principles of personal hygiene, childhood behavior, and teething, as the basis of modern child rearing. Further, he solidified the physician's position as expert adviser on the changing practices of child care.

Mothers and physicians alike were concerned with the care of individual children, but increasingly they addressed the social and political problems that confronted families and professionals across the nation. In addressing issues such as women's suffrage, child labor, children's health, and child advocacy, lay and professional spokespersons called on the moral duty of Americans to support their country and its children. By focusing what Florence Kelley called this "moral power"[18] on children's health, not only was social and political change achieved, but also within American society children came to be valued more highly.[19] On one level their value was priceless, but on another reductions in infant mortality and fewer deaths from smallpox and diphtheria suggested that specific social, medical, and political actions could increase their value. As a result of these efforts, individual mothers, the 190,000 members of the Congress of Mothers, pediatricians, and social reformers all recognized a new impetus for the promotion of children's health.

As mothers and their professional advisers jointly considered the problems of children's health, they addressed many new health problems about which there had previously been little concern. The accidental death of children was an important example. By 1900 fatal accidents involving children were no longer attributed to God's will, but rather "mothers were urged to take the burden of death off the shoulders of the Lord." The growing sense of social responsibility for such problems was demonstrated in the Newark episcopal rector's admonishment to his parishioners that God did not take these children "out of the world," but that they were "thrown out of it by those responsible for the crime."[20] Professional societies that promoted children's health, like the American Child Health Association, sponsored programs that reduced such needless tragedies. Increasingly, the public also accepted social responsibility for such problems and helped alleviate the personal burden of such losses. For example, a New York City family, whose nine-year-old daughter was killed by a trolley, received more than $87 in contributions for her funeral. These efforts were a response to a story in the *New York Times* that publicized the family's financial plight. "The last money we had was in Marion's hands when she was killed. She was going to the store to buy five cents of milk."[21] Professionals and citizens recognized that improved public safety measures, like school education programs and public notification about the dangers of trolleys, automobiles, and a myriad of other complexities of urban, industrial life, reduced accidental death. As a result, fewer children were killed or maimed, and fewer families needed emotional and financial support for their injured and dead children.

Children also died from accidental poisoning from teething syrups, cough remedies, anodynes, and any number of other medical elixirs. Many of these compounds, like Mrs. Winslow's Soothing Syrup, contained opium or chloroform, and some contained cannabis. Improper dosing or accidental ingestion of these potent active ingredients caused unnecessary deaths. A Mankato, Minnesota, health officer reported an 18-month-old child with the measles who was "peevish and cross." Over the 12 hours before death the child received more than "half the contents of the bottle" of a cough remedy, the composition of which the attending doctor was unaware. A subsequent analysis of the soothing syrup, performed by the state board of health laboratory, "found morphia." The child died from an opiate overdose, a diagnosis that this practitioner made with the aid of the best laboratory science of the day. In short, the "whole official and sanitary powers ha[d] been invoked in favor of little children."[22] Science prevented deaths from infectious diseases and, when directed in the service of other social problems, also reduced needless deaths and injuries.

Mothers, like physicians, applied scientific principles to the health care of their children. As governmental programs became available, mothers requested infant and children's health advice from these new sources of expert opinion. At the end of World War I, one woman advised the Children's Bureau of her needs in this regard: "I want very much a pamphlet of some kind containing instructions on the first things to do when the Baby arrives. . . . It's quite a distance in winter, when roads may be bad. . . . I want to get some practical directions so that a woman could do all the necessary things if the Dr. was not in time. I thought that you would have the latest and best information and would know just what to send me."[23] No longer were the traditional maternal virtues of "spirit, wit and resourcefulness" sufficient for child rearing, but "scientific reason" and the advice of experts supplemented maternal instinct as the basis for the daily care of children.[24] The "proper management of children" that formerly was "greatly neglect[ed]" became, as the popular medical writer Samuel Pancoast of Philadelphia advised his readers in 1901, the "most important subject that can be brought to the consideration of a parent."[25] Parents who followed the advice of their physicians were increasingly more successful with their children's health problems, and as they and their professional advisers addressed the larger social problems of children's health fewer children suffered from illnesses and died of accidental causes.

Physicians and lay advisers increasingly relied on the expanding body of children's health literature grounded in the scientific observation and study of the child. Physiology and psychology replaced domestic science as the basis for an understanding of children's health. The development of the child's emotional, social, and psychological worlds, not just the physical and moral worlds became important. According to *The Mother's Book* (1911), the application of these ideas was "intended to help the mother to develop and train her children in the best and wisest way from their babyhood until they reach adult years."[26] These efforts were necessary, as then Secretary of Labor Herbert Hoover concluded, because "the economic and social progress of the nation" was based upon the "physical, mental and moral health" of its children.[27] Only a partnership among mothers, physicians, social reformers, and politicians offered the social, economic, moral, and scientific tools needed to address the health problems of America's children.

The Science of Children's Health

The science of children's health began with an understanding of the normal growth and development of children. Standard tables and normal growth charts were published, and mothers were given detailed directions for weighing and measuring their children. When children were properly weighed and measured, comparison with "normality" easily followed, and mothers were able to demonstrate to themselves and society the successful completion of their maternal duties. Mothers who provided "the best hygiene possible" during the key years from two through six regularly demonstrated the adequate growth and development of their children.[28] By managing the "details of daily life," the feeding and care of their young charges, mothers promoted the health and well-being of their children.[29] Pediatricians provided mothers with both the methods of child rearing and the standards of success. Mothers needed advice; one woman noted that she was "going to live in a new oil field twenty-six miles from a Doctor, five miles from a telephone and a quarter of a mile from my nearest neighbor."[30] While some mothers needed advice that permitted their independent function without physicians, most advisers, in contrast to their nineteenth-century predecessors, did not intend "in any way to take the place of a physician, when a child is ill, but simply to enable mothers to take better care of their children."[31] The partnership that women and physicians formed extended from the tenements of New York to the Wyoming oil fields. With the expert pediatrician as the central authority on children's health, the most significant question for mothers, fathers, and teachers—"in fact, to everyone interested even remotely in children"—was "shall we send for the doctor?"[32]

From colic and thumb sucking to the common cold and fits, the troubled mother "must not trust to her sense of touch alone," but the thermometer and the measuring spoon were essential for the diagnosis of fever and for providing the proper dosage of medication. The reports of these technological tools were written in a scientific script that the expert physicians deciphered and from which in turn they dispensed the advice that benefited the nation's children. Such scientific analyses explained the often vague details and methods of complicated problems like infant feeding. In 1930 McKim Marriott, professor of pediatrics at Washington University in St. Louis, recognized the confusion of this seemingly simply task. He called his fellow pediatricians to task for the "bewildered" diversity of feeding methods. At the same time, McKim recognized that this confusion was not necessary, for the "fundamental facts" and requirements were "fairly well established."[33] Pediatricians understood the problems and the necessary solutions; what remained was the simplified translation of this knowledge and its daily application by mothers to the care of their children.

Parents, and especially young mothers, increasingly accepted the advice of pediatricians. So popular was this subject that it provided a basis for daily conversation, continuing education, and the foundation of a social cause.[34] During the post–World War I decade the promotion of motherhood offered women an alternative to the political endorsement of the suffragist movement. Full-time motherhood was socially approved, even sanctioned, "in the names of science and progressive education."[35] Republican motherhood beneath the gown of science remained at the heart of the health care of America's children. This renewed emphasis on motherhood also placed mothers and the family at the center of cultural assimilation. Many immigrants and native-born Americans accepted this new emphasis on mothers and children's health, and in the process the scientific principles of bacteriology and statistics shaped American lives and encouraged the acceptance of the broader aspects of American culture. Children benefited from these efforts with fewer illnesses, and their mothers more frequently recorded normal growth and development for their offspring.

As pediatricians and mothers accepted a scientific basis for children's health, so did the general public. Science provided solutions, according to the mayor of Milwaukee, for the central problems of children's health. Science enabled the smelting of ore into metal, and its manufacture "into the necessities of life."[36] Electrical appliances in the home, municipal supplies of water and natural gas, and public sanitary sewers all reduced the burdens of domestic life, while fewer births and less frequent infant deaths reduced the physical and emotional burdens of childbearing and child rearing for "small household saints,"[37] and fewer mothers to "look old at thirty."[38] In short, scientific advice in the form of public health measures improved children's health and reduced infant mortality. Yet, ignorance and poverty remained central complicating factors.

In the postwar decade, broader public health measures were needed not only in the tenements of New York and Boston, but in the rural south and the west as well. As one Mississippi mother whose husband was only paid twice a year noted, "if the children get sick between seasons they have to get along."[39] Poverty and poor sanitation, common for both black and white southerners, caused the "filthesome diseases" that available children's health advice could prevent.[40] Professional advice alone was not sufficient to correct such immense social problems, and death and illness remained high for both poor white and black infants and children, but especially for black children. Many social problems, like poverty and substandard housing, were greater among blacks. Throughout much of the south, "public sentiment" opposed programs that "cut down the death rate of the Negro."[41] Nutritional deficiencies were also common and not easily remedied when fresh vegetables and fresh meat were infrequently available. One observer concluded that one of every two American children had rickets. Skeletal deformities resulted from the weak bones that calcium and vitamin D deficiency caused. Infants died with pneumonia, and mothers, who had had rickets as children, died in childbirth because of deformation of the pelvic bones.[42] A southwestern mother reported that her 28-month-old son was "very sallow looking, tongue is always coated, sometimes constipated, altho I give him castor oil and castoria; these help temporarily. His eyes are yellow looking, no blood seems to be in them. He looks to be anemic but I really don't know what to feed him."[43] The child died with rickets and other nutritional deficiencies, as did others whose diet was based upon pork fat, grits, and molasses. The nutritional knowledge of the day could have prevented these problems, yet the immensity of the social problems complicated easy solutions.

When "mere ignorance" was responsible for infant death, mothers aware of the new scientific basis of child care often helped educate less-informed women. Mothers who had experienced the death of a child also furthered their own educations. One such mother reported that since her son's death "I've read and studied everything I could get. I've visited public clinics and hospitals, I've attended baby welfare lectures. But I find so few people who are ready to believe in better baby care, and most of all the mothers with families. They are ready as a rule to laugh in your face."[44] Not all women had accepted the scientific basis of mothering, especially when their own children were apparently healthy without the advice and attention of child health authorities. At the same time other mothers, who had "religiously" followed the scientific advice of the experts, did not understand their own children's death. A Missouri woman whose child was stillborn concluded: "I took such splendid care of myself, that I had not even the slightest doubt as to the outcome, regarding either the baby or myself and of course the shock was almost more than we could stand. Instead of the sparkling baby boy we have only a beautiful memory."[45] Medical science was not infallible, and since its widespread application to the daily care of children was more problematic, death and disease could result despite attention to the rules of children's health.

By the 1920s the health of American children was improving. Because of improved living conditions, wide-scale vaccination, better nutrition, improved prenatal and obstetrical care, as well as specific health reforms, like milk stations and the pasteurization of milk supplies, fewer children died from the common diseases of childhood. In Chicago, for example, only one tenth as many children died from measles and diphtheria, while nearly 500 times fewer children died of smallpox.[46] By 1950 the number of surviving infants was even more dramatic. Of 10,000 live-born female infants in 1880, only 8,489 survived the first year of life, while in 1950, out of 10,000 infants, 8,736 are expected to live to age 55. These dramatic improvements in health resulted from the application of public health measures to the daily lives of the nation's families. As a result both the public and professionals recognized medical science as an "authority of higher law."[47] Medical science was the solution to many of the problems of daily living and a promising means for solving social problems.

The Organization of Child Advocates

During the first decade of this century, physicians and social reformers combined efforts and formed professional organizations that promoted children's health. The American Association for the Study and Prevention of Infant Mortality, founded in 1908 "to prevent the loss of infant and child life and to promote child health," was an important early example.[48] This organization eventually became the American Child Hygiene Association. Its members were not only concerned with the study of infant death but also with the "dissemination of knowledge" and the "encouragement of methods for the prevention of infant mortality." By means of annual meetings, publications, public exhibits, and, according to Dr. Josephine Baker (1873–1945), "various other types of propaganda work," the public and the profession were advised of educational efforts and service programs that Baker concluded were of "the utmost service in raising the standard of health of the children of the country."[49]

In 1917 the health of school-age children became the focus of the Child Health Organization and its early leader, Emmett Holt. While no specific professional program was offered, teachers were encouraged to promote the health of their pupils, and school programs for nutrition, including free lunches, and the study of the health of schoolchildren were fostered. Children became active participants in these programs, and as they were educated about the science of health, they carried health advice home to their parents and families. Children were not only the object of interest in health promotion but also the conveyors of the scientific principles of health to their families. Health authorities recognized that the education of schoolchildren promoted not only children's health but also general health.

Schoolchildren were taught, as Josephine Baker advised, "living health,"[50] and thus they avoided "the habit of dullness, begotten by the unsanitary conditions" that poverty spawned for "a whole generation of citizens."[51] As more American children attended school, schools offered, as a Kansas City administrator noted, the opportunity "to unfold the natural and symmetrical beauty of the human body, making it fit and capable, in every phase of moral life."[52] These wide-ranging goals required better educators and facilities. To meet these ends, school inspections and improvements of facilities were undertaken. The routine physical examination of schoolchildren was expanded, and public health measures, like mandatory vaccination and the exclusion of sick children from school, were started. These measures established a more healthful environment in which the nation's schoolchildren learned and saw the scientific principles of health in action. By both seeing and doing, children were given a model of healthful living, which they in turn could provide for their own families and friends.

In order to model healthful practices, the school building and its environs had to meet sanitary criteria. Some schools, however, did not have sanitary or healthful facilities. Before World War I, a New Hampshire doctor reported that "not a few of our schools, even in the principal cities boasting of their refinement and culture, are filthy and unhealthy, and in so far as uncleanliness goes give reason for the accusation made at times that they are ungodly."[53] By 1917 New York State, with more than 22,000 school buildings, could only claim a quarter of its facilities met minimum sanitary requirements, according to Josephine Baker.[54] Some schools had no running water or indoor plumbing, only outdoor privies. Many were dirty, poorly ventilated, and a potential source of disease transmission. These problems required correction, if children's health was to significantly improve. More important, these problems required significant attention, if the school was to become a model of health for the education of children and their families.

In 1910 New Jersey became the first state to enact a statute for the general physical examination of schoolchildren. In so doing New Jersey physicians and educators were employing, as a New York educator noted, "all means in our power to prevent diseases" and remedy children's health problems.[55] These evaluations emphasized remediable conditions, especially dental caries, visual loss, hearing difficulties, postural defects, and other preventable or readily treated ailments. Not surprisingly, when large numbers of children were examined, ill health was regularly reported. In 1922 a Children's Bureau study in rural Kentucky found dental caries and "tonsil problems" for more than three-quarters of examined children. Nearly one-half of these children lived in homes "incapable of providing the essentials of a simple standard of living."[56] Similar results were found in New York, where only 481 of 1,027 examined children were "normal."[57] During the following decade, in a single study from suburban Hyde Park, Illinois, at least one of 1,882 identified defects were found in each of 1,139 students examined.[58] Clearly, as the Child Health Organization had emphasized and the 1919 White House Conference on Children had recommended, school health standards were needed. While these programs identified sick children, often with correctable medical problems, the larger social factors contributing to disease were present in too many American homes. School health programs promoted parental education about these circumstances, but larger social solutions were required if these central problems were to be resolved.

A step toward the solution of the social problems at the root of the problems of children's health was taken in 1922 when the American Child Hygiene Association and the Child Health Organization merged to become the American Child Health Association (ACHA). Under the official sponsorship of Herbert Hoover, the new organization flourished by promoting political solutions for the problems of children's health. In proclaiming the child's Bill of Rights at the inaugural meeting of the association, Hoover both identified and mandated solutions for the problems of children's health: "There should be no child in America that has not been born under proper conditions, that does not live in hygienic surroundings, that ever suffers from undernutrition, that does not have prompt and efficient medical attention and inspection, that does not receive primary instruction in the elements of hygiene and good health."[59] Hoover placed a new light upon children's health not only by emphasizing its importance and calling for national political solutions but also by proclaiming medical science as the basis for promoting and maintaining children's health, thereby providing official sanction to physicians as the nation's authorities on children's health.

With the support of leading pediatricians, like Baker and Holt, the support of leading politicians, like Hoover, and the capable direction of public health authorities, like Samuel J. Crumbine, the ACHA rapidly designed and implemented programs that furthered children's health. The association initially completed a survey of health conditions in 86 American cities. In a letter to Hoover, Crumbine concluded that this effort was "the most important single contribution to public health administration and practice in a decade."[60] One-fourth of these cities had no board of health and no public health nurses. Each city had a health officer, but only two such officials had diplomas in public health. One-third of these cities had no clinics, facilities, or public services for preschool children. While almost all offered physical examinations for schoolchildren, they were mostly "superficial." Improved delivery of children's health services was needed if American children were to reap the benefits of the scientific principles of health. This need was more dramatically defined the following year when the milk supplies from 650 American cities in more than 30 states were surveyed by the association. Nearly one-half of the milk samples analyzed were "dirty" and 85 percent were delivered without ice or refrigeration.[61] Crumbine, Hoover, and the other officers of the association recognized that further political and social solutions were necessary.

Public education was the major means by which the ACHA promoted children's health. As problems were identified the association mounted public education programs. These efforts included publications and, eventually, popular radio shows and motion pictures. In early 1921 the regularly published *Mother and Child* reached more than 50,000 American homes. Pamphlets, circulars, and flyers on diverse aspects of children's health were freely distributed throughout the nation. In 1924 the society first promoted May Day as Child Health Day. One observer concluded that, after the Dempsey-Tunney fight, the Lindbergh flight, and the World Series, Child Health Day had more publicity than any other event of the day. Popular magazines, including *Good Housekeeping, Collier's,* and *McClure's,* all supported these efforts. By 1925 nearly all the nation's governors had endorsed the program as well. Through the efforts of the ACHA, Hoover and others raised the American conscience about children's health and urged political solutions for its central problems.

During the last years of the 1920s, the rising popularity and availability of radio broadcasting offered a new means of promoting the healthy practices. In 1928 the ACHA sponsored the "Cheerio" radio program that both entertained and informed the public. These factual programs were carried by the NBC radio network from the eastern seaboard to the Rocky Mountains. Programming was often presented as a drama geared toward children, with a moral message. Children, but more importantly mothers and fathers, as the care givers and advocates for their children, became the vehicles for the understanding and implementation of principles of good health. As Angelo Patri (1876–1965) told his radio audience for more than 15 years, it was "disgraceful," as well as unnecessary, "to be so unintelligent as to allow children to form the habit of having colds."[62] In the view of Patri and others, parents had a moral obligation to provide an environment that fostered children's health. This moral responsibility pertained to professionals and politicians, as well.

Child Advocacy in the Twentieth Century

The moral and philanthropic support of children's issues did not end with the nineteenth century. Rather, efforts were intensified and expanded nationally. Milk stations were founded, and children spared the ravages of preventable diseases. Prevention by means of the scientific principles of public health was the basis of child saving. Mothers, professionals, and politicians agreed with Mrs. Campbell Forrester, who told the Huron County Federation of Women's Clubs in June 1924: "Where we have always waited for the individual to become ill and then endeavored to cure the disease, we now are making the effort to reach the individual before he becomes ill. We are trying to prevent instead of cure. We have been starting our fight after all need of fighting was past, when the diseased organs were beyond repair and we could only hope for a few days or weeks to the life."[63] Children's health was most successfully promoted by disease prevention rather than disease treatment, especially when the scientific basis of prevention was well defined and wider application only required more extensive political and social action.

At the same time that prevention was emphasized, the "existing" social conditions that promoted ill health were, as Dr. Kate Barrett told the Eighth Special Purity Congress in 1914, "nothing that the experienced individual worker has not always known."[64] If poverty was not easily reversed and if institutional care did not readily promote health, other solutions were available. Proposed solutions often included individual action and the daily assistance of mothers and families. The placement of "delicate foundling babies" in private homes for "mothering and cuddling" under the direction of foster mothers with "a strong maternal instinct" was one alternative method of promoting children's health. Maternal efforts were assisted, when necessary, by professional advice. Both doctors and nurses were available for home visits. The eye of the "expert" ensured that "the little ones progress[ed] properly."[65] These homey efforts were supplemented in some urban areas, like Chicago and New York, by country vacations for recovering children.

Other new programs for children's health were run by neighborhood settlement houses. These programs combined a maternal interest with professional advice and the physical facilities of the institution for the benefit of neighborhood children and their families. The emphasis, according to Jane

Addams of Hull House, was maternal efforts assisted by educational programs directed by the "stern mandates of science."[66] Settlement houses also
provided training grounds for future leaders of the children's health movement. Lillian Wald and Grace Abbott, founders of the Children's Bureau,
gained valuable experience in this manner. More important than such training was the education of mothers about children's health. These efforts at
Hull House included lectures by physicians, nurses, and university professors. In March 1897 a University of Chicago professor lectured to a group of
Italian women about "Bacteria and Disease."[67] Other classes on physiology
and hygiene were offered and often illustrated with the stereopticon, an opti-
cal device for the three-dimensional viewing of photographs and illustrations. Addams concluded that these efforts taught some of the neighborhood
"women to feed their children oatmeal instead of tea-soaked bread, but it
has been done, not by statement at all but by a series of gay little Sunday
morning breakfasts given to a group of them in the Hull House nursery."[68]
Science provided the principles, but the daily solution to children's health
problems was directed as much by gentle persuasion as by scientific theory
and argument.

Addams and her colleagues recognized that ignorance and traditional
beliefs were best addressed by subtle example without confrontation. Italian
mothers on Chicago's West Side learned about rickets and its treatment in
this way. The crooked legs of children with this condition were aided with
baths and cod liver oil, but not by damning the evil eye that many of these
women believed caused the disease. None of the women, however, was
asked to remove the bag of salt used to ward off the evil eye. Success was
attained "without mention that disease was caused not by the evil eye but by
lack of cleanliness and nutrition, and without passing through the intermedi-
ate belief that disease was sent by Providence[;] the women form a little center for the intelligent care of children, which is making itself felt in the
Italian Colony."[69] By presenting medical knowledge and advice without
appearing to contradict cultural traditions, women taught each other just as
they had done for centuries, and with the expert aid of physicians and visiting nurses and the facilities of a circulating library of books, posters, and pictures, immigrant women learned the scientific principles behind children's
health. As a result fewer children died on Chicago's West Side and throughout the nation.

Public education about children's health became a central activity for
many settlement houses and neighborhood organizations. In 1910 the superintendent of the Milwaukee Visiting Nurses Association noted that their
efforts were directed at reaching "babies before they are ill, teaching the
mothers to care for the child and avoid the preventable diseases which claim
so many."[70] The Maternity Center Association of the borough of Brooklyn
(New York) undertook both prenatal and children's health educational pro-

grams. These efforts were sponsored by "some very influential Brooklyn people."[71] Lectures were given at schools, hospitals, and public meetings. Pamphlets published and distributed by social workers and some merchants provided a means for demonstrations of children's health practices. "Mothercraft" clubs were formed where both experienced and new mothers learned about scientific health practices.

Documentation of the benefits of settlement house child health programs was difficult, but some efforts were undertaken. This process was more easily performed at the Henry Street Settlement in New York City, because patient care services in the form of "skilled nursery care" were a major feature of their programs. Visiting nurses not only educated families and tended the sick but, where possible, "solve[d] social and economic problems" that caused poor children's health.[72] In 1900 the program included 15 nurses but by 1926 employed 164 nurses and treated 49,120 patients. Ultimately, the success of these efforts encouraged Josephine Baker, director of the New York City's Bureau of Child Hygiene, to include visiting nurses as a central feature of the city's efforts.

In 1914 Lillian Wald reported that the staff of the Henry Street Settlement cared for 3,535 cases of childhood pneumonia in the home. Eight percent of these children died, which was a marked improvement over the 30 percent of hospitalized children who did so.[73] In spite of these early impressive results, Wald reported that her efforts "encountered the inevitable opposition which the unusual must arouse."[74] Although she was too gracious to provide details, Wald attributed much of the problem to the opposition of local physicians. Wald and her corps of nurses challenged the professional position of physicians by taking an active professional role in the daily care of sick children. Likewise, the incomplete success of the Maternity Center of Brooklyn arose partly from a lack of "the active support of the physicians of the community."[75] Neither of these organizations offered programs that physicians generally provided; rather they promoted education and daily home care, which poor mothers desperately needed for the benefit of their children. Nonetheless, some physicians opposed these efforts for professional and ideological reasons. Physicians did not want to share the professional fees from the care of sick children with other health care providers, nor did they want to dilute their authority as the spokespersons for the health of the nation's children. Their actions suggested that professional interests compromised their support of children's health and instead placed narrow economic and ideological interests before the needs of some sick children.

The fact that children's health was effectively promoted by broad-based educational programs was not lost on some professional and philanthropic organizations. During the 1920s the Rockefeller family's Commonwealth Fund supported Child Health Demonstration projects in several states, including Georgia, Tennessee, and North Dakota. These programs were designed to increase local children's health services, to educate mothers and the community generally, and to emphasize the importance of children's health from birth through the school years. In short, the programs were established as "a model child health unit in a small community" and as a means of determining "the best methods of child hygiene work for the future."[76] As Josephine Baker noted in her review of the project, the prevention of infant mortality was "successful only in proportion to the education of the community as a whole." Consequently, educational efforts included local organizations, like the Parent-Teacher Association and the Red Cross. Chambers of commerce, boards of education, and city councils were involved, as were civic clubs, like the Rotary and the Kiwanis clubs. These efforts were successful, just as settlement house programs had been, and as a result infant mortality rates declined more dramatically for families participating in the projects than for other local families. In Athens, Georgia, for example, from 1920 to 1926 infant mortality declined by one-third for white participants and by nearly 45 percent for black families. The Commonwealth Fund found that the babies of participating families had "a firmer hold on life" during their first months. Children's health improved when professional experts educated mothers about the principles of children's health and when social programs were established that provided necessary services.

The Public Education of a Nation

During the first half of the twentieth century, perhaps the single most important federal institution that promoted the health of American children was the Children's Bureau. The bureau was primarily a product of the efforts of the female leaders of the National Child Labor Committee. These women included Florence Kelley, a factory inspector from Illinois, Grace Abbott, head of the Immigrant's Protection League, Julia Lathrop, an associate of Jane Addams at Hull House, and Lillian Wald, founder of the Henry Street Settlement. The bureau was established in 1912, and Lathrop, its first director, became the first female director of a federal bureau a decade before women obtained the right to vote. As a result motherhood, which Lathrop considered the "most essential of employments," was emphasized, and the promotion of maternal and children's health became essential features of the social and political movement for women's rights.

The initial proposals for the establishment of the Children's Bureau were controversial because some opposed the expenditure of federal funds on the problems of maternal and children's health and others opposed the official recognition of problems they considered best managed in the nation's homes.

Most observers, however, agreed that there was need for greater concern about children. Child laborers in many industries from papermaking and printing to carpet and dye production were singled out for special concern. In the *Bitter Cry of the Children* John Spargo chillingly reported juvenile match makers who suffered from "phossy jaw," gangrene of the lower jaw from phosphorus poisoning. Alexander McKelway, a clergyman, reformer, and speaker for the National Child Labor Committee summarized the need for the bureau. He noted that it was a "national disgrace that nobody knows how many children in America die under one year of age." At the same time he estimated that 200,000 mothers and an equal number of fathers, "to say nothing of the suffering of the children," were needlessly bereaved each year.[77] Professionals, more than 200 "recognized experts," endorsed a federal Children's Bureau. The initial legislation for the bureau was introduced in the previous decade during the 59th Congress, but only in 1912, with the support of groups as diverse as the Daughters of the American Revolution, the American Prison Association, and the Farmer's Education and Cooperative Union, was the measure finally enacted and funded with an initial appropriation of $25,640 for the inaugural year's operation.[78]

The Children's Bureau immediately filled a void because no other federal office was involved with children's health. The bureau's mandate was "to investigate and report upon all matters pertaining to the welfare of children and child life among all classes of people."[79] Such a broad charge offered almost unlimited horizons for the bureau, but, importantly, Lathrop placed the initial emphasis upon infant mortality, a frequent and preventable problem. Lathrop's previous work at Hull House had given her personal experience with the magnitude of the problem, and the 1910 British public health study of infant mortality provided a guide for the relevant methodology. By recognizing the frequency of preventable deaths, Lathrop acknowledged the importance of this study. She noted that during the first decade of the twentieth century, two and one-half million children died and that "sanitarians assure us that by methods already available it would have been possible to save the lives of half these children. Such methods of safe-guarding life are understood to include, not only medical care, but especially various forms of social betterment, sanitation, and prevention."[80] If, as Grace Abbott, a future director of the bureau, concluded, "the progress of a state may be measured by the extent to which it safeguards the rights of its children,"[81] then the monumental effort against infant mortality embodied in the establishment of the Children's Bureau was a major sign of progress for the American nation.

Lathrop wisely recognized that before prevention and educational campaigns could be undertaken, the exact magnitude of the problem of infant mortality must be defined. Thus, collection of vital statistics and mandatory birth registrations were essential because "you cannot find out why babies are dying unless you know what proportion of babies are dying."[82] As Lathrop concluded in the first annual report of the bureau, this work was "fundamental to social welfare, of popular interest, and serve[d] a real human need."[83] This effort, as Grace Abbott recalled two decades later, was undertaken with "no narrow or timid spirit."[84] Lathrop was "prepared to go wherever the interests of the child might lead her and to accept whatever conclusions flowed from an honest interpretation of facts assembled with meticulous accuracy."[85] The humanitarian needs of children were at the heart of the bureau's efforts, but its approach was based on the scientific principles of public health measures.

While statistics were essential for definition of the problem, educational programs were foremost in the campaign to prevent infant death and disease. Although the bureau had no medical staff, by 1914 it had published *Infant Care,* a manual detailing the practical aspects of child care and emphasizing the prevention of childhood illness by the application of the scientific principles of public health and personal hygiene. By 1921 more than one and a half million copies of the book were published and distributed. In its first 50 years the text, which went through numerous revisions but was always written for the "average mother," was distributed once for every three infants born in the country. Within the first decade of existence the bureau issued one hundred formal publications and numerous other educational brochures, pamphlets, flyers, and informative notices.[86] This tabulation did not include the thousands of responses to individual questions that women addressed to the bureau's experts on infant and child care. In a single year as many as 100,000 women queried the bureau about diapering, feeding, clothing, and rearing their children. Most found the advice and the government publications useful. For example, a Minnesota woman recalled that the government book "did me more good than the Doctor I had at the time my baby was born, I did not have a great deal of money and the information in these booklets was [concise] and helpful. I just felt that I should write and tell you how grateful I was that I can get even this little bit of free advice from our government. We should be able to get more medical help and advice from our government regarding babies and child raising."[87]

In 1917 the inclusion of medical information in the new edition of *Infant Care* was questioned by some physicians and politicians who believed such knowledge was beyond the comprehension of many mothers and rightfully in the domain of the physician. Dorothy Reed Mendenhall, who filled the new position of medical officer, however, in a letter to Lathrop clearly noted the necessity of its inclusion: "I believe mothers have a right to know the scientific reasons which underlie infant feeding and that the mothers our bulletins reach are capable of understanding such information. The farmers of our country are educated by bulletins from the Department of Agriculture in regard to infectious diseases. . . . Why then, should references to marasmus and scurvy and their treatment, which often result from improper feeding in infancy, be cut out of a bulletin sent to mothers by the U.S. Children's Bureau?"[88] Accurate information about child rearing was, according to one contemporary author, "the passion of the day."[89] A passion sufficiently strong that 1918 was designated by presidential decree as the Children's Year.

The awakening of the public mind "to the value of human stock" led to a multitude of state and local efforts that promoted children's health.[90] Many of these efforts paralleled federal programs. City and state divisions and bureaus of child health were established with the aid of women, doctors, nurses, public health officials, clergymen, and politicians. Often child welfare statutes were passed, as in the case of the first statute in Minnesota (1917), because of an emphasis on social justice and laws to protect children, without specific reference to children's health. Child labor laws were enacted, and by 1920 nearly 30 states had established programs specifically promoting children's health. No longer was it possible to conclude that governments spent more money to fatten hogs, raise cattle, or feed milk cows than they spent on programs for children. Instead the emphasis was now upon protecting "children from the ravages of the insidious, slow, far-reaching, terribly prevalent, and fearfully fatal diseases."[91] These new programs rapidly expanded and became an increasingly important aspect of local and state health projects. The Bureau of Child Hygiene of New York City became, under Josephine Baker's direction, the most expensive department in the city's health program.

The second Children's Bureau in the nation, established in Kansas in 1915, illustrated the services provided by these new state and local programs. The first director of the bureau, Lydia Allen DeVilbiss, was reported by a Kansas newspaper to "probably have done more work in child hygiene than any other person in this country."[92] Perhaps this was an overstatement, but DeVilbiss's training with Baker in New York City gave her excellent credentials with which to undertake a project that included efforts designed "to see that every baby has a chance."[93] To achieve this goal, organizers published posters, pamphlets, and certificates and erected public exhibits and displays promoting children's health. Children's health fairs and baby programs were conducted at county fairs, lectures by members of the state medical society were given, and baby weeks were held in local communities. Mothers registered their pregnancies and became members of the Kansas Mother's Club. Membership meant receiving the 160 pages of advice found in the *Kansas Mother's Book*, participation in lectures and baby contests, and competition for the Governor's Trophy as a representative of the healthiest county in the state of Kansas.[94] If these efforts were not sufficient, the specially equipped railroad car, "Warren," toured the state with educational exhibits about children's health and provided daily well-baby clinics.[95] Adolescent girls were also encouraged to learn about child care by joining

Little Mothers Leagues. One journalist described this organization as the "largest volunteer life saving corps" in the world.[96] With the aid of dolls and other educational devices, participants learned the basics of child hygiene and infant care. These young women helped reduce infant mortality by becoming more knowledgeable future mothers. Throughout the nation many of these same programs were adopted.

These educational efforts reached and eventually involved many Kansas women. More than 400 well-baby celebrations were held, including the issuance of more than 3,000 certificates of infant health. Five thousand girls became members of the Little Mothers Leagues. Tens of thousands of educational pamphlets and booklets were issued on topics ranging from infant feeding to toilet training. These educational programs, while not solely responsible for reducing infant deaths, contributed to lower infant mortality in the state. By the 1920s the infant death rate in the state was 16 percent below the national average.[97] Kansas, as well as other states, successfully reduced infant mortality by the application of public health measures and the provision of widespread public education about children's health.

Nationwide Programs

By 1921 most states wanted more help in the coordination of their children's health activities. A survey by the Russell Sage Foundation concluded that only 4 of 22 states surveyed did not desire help in the establishment of better health programs. As the health officer of Delaware noted, the benefit of such information was "to know the best that is being done in other states."[98] While the "pooled experience" of other states was a "wonderful guide" for new programs, most states reserved their own sovereignty. Innovation might be sparked by knowledge of successful outside programs, but decisions about program implementation remained strictly a local and state matter. While federal control was not welcome by most states, the cooperative interaction among states and with federal programs, but under state control, promoted the health of American children.

In spite of new state and federal programs, the high rate of maternal and infant death that marked the late nineteenth and early twentieth centuries continued in the post–World War I era. In response female reformers and public health officials supported programs for American mothers and their children. Both urban and rural families, and especially the poor, received assistance. These activities culminated in the sponsorship and passage in 1921 of the Sheppard-Towner Maternity and Infancy Act. This was not only the first major act of federal social legislation, but also the first piece of women's legislation passed after women obtained the vote. The act did not

provide medical care for all women and children as its sponsors had originally hoped, but rather required matching state funds coupled with federal
funds for the education of midwives, nurses, and mothers about maternal
and children's health. In effect, the program supplemented and expanded
previous state and local programs with federal monies, while emphasizing
the educational methods and scientific principles of earlier successful public
health and children's bureau programs.

Not all agreed that expanded federal programs were the solution. Many
physicians opposed these efforts, but most agreed that the high rate of
maternal and infant death required that some measures be undertaken with
"dispatch and efficacy."[99] The editor of the *Medical Women's Journal* concluded: "The protection of the child must begin with the protection of the
mother. . . . [T]here is little prospect of providing adequate care until the
problem is recognized as a national problem and met in a national way."[100]
Senator Harding, a supporter of the proposed maternity and infancy legislation, concluded, "who can suggest one of these tasks which can supersede in
our hearts, or in the rank which foresight and wisdom will give, that of protection of maternity?"[101] Proponents of the Sheppard-Towner Act continued
this argument. After citing the quarter of a million childhood deaths in
America, Florence Kelley asked a congressional committee in 1920, "why the
issue was not taken seriously?" and "why does Congress wish women and
children to die?"[102] The stumbling block for Congress and the political leaders of the nation was the enactment of federal funding for local and state
programs. Many politicians and physicians remained unconvinced that federal programs were the answer to what they felt were the personal problems of
maternal and children's health. Many physicians, in fact, agreed with the editor of the *Illinois State Medical Journal,* who concluded that the proposed
legislation was "a menace and represents another piece of destructive legislation sponsored by endocrine perverts, derailed menopausics and a lot of
other men and women who have been bitten by that fatal parasite, the uplifts
putrifaciens, in the guise of uplifters, all of whom are working to devise
means to destroy the country."[103] Many physicians and organized medical
societies, including the American Medical Association, opposed the legislation because they recognized infant and maternal deaths as state and local,
but not federal, problems. In addition, they opposed what they saw as the
confusion of medical and social problems. At issue, according to Senator
James Reed, was that "a few simple ladies holding government jobs in
Washington" were teaching mothers how to become better mothers.[104] For
opponents of this legislation, these political issues were more important than
expanded programs for the health of the nation's children.

Despite the reservations of some politicians and physicians, in November
1921, when the legislation passed the Senate by a nine-to-one margin and
the House by a seven-to-one margin, America's mothers and children were

the victors. The Sheppard-Towner Act, in the words of Florence Kelly, was of "fundamental importance" for the nation. More than "treating sick people," the program taught "people how to keep well and readjust . . . the bad effects of wrong environment."[105] The legislation addressed, as Josephine Baker recognized in publications and addresses to a nationwide audience, the fundamental social and economic factors in children's health, but the basic issue of poverty that faced many American families remained unresolved. Nonetheless, within six months of the passage of the legislation, expanded state maternal and children's health programs were under way. The act mandated that participating states create a children's bureau to cooperate with the federal Children's Bureau, and that each state create detailed plans of the children's and maternal health projects it planned to undertake. Federal monies became available to the states only when state matching funds were authorized. The legislation did not specify the nature of state programs, other than precluding the removal of children from the custody of their parents. According to Emmett Holt, federal funding and the programs it enabled "made possible in very many states a much wider field of service than has heretofore existed."[106] More mothers and their children received the benefits of an expanded number of successful health programs.

While many professionals were convinced of the benefit of the new legislation, some women wondered how their families would benefit. One woman wrote to Julia Lathrop of the Children's Bureau: "Will you please write me a letter and tell me please what will the Child Welfare and Maternity Bill that has passed in Congress do for us mothers and wives of farmers and working men? Will it be possible to get those necessary things such as medicine, bed dressings, etc.?"[107] The Sheppard-Towner Act provided few services for direct patient care. Medical services were not widely expanded; however, educational efforts were significantly increased. Programs were enacted throughout the nation, and thousands of families benefited from the wider provision of expert children's health advice. By 1929, when only three states did not participate in Sheppard-Towner programs, 22 million educational publications had been distributed, 183,252 health conferences conducted, 2,978 prenatal centers established, and three million home visits completed.[108] During the eight-year term of the Sheppard-Towner legislation, public health education, but not the provision of personal medical services, enhanced American children's health.

In 1928 the Chicago-based Elizabeth McCormick Memorial Fund, in reviewing the Sheppard-Towner legislation, concluded that state children's health programs had "profited greatly by the pooling of experience . . . and by advice received from the [Children's] Bureau."[109] Women also provided individual testimonials supporting the educational benefits that resulted from the legislation. A Wisconsin mother concluded that by "taking care of myself the way you told me to do," she was able to successfully nurse her third child longer than the first two. Another mother reported that her boy's health was due to similar advice made possible by Sheppard-Towner funded programs. A third woman reported that her second child survived, whereas her first died because she "knew nothing about caring for [her]self."[110] Perhaps a New York woman best summarized the benefits of this important piece of social legislation: "When people stop me on the street and ask the whys and wherefores of my so obviously healthy baby I always say, 'He's a Government baby,' giving all credit to your bulletin (*Infant Care*). I was lucky enough not to know anything about babies before and not to have any relatives who thought they did."[111]

In spite of the apparent benefit of broader federal maternal and children's health programs, Congress, with the active support of the American Medical Association, did not renew the legislation in 1929. This withdrawal of federal financial support, just as the Great Depression was beginning, resulted in a shift from federal to locally funded and privately financed programs. As a consequence, important medical services for women and children were no longer available. In fact, as the depression expanded "the first reductions in the health budgets" were in programs that provided services for children and public health projects. These reductions were accompanied in New York City, and elsewhere across the nation, by an increase in the number of children with rickets and in the number of malnourished babies. From 1928 to 1932 the New York City health department reported a 50 percent increase in malnourished schoolchildren. By 1932 one in five New York schoolchildren suffered from malnutrition.[112] As the depression continued, 14 states each provided $3,000 or less for maternal and children's health services.[113] Many children, and many adults as well, suffered the ill effects of frugal times. Death and disease became more frequent, and the pain and suffering experienced by many sick American children remained unattended.

Despite the limitations of federal and state funding, by the 1930s children's health care became more institutionalized, with the construction of new facilities and with the establishment of more encompassing government programs. Physicians became stronger spokespersons about children's health, and their statements in the legislative chamber and at the bedside were regularly accepted as authoritative pronouncements. Children's hospitals expanded, general hospitals admitted sick children, and more local clinics and dispensaries opened. There were 20 infant and child welfare clinics in 1900, and more than 1,500 by 1930. In addition, more than one hundred cities had maternal and infant health bureaus that expended one-third of the health department funds in the nation.[114] In 1919 Michael Davis, administrator of the Boston Dispensary, which had reportedly started the nation's first well-baby clinic four years before, concluded that such facilities were "not only for treatment, but for the control and prevention of disease and for the education of the community." This "positive and aggressive force" was responsible for more than a 50 percent reduction in infant deaths for babies that attended the clinic compared with Boston as a whole.[115] Successful programs and documented results, such as those Davis reported in Boston and Lathrop tabulated in Washington, furthered children's health, but poverty and social circumstances prevented many American children from experiencing the benefits of these programs.

As the condition of American children's health became more dependent on institutions established by federal, state, and local governments, the ideology of children's health was increasingly codified within the domain of "economic conditions."[116] More often physicians, mothers, and politicians recognized that poverty was the root cause of many of the health problems of children. The health care of children represented more than the treatment of sick children and the dispensing of medications. Instead, an "intricate, interwoven and an interdependent social and economic system,"[117] which included prepared food, kindergarten classes, playgrounds, health clinics, immunization programs, and school physical examinations, was established by mothers, scientific experts, and public officials. Many problems were solved, and fewer children died of preventable diseases and injuries. As World War II commenced, Eleanor Roosevelt told the National Maternal and Child Health Council that "there was no question more important at the present time than child care."[118] Clearly, there were essential military and political questions of the day, but nonetheless, children's health remained a central issue.

7

The Whole Child, Body and Soul

In April of 1937 a seven-year-old Cincinnati boy developed the measles. In less than a week, he complained of an earache for which a myringotomy (incision of the eardrum) was performed. Within days, as the infection spread, his fever climbed to 105 degrees, and he complained of hip and leg pain, even neck soreness. X-rays were taken, and samples of blood, urine, and cerebrospinal fluid obtained and analyzed. Blood counts were completed, and bacterial cultures started. Surgical drainage of pus from the ear and mastoid bones, as well as the affected hip were necessary. Five blood transfusions were given, and the boy received oral and intravenous antibacterial therapy. He was given prontosil intravenously and 228 tablets of prontylin orally, without "apparent toxic symptoms" from the use of these early forms of sulfa medication. This boy lived, a contrast to what usually occurred during the preceding 14 years at the same hospital, when only 1 of 57 patients with severe streptococcal infections survived.[1] He was among the first children in America successfully treated with antimicrobial drugs. Within a decade penicillin was available, and soon streptomycin and a myriad of other new antibiotics offered therapy for many previously fatal bacterial infections. In the process the diagnosis of specific bacterial infections by precise microbial methods and therapy with antibiotics became accepted scientific practices.

Contemporary pediatric practice, and medicine in general, became centered on the wider application of science to the health problems of American children. At the same time, the traditional influences on children's health, from mothers to institutions, remained active; but increasingly medical science provided the means by which infant mortality was reduced, feeding problems eliminated, and leukemia cured. More physicians employed drugs for cancer chemotherapy and utilized surgical instruments and principles that correcteded congenital anomalies and repaired traumatic injuries.

Children's hospitals employed the rapidly expanding medical technology of computerized tomography, isolation rooms, and automated biochemical analyses of blood and urine. Parents, as well, relied upon medical science to protect the health of their children.

As pediatricians expanded the boundaries of their practices, they actively defined and accepted social problems as medical problems. The biosocial model of pediatrics that Abraham Jacobi and his colleagues championed at the dawn of the twentieth century became the basis for children's health care at the end of the century of the child. Child abuse, delinquency, and behavior problems were accepted in contemporary pediatric practice as medical problems. In essence, physicians, parents, and public officials recognized that this broader view provided for the care of the whole child, body and soul. In the process there was a development of an ideology of children's health that in many ways resembled colonial ideas on the subject. Admittedly, the soul was now more secularly and perhaps more accurately defined as the mind, but, nonetheless, the care of the whole child was the duty of parents, physicians, and society. The widespread implementation of broad-based social programs that prevented child abuse and reduced the transmission of infectious diseases demonstrated the codification and acceptance of this view of children's health. In effect, modern child advocates from parents to physicians to social workers placed themselves within the world of the child. Perhaps they had not gone as far in dealing with a child's soul as Cotton Mather proposed in *A Man of Reason* (1718), but, increasingly, resolutions to children's health problems took into account the child's social world.[2]

The concluding chapter of this work is not an attempt to recount all of the scientific advances that have accompanied the medicalization of the health and social care of American children, but rather an integration of the major themes that have defined the whole child as the object of attention and study by contemporary pediatricians and society. Medical science does not occupy the center of this stage. Instead, the recognition of the psychological nature of many children's health problems and the move to a biosocial model of children's health care will occupy the center of this chapter. This chapter begins with a discussion of institutional and social efforts in child advocacy as a prelude to the later discussion of the science of the body and the science of the mind. It concludes with the recognition that many of the root causes of today's child health problems are the same as they were a century ago.

The Central Role of Science in Child Rearing

Twentieth-century American mothers increasingly relied on science and the advice of expert physicians in rearing their children. From the selection of footwear to diaper changing, feeding schedules, and the prevention of tooth decay, advisers offered a scientific basis for maternal decisions. At the same time, nearly all recognized, as did children's health adviser Norma Selbert, that "mothercraft" was "a practice learned by actually caring for children." Advisers counseled mothers, but the day-to-day work of child rearing required that mothers learn the scientific "rules, rules, rules" of caring for their children. As they did so, American mothers increasingly placed reliance on medical advice rather than traditional lore.[3] A Bellingham, Washington, mother emphasized her dependence on the Children's Bureau publication *Infant Care:* "Unless I learn it by heart it will do me little good, for, as was the case with the first monograph, I am so constantly lending it, that I never have it on hand for quick reference."[4] When advice was not available, or when it was contradictory, the wise and successful mother followed the "only safe policy": she obeyed her "own doctor."[5]

From the need for prenatal care to the selection of a summer camp, advisers defined the details of scientific child rearing. As the biosocial model of children's health care was accepted, and as public health and medical measures were more widely practiced, fewer children died, and a greater emphasis upon the broader aspects of child rearing was possible. According to many advisers of the day, wise mothers practiced the expanded scope of their duties based on the advice of their physicians, lest their children remain "unfinished product[s]."[6] If verbal advice alone was insufficient to complete this process, mothers were offered photographs that explained, demonstrated, and reinforced the best methods of child rearing.[7] The end result was that children ate better, suffered from fewer diseases, recovered from illness more rapidly, and died less frequently.

This emphasis on science was not without some danger. Dr. Benjamin Spock (b. 1903), perhaps the most popular children's health adviser of this century, concluded that science alone was not sufficient for child rearing: "The rearing of children is more and more puzzling for parents in the twentieth century because we've lost a lot of our old-fashioned convictions about what kind of morals and ambitions and characters we want them to have. We've even lost our convictions about the purpose of human existence. Instead we have come to depend on psychological concepts. They've been helpful in solving many of the smaller problems, but they are of little use in answering the major questions."[8] In short, successful child rearing required the supplementing of science with a traditional moral emphasis. This was a task, as Spock indicated, that most experts left to parents, especially mothers, who provided, as they always had, the human means of child rearing that were essential for the complete health of American children.

While mothers and physicians alike accepted the scientific basis of child rearing, even mothers who were themselves trained physicians found the application of this new knowledge to their own children difficult. Dorothy

Whipple, a Johns Hopkins medical graduate, mother, and the author of the popular *Our American Babies: The Art of Baby Care* (1944), noted the often difficult application of science to personal child care: "I started in to apply to my own child what I had learned. I soon found that it made a lot of difference to me whose baby was crying. I had been able to go away with equanimity from some other mother's screaming child, with the knowledge that a skilled nurse would see that he lacked nothing, but to go away from my own crying baby, and stay within earshot for an hour or more before the clock said I could give him the milk I knew he wanted, that I confess, I found to be a different matter."[9] As this physician-mother indicated, the scientific care of children left little room for the emotions of caring mothers. Consequently, despite the scientific words of their advisers, most mothers, and fathers for that matter, did not completely cede the rearing of their children to the experts. While some parents concluded that they were losing influence over their children, most remained the central figures in their lives. Mothers fed, clothed, and bathed their sons and daughters, and they tucked them into bed at night.

Mothers continued to play the central role in the rearing of their children, but increasingly twentieth-century fathers expanded their contribution to child care. Elizabeth Lowell Putnam concluded in her presidential address to the Ninth Annual Meeting of the American Association for the Study and Prevention of Infant Mortality in 1918 that "one of the very serious mistakes" that was made was that "of assuming that fathers care little or nothing for their children." She proposed a resurgence of interest in fatherhood so that the task of motherhood "will become far easier of accomplishment."[10] Few experts and physicians of the day recognized the wisdom of this advice, and only later in the century did child psychologists and pediatricians emphasize the central role that fathers and family relationships played in the normal psychological development of children and the furtherance of children's health.

The Actions of Medical Advisers

By the middle third of the twentieth century, artificial feeding was recognized by many advisers and mothers as the best means of infant nutrition. Science provided an understanding of the principles of infant feeding that enabled the precise production of artificial formulas. When these principles were applied by the commercial food industry in accordance with sanitary measures dictated by the germ theory, artificial feeding became a viable option. By 1930 many American mothers accepted that artificial feeding was better than breast feeding, having been convinced of its validity by advertising, testimonials from other mothers and professionals, and the provision of free samples, and, perhaps most important, with the "proper authority" from physicians. As a result artificial feeding replaced breast feeding as the accepted nourishment for American infants.[11]

The scientific mystique surrounding artificial feeding was enhanced when several manufacturers, including the Nestlé Company, announced that their product was "sold only on the prescription or recommendation of a physician."[12] Many physicians, as well as infant formula companies, felt formula should be available on a prescription-only basis. Otherwise some mothers would not be able to feed their infants safely and physicians would lose an important opportunity for the control of their patients' health. In 1932 the American Medical Association Committee on Feeding refused approval for formulas advertised and sold directly to the public. Both manufacturers and professionals recognized that professional control of infant feeding promoted the scientific basis of children's health care and enhanced the professional position of the pediatrician. The medical and professional basis for artificial infant feeding were "fundamentally sound," but as a Yale pediatrician advised his colleagues, the "personality of the child" required attention as well. The doctor concluded that the physician and parents should "worship the baby more and the measuring stick, the scales, the graduate and the clock less."[13] In effect this physician, and undoubtedly others who agreed with him, recognized, as had mothers for generations, that infant feeding and child rearing were as much an art as they were a science.

By 1950 infant mortality in the United States had decreased more than 75 percent from the 114 deaths per 1000 live-born infants that occurred in 1910. Not only were total deaths dramatically reduced, but childhood infectious diseases no longer were the dominant cause of infant death. Improved sanitation, healthier infant feeding, better housing and living conditions, along with public health measures, and, by the late 1930s, the introduction of the first antibacterial medications—the sulfanamides—decreased infant mortality. Where infant mortality remained high, poor living conditions were often the cause. At mid-century the "blighted areas" of Chicago, for example, had infant mortality rates that were 25 percent higher than elsewhere in the city. A professional review of hospital records at the city's Cook County Hospital "revealed that hospitals and clinics cannot contribute their utmost to the community's health as long as patients must be returned to substandard living quarters."[14] The release of one of every six infants at the facility was delayed because of substandard housing or similar social problems.

By the 1940s premature birth was the single most important cause of infant death in the nation.[15] While "general ignorance or carelessness," including a lack of adequate prenatal care, was responsible for many of these deaths,[16] most occurred because neither obstetricians nor pediatricians understood the normal birth process sufficiently well to prevent premature

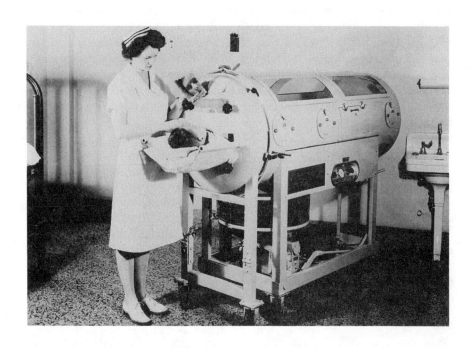

Epidemics of poliomyelitis were frequent before the 1950s, commonly resulting in respiratory paralysis. Before the routine availability of immunization, the iron lung, now a forgotten piece of medical technology, provided breathing support for many polio victims.

Hospital Archives, University of Kansas Medical Center, Kansas City, Kansas births. They did not recognize that poor nutrition, inadequate personal hygiene, and poverty resulted in premature births more often than abruptio previa (the separation of the placenta from the wall of the uterus) or kidney disease. In 1949, in order to understand the causes of prematurity more completely, Dr. Leona Baumgartner of the New York Health Department recommended "a careful clinical study" that would "at least open our eyes to the areas in which basic research should be done."[17] When answers to the problems of children's health were incomplete, most physicians and health officers agreed with Baumgartner—that science offered the means for their successful resolution. Yet, after a half century of scientific investigation, premature births remain a primary cause of infant death in this country. The public and professionals, as a *New York Times* editorial concluded, recognize that "the causes of the country's intolerably high rate of infant deaths are well understood."[18] Quality medical care, in its "broadest sense", for many mothers and children of poverty status remains unavailable. The solution is relatively simple: the provision of comprehensive medical care, including prenatal care, adequate nutrition, social support, and health education.[19] But financial, institutional, political, and logistical constraints prevent easy implementation. Nonetheless, the biosocial model of the whole child, with its emphasis on social as well as medical factors, offers a means of implementing programs, like immunization against infectious disease and the fluoridation of water, that prevent rather than merely treat disease.

By mid-century pediatricians tackled more complex children's health problems that required more and more specialized scientific and medical knowledge. Most of the advances in pediatric medical practice followed general medical advances, like the development of surgical techniques and the refinement of the technology for performing X-rays. Immunologic methods that immunized children against childhood infectious diseases were especially important and successful. By the 1960s, immunization against measles, mumps, rubella, and polio was routinely completed. Rather than the widespread epidemics of the early years of the century, which caused frequent childhood deaths, most children were protected against these common yet serious infectious problems. During 1958 more than one million doses of the Salk polio vaccine were administered to suburban Chicago residents. The benefit of these scientific efforts was demonstrated across the city, where only 16 cases of poliomyelitis with three deaths occurred. The dramatic results of this seemingly simple procedure stood in sharp contrast to the frequent deaths that polio had caused half a century before.

The practice of routine immunization was an example of the important changes that more complete medical knowledge, generated from the study of the physiology and biochemistry of infants and children, provided. Endocrinologists isolated hormones and treated diabetes and growth failure, while cardiologists recognized an increasingly complex variety of heart defects and offered the means of their surgical correction. Previously unrecognized medical problems, like Cooley's anemia and cystic fibrosis, were described, and the means of maintaining salt and water balance with intravenous fluids understood. Not only was the biochemical basis of many of the major children's health problems identified, but an understanding of the methods of medical treatment was established. Rickets, for example, long recognized as a cause of ill health and deformed bones, was identified as a problem of calcium deficiency in growing bones. Better living conditions that provided children with sunlight and improved sources of calcium and vitamin D readily prevented the disease. In short, science provided pediatricians with the tools to diagnose disease more accurately and treat its ill effects more adequately. Unfortunately, despite such medical successes, measles cases today are increasing, whooping cough is more frequent, and a growing number of children, mostly victims of poverty, are incompletely immunized against preventable childhood diseases, all because of inadequate knowledge or finances and limited availability of medical services. This resurgence of avoidable health problems is symptomatic of the unresolved social problems that cause ill health for many American children.

The Provision of
Children's Health Care

During the second half of the twentieth century, institutions have played a central role in the provision of health care to American children. These efforts were motivated, as the Third White House Conference on Child Health and Protection held in 1930 stated, by the desire "to set forth an understanding of those safeguards which will assure to [children] health in mind and body."[20] Hospitals provided birthing facilities and beds for sick children, and specialized laboratory and X-ray capabilities were developed. In addition, clinics, dispensaries, and neighborhood agencies were established to treat both sick and well children.

Neighborhood agencies, including federal, state, and local children and youth projects, were started and often modeled on previously successful settlement houses, like Henry Street Settlement in New York, Hull House in Chicago, and Hale House in Boston. These public facilities, generally operated at little or no cost to the families they served, were frequently overwhelmed with the needs of sick children. Many of these facilities' services included well-child care, immunizations, nutritional advice, and counseling. These preventive measures more effectively and economically promoted children's health than did the mere treatment of disease. Despite federal and state programs that provided aid to dependent children, promoted the health care of pregnant women, established welfare services for homeless, neglected, and delinquent children, and started crippled children's services, many children still received incomplete health care because of limited family and public resources and ignorance of the usefulness or availability of existing programs. Many of these endeavors began as part of the Social Security Act of the Depression era, when the health of many American children was threatened by poverty. In fact, by 1937 Grace Abbott counted more than 527,000 American children among the recipients of aid to dependent children, and many more whose health could have benefited from such aid.[21]

Increasingly during the 1940s at children's health clinics, preventive measures and patient education were more important than the treatment of acute medical problems. The effectiveness of such efforts as Samuel J. Crumbine reported was difficult to assess: "It is like trying to explain to a group of taxpayers the usefulness and wisdom of 'Fire Prevention Week,' when all the old rubbish and rags in the cellar and attic were cleared out and the alley cleared of its trash, with the result that there were no fires from that sort of hazard that year. Nothing happened, so nothing can be said, except there was no fire, altho one must admit that there might not have been a fire, without all the work and expense of cleaning."[22] Parents and politicians may have had difficulty identifying the benefits of disease prevention for individual children, but public health officials had no problem appreciating longer lives and fewer cases of infectious and nutritional diseases.

In addition to more facilities, the training and expertise of children's health professionals were expanded. More physicians trained more rigorously for longer periods of time as pediatricians, and a larger number of practitioners concerned with children's health sought additional training in public health and preventive medicine. Pediatricians increasingly played a more active role in state and county health departments. They supervised increasingly complex service organizations that required expertise in obstetrics, pediatrics, dental care, public health, orthopedics, nursing, nutrition, accounting, law, administrative procedures, and hospital standards. In 1939 public children's health services were available at 2,394 centers in 41 states. Two-thirds of the counties in the nation had the services of public health nurses.[23]

While these results were encouraging, the rejection of nearly 50 percent of military inductees during World War II, the same percentage that was rejected in World War I, was evidence that many aspects of children's health required attention. Dr. Martha Eliot, associate chief of the Children's Bureau, told a Senate subcommittee in 1944. "It takes such a catastrophe as war to show us how poorly we have measured up to our responsibilities to the 40 million children of the nation in fitting them physically and mentally to take their places in the work of the Nation."[24] The doctor called for a nationwide federal program that provided personnel, services, and facilities for better children's health care.

Improved care required not only better services but also, as participants at the Mid-Century White House Conference on Children and Youth were advised in 1950, the ability "to develop in children the mental, emotional and spiritual qualities essential to individual happiness and to responsible citizenship."[25] Increasingly, these efforts included the whole child and were centered not only on normal children but on handicapped children as well. As many as half a million children were affected with rheumatic fever, poliomyelitis, orthopedic problems, cleft lip or palate, and a myriad of other handicapping conditions that required special services. Others, who increasingly became the subject of medical attention, suffered from cerebral palsy and mental retardation. Statewide programs for handicapped children aided many of those affected, but it was not until the 1960s that the National Institute of Child Health and Human Development was established as part of the National Institutes of Health. This important center for scientific research about children's health further promoted the understanding of normal and sick children. Along with other federal and state programs, the National Institute of Child Health and Human Development also provided the means to study the social, emotional, and mental problems of the nation's children.

The Mind of the Child

Just as pediatricians dissected and analyzed the anatomy of the child's body, so they also probed the corners and realms of the child's mind. When Felix Adler and five mothers founded the Child Study Association in 1888, they singled out for study, not only the physical problems of the child, but the "mental" and "moral" as well.[26] By the early twentieth century these initial efforts, stimulated by exposés, like the publication of former mental patient Clifford Beer's *A Mind That Found Itself* (1908), sparked the formation of the mental hygiene movement. By 1916 a leading Illinois public welfare official concluded that "the study of the child from the standpoint of the scientific interpretation of mind and its making is a new science—but it is here to stay."[27] Professional experts, like G. Stanley Hall (1846–1924), Sigmund Freud (1856–1939), and John B. Watson (1878–1958) emphasized behavioral approaches to children's health. In addition, many lay organizations from the Parent-Teacher Association to the American Association of University Women helped foster public support for this new emphasis on children's mental health.[28]

Psychology, which William James (1842–1910) called the "science of mental life," formed the foundation for the understanding of the mind of the child.[29] When John Dewey (1859–1952) linked this new science with the reforming progressive spirit of the day and his own pragmatism, "new views of the child and new views of the world" came into focus.[30] By emphasizing both the physical and the mental development of the child, in effect the whole child, and promoting practical, effective solutions to the problems of child rearing, Dewey offered pediatricians an important example of the usefulness of the biosocial model of child health and development. When practitioners and mothers followed Dewey's advice, a child could "fulfill its own destiny" with a healthy mind and a healthy body.[31]

In order to understand the development and functioning of the child's mind, the quantitative study of behavior was needed. Alfred Binet (1857–1911), for example, began his work "to serve the interesting cause of the education of subnormals"[32] but, subsequently, developed the means for the quantitative study of human intelligence. According to Binet, the scientific study of children required a method of measuring intelligence. This study of the diversity of "intellectual attitudes" ultimately enabled the formulation of a statistical interpretation of intelligence, the "law of the intellectual development of children."[33] Binet, among other experts of the day, opened the mind of the child to scientific scrutiny and, in the process, developed new means for understanding child development and behavior.

An important early participant in the study of child psychology and an active member of the Child Study Association was the Clark University professor and educator G. Stanley Hall. Hall, who was strongly influenced by Herbert Spencer and Charles Darwin, viewed education and child development as preparation for "complete living."[34] Children's mental development, just like its biological corollary, embryogenesis, was a natural process. In essence, as Hall stated in *Evolution and Psychology*, this included "nearly every act, sensation, feeling, will and thought of the young child."[35] While Hall and other psychologists of the day recognized that the development of the child's mind was a natural process, they also reported it was frequently adversely influenced by adults. In part, developmental problems, psychological conflicts, and mental illness arose from interference with the normal psychological development of the child. Only when parents and physicians understood normal mental development could they adequately foster the mental health of their children.

Hall also first recognized adolescence as a unique developmental transition from childhood to adulthood. Hall placed this "new birth," when "the higher and more completely human traits are now born," within the realm of normal child development, and as a result pediatricians incorporated adolescent health care into pediatric practice.[36] The developmental process that began in infancy logically extended to adulthood. While the first clinic specifically designed for adolescent patients was not established in the United States until 1951 at the Boston Children's Hospital, Hall's early work called attention to the problems that the events of recent decades have highlighted. Adolescents were physically and sexually mature, yet socially immature and confined by social dictates to an uncertain existence between youth and maturity. During the second half of this century, pediatricians have advised, treated, and helped ease many adolescents' transition to an adult world.

If Hall defined child development as a natural event, the Johns Hopkins professor and behaviorist John B. Watson situated the process within the realm of the "natural sciences." Watson based his observations on the "human animal" and required that "everything which cannot be stated in the universal terms of science" be discarded.[37] He believed that when human behavior was sufficiently well understood, it was predictable and thus subject to control and manipulation. Without the knowledge essential to this understanding, "the tender years of infancy" were almost "a dangerous experiment" in child rearing:[38] "Remember when you are tempted to pet your child that mother love is a dangerous instrument? An instrument which may inflict a never healing wound, a wound which may make infancy unhappy, adolescence a nightmare, an instrument which may wreck your adult son or daughter's vocational future and their chances for marital happiness."[39] Watson believed that the scientific principles of child development enabled parents and pediatricians alike to convert the "dangerous experiment" of childhood into a defined and predictable developmental process. The end result was, according to Watson, the prevention of developmental dilemmas and the resolution of many of the daily problems of child development. The price adherents of Watson's beliefs paid was the elimination of touching, emotional contact, and bonding between parent and child.

When viewed from the behaviorist's perspective, an understanding of child development became a tool for the control of children's behavior. Watson concluded: "Psychology as the behaviorist views it is [a] purely objective experimental branch of natural science. Its theoretical goal is the prediction and control of behavior. Introspection forms no essential part of its methods, nor is the scientific value of its data dependent upon the readiness with which they lend themselves to interpretation in terms of consciousness. The behaviorist . . . recognizes no dividing line between man and brute. The behavior of man, with all of its refinement and complexity, forms only a part of the behaviorists total scheme of investigation."[40] Behaviorists believed that human development was no different from animal development.

Watson espoused these principles in popular articles that appeared in numerous magazines, including *McCall's, Ladies' Home Journal,* and *Good Housekeeping.* He concluded that the scientific principles of behaviorism, based upon the conditioned response, led not only to healthier babies but "better brought up babies."[41] These measures were necessary because "once a child's character has been spoiled by bad handling which can be done in a few days, who can say that the damage is ever repaired."[42] While many might disagree with Watson's rather sterile application of science to child-rearing practices, the identification of behavioral problems as developmental in origin and the possibility that they were amenable to expert intervention further promoted the medicalization of the treatment of the child's mind. These efforts offered the possibility of prophylaxis and control of deviant or unaccepted behavior by physicians, psychologists, other expert professionals, and parents.

In 1909 G. Stanley Hall persuaded Sigmund Freud to lecture at Clark University. These five lectures introduced many Americans to Freud's psychoanalytic conception of the mind. The unconscious and Freud's emphasis on sexuality were new, but like Hall and Watson, he saw human nature as an extension of animal nature. For Freud, humans were irrational beings, and when they were confronted with conflicting circumstances, often based upon unresolved childhood sexual conflicts, psychopathology could result. The psychological development of the child carried with it "the seed of a pathological disposition."[43] While Freud offered an alternative theory of child development, he agreed with most other child psychologists that professional intervention, in Freud's case based upon the principles of psychoanalysis, facilitated child development and enabled the treatment of ill health.

By 1916 all of Freud's completed works had been translated into English and were available in America. Certainly the most controversial aspect of this body of work was its emphasis upon sexuality. According to Freud, even children were sexual beings. This was a view that many early twentieth-century Americans were not willing to accept. Nonetheless, Freud emphasized its importance and held it up for "thorough study":

> One feature of the popular view of the sexual instinct is that it is absent in childhood and only awakens in the period of life described as puberty. This, however, is not merely a simple error but one that has had grave consequences, for it is mainly to this idea that we owe our present ignorance of the fundamental conditions of sexual life. A thorough study of the sexual manifestations of childhood would probably reveal the essential characters of the sexual instinct and would show us the course of its development and the way in which it is put together from the various sources.[44]

Freud believed that when this process was adequately understood, the natural basis for child development was readily apparent. In fact, this understanding was essential for psychoanalytic intervention, which was, as Freud told his Clark University audience, "no more than a prolongation of education for the purpose of overcoming the residues of childhood."[45] Freud, like Watson and Hall, placed the correction of developmental problems within the natural process of child development. Without an understanding of normal development, neither parents nor physicians were capable of addressing the developmental and behavioral problems of the nation's children.

While many were attracted to Freud's ideas, others were repelled by his emphasis on sexuality. Many Americans, lay and professional alike, agreed that "only a depraved person could interpret the pleasure of the babe sucking at its mother's breast as erotic, much less incestuous, or connect in any way the child's wish to romp in the fresh air without clothing with the perverted exhibitionism of degenerates."[46] Recognizing this problem, Freud told his Clark University audience that "even workers who are ready to follow my psychological studies are inclined to think that I over-estimate the part played by sexual factors."[47] Despite the controversy surrounding Freud's emphasis on sexuality, his theories and the ensuing discussion created a new openness about sexuality that questioned the objectivity and reason of previous psychological theories.

During the 1920s and 1930s Freud's influence was much greater among artists, writers, and intellectuals than it was among the public, physicians, or child health workers. At mid-century, Alfred Kazin, an early advocate of Freud's work, summarized the master's contributions: "Freud's extraordinary achievement was to show us, in scientific terms, the primacy of natural desire, the secret wishes we proclaim in our dreams and the mixture of love, and shame and jealousy in our relations to our parents, the child as father to the man, the deeply buried instincts that make us natural beings and that go back to the forgotten struggles of the human race."[48]

Freud offered explanations for human behavior that a growing number of American professionals found attractive. But only 1 of 42 child rearing manuals of the 1920s readily accepted the Freudian perspective on child development.[49] Freud's theories were neither as popular nor as influential as the behavioral model offered by Baltimore's Watson. Yet both recognized the essential role that child development played in children's and adults' health.

Although several theories of child development existed, all psychologists and pediatricians agreed that "normal" development followed certain psychological norms. Arnold Gesell (1880–1961), a pediatrician and the director of the child development clinic at Yale University for nearly 40 years, concluded: "It is important to recognize that such psychological norms are attainable, and that the standards of mental health are as legitimate and as feasible as standards of physical status. Even in our present state of comparative ignorance, it is possible to lay down for various ages of infancy and childhood certain concrete minimum essentials of mental health expressed in tangible behavior terms."[50] Drawn from several theories of child development—behaviorist, psychoanalytic, learning-based—a scientific understanding of the normal developmental process provided a basis in the mid-twentieth century for the prevention of mental illness and the treatment of behavioral problems.

The child guidance movement, which was directed by physicians and other experts, began during the 1930s with an emphasis on the scientific understanding of the child's mind and its control as a way of preventing delinquency and maladjustment. Many believed that the principles of child development provided "an orderly, systematic scientific approach" to "overcoming undesirable habits and straightening out twisted personalities."[51] The "total transactions of living" controlled the development of the adult, and only when the expert guided the developmental process was success likely.[52] Increasingly, these measures were deemed appropriate not only for understanding the normal developmental process, but they also provided the tools for guiding child development within specific expected limits. Just as the fundamentals of nutrition promoted the physical health of children, so attention to the principles of child development fostered their mental health. Physicians, and particularly pediatricians, who "almost entirely" controlled the crucial first two years of life, were uniquely placed to provide such care. As Gesell reported to the American Academy of Pediatrics in 1939, the mental health of the nation's children was so essential that adequate training about child development and mental health was an "important part of every pediatric teaching program."[53] By promoting professional training, physicians officially accepted the mind of the child as being within the domain of medical responsibility. By mid-century pediatricians, like their colleagues of three centuries before, were regularly attending to matters of body and soul.

Medical science had dramatically reduced the incidence of infectious diseases by preventive methods, and practitioners of child guidance hoped to do as much for mental illness and behavioral problems. Prevention was easier than curing illness, and, as a *New York Times* editorial noted, it was applicable "to children, who, though they might never become criminal or insane, have clearly marked mental attitudes and habits which if allowed to become fixed will render them unnecessarily unhappy and ineffective in adult life." By understanding and applying the norms of child development and by the "intensive study and treatment" of not only children, but their parents, families, and social circumstances, child guidance authorities predicted that healthier children with fewer behavioral problems would result.[54]

The Whole Child

Contemporary pediatric practice is grounded within the scientific study of the whole child—body and mind, psyche and soma, flesh and soul. Today pediatricians employ the principles of renal physiology as much as they do behavioral modification and drug therapy for the hyperactive child. Disease prevention relies as much upon theories of child development as on the principles of the germ theory. Pediatricians attend the physical, behavioral, emotional, and social problems of their patients.[55] Popular child advisers, from Benjamin Spock to T. Berry Brazelton, advise parents of the wide and varied role of the pediatrician in baby and child care. In essence, they continue the biosocial role of the pediatrician that Abraham Jacobi favored at the dawn of the century of the child. By so doing, pediatricians, with the aid of parents, help, according to a popular pediatric textbook, "each boy and girl to reach maturity equipped physically, mentally, and socially to function as responsible members of society within limits approaching his or her own potential and to have had the opportunity of thoroughly enjoying the years of getting there."[56] In short, the role of the pediatricians is to foster the growth, development, and maturation of the whole child.

Scientific, public health, legal, and social action was necessary for the effective diagnosis and treatment of the whole child. Beginning in the 1960s, an especially important effort for many physicians was the correction of social factors that often impaired children's health. The importance of social problems, especially poverty and substandard living conditions, received emphasis during the depression years when American society increasingly focused on the welfare of the child.[57] Children still died of malnutrition, smallpox, and pneumonia, but as the physician and former Hull House resident Alice Hamilton noted in 1930, "certainly if the social part were eliminated the work would be not nearly so effective."[58] Many of Dr. Hamilton's colleagues, especially male physicians, did not agree that the health care of American children required attention to the broader social problems of the nation. In fact, many considered such concerns beyond the realm of medical practice. Yet, the results that Hamilton and her colleagues reported provided evidence that medical attention directed at the problems of the whole child benefited the health of the nation's children.

The renewed focus on child abuse in the 1960s exemplified the use of the biosocial model of children's health care and included not only physical injury, but also emotional trauma, sexual abuse, and neglected medical care. Professional recognition of child abuse as a medical problem for American children emphasized the magnitude of the problem to the American public.[59] Each year from 1961 to 1974, nearly one hundred infants and children were reported to have been killed by their parents. These deaths represented more than 3 percent of childhood and adolescent homicides in the nation. Clearly, the traditional medical model for children's health was insufficient to deal with a problem of this nature or magnitude. Rather, according to one pediatric authority, maximal effectiveness in combating child abuse required that pediatricians provide "attractive, accessible, noncoercive health (both physical and mental) and social services that strengthened parents' autonomous efforts to nurture and protect their children."[60] Effective intervention included not only the treatment of physical injuries but also counseling, homemaking, and parent aide services, psychotherapy, economic and employment assistance, and developmental evaluation and guidance. Prevention required attention to the whole child and the fostering of his or her individual health by addressing the larger social and emotional problems that faced the child's family. If molecular genetic science could probe the inner recesses of the cell for the diseased genes of cystic fibrosis or Duchenne's muscular dystrophy and if public health measures could eradicate smallpox from the farthest corners of the globe, then children's social problems should be equally amenable to effective solution. Successful remedy of social problems required, as Dr. Samuel Levine of Cornell University and president of the American Pediatric Society concluded, using the biosocial model of children's health: "Why should a case of primary aldosteronism [a hormone disorder of the adrenal gland] be considered to be more exciting, challenging, and complex than a major reading problem or an incipient case of juvenile delinquency? Actually, I suspect the latter could be equally challenging if we were willing to admit our present ineptitude in the realm of social, cultural, and personality factors and if we tried to fill the gaps in knowledge in the behavioral sciences with the same vigor used to attack the biologic problems of organic disease."[61] Levine proposed that the same scientific methods and careful analysis that identified and solved rare endocrine problems of the kidney are potentially equally successful against the behavioral and social problems of delinquency and learning disabilities.

The general acceptance and widespread implementation of the biosocial model of children's health required that physicians and medical students receive a fundamental grounding in its principles. Just as anatomy and physiology were essential for an understanding of the health of the body, study of "the social sciences—sociology, cultural anthropology, psychology, economics and urban planning, among others"—was basic to an understanding of child development.[62] By the 1980s most American medical schools emphasized the biosocial model; yet, as the 1981 report of the Select Panel for the Promotion of Child Health (*Better Health for Our Children*) concluded, the problems of children's health in America were incompletely addressed. Perhaps the most striking criticism in this multivolume assessment of the health of America's children was the highlighting of "the contrast between how much we know about promoting the health of pregnant women and children and how little is actually reaching some of the most vulnerable among them."[63] In effect, the panel called upon the American public, the medical profession, and Congress to assume a broader role in promoting the health of American children. Only when the public at large recognized that social factors were significant impediments to improved child health and then acted to remedy those problems would more American children obtain the benefits that accrued from a century of efforts designed to promote their health.

To take but one example, lead toxicity—that "blunter of children's cognition and silent thief of their futures"[64]—is both a common and an important problem of children's health that despite available resources has been only partially addressed by American families, physicians, industry, and society. Today, nearly one American child in six has toxic levels of lead in his or her bloodstream. More than one-half of black children of poor socioeconomic status have abnormalities due to lead poisoning, while only 1 in 14 white, well-advantaged children are affected.[65] The lead problem continues not because of a lack of knowledge about the toxic effects of lead, for these have been known for years, not because of a failure of legislative resolve, for lead-based gasoline additives have been eliminated, not because of a lack of industrial alternatives, for lead-free paints are widely used, but largely because of societal inaction. Since the toxic effects of lead are slow and subtle, it is all too easy for society to ignore the magnitude of the problem. Too often, as authorities on child health recently concluded, the "moral" necessity of the problems of children's health remain unanswered within the "self-satisfied pragmatism" of a society that bases decisions on economic rather than human benefits. As a result children's health is endangered and a potential economic benefit of an estimated $28 billion from the avoidance of preventable lead toxicity remains undelivered to the American economy.[66]

While society, through neglect or limited knowledge, may endanger the health of children, children themselves, particularly adolescents, often engage in potentially dangerous behavior. Consequently, too many children die preventable deaths. Experimentation with drugs is common; motorcycles are ridden without safety helmets; and AIDS, gonorrhea, and other sexually transmitted diseases are acquired through unplanned or unprotected sexual encounters. Before birth, teens' babies are exposed to crack, angel dust, and other substances of abuse. And perhaps nowhere are the risks and violence in the lives of American children more dramatically depicted than on city streets where drive-by shootings and drug deals are part of daily life.

Violence is a central feature of twentieth-century America. Over the past two decades, the rate of violent death for American children has nearly doubled. Seventy percent of teenage homicides, and nearly as many suicides, are associated with firearm use. This translates each year into the death of nearly 3,200 American adolescents age 15 to 19. Nearly one of every two deaths of black male adolescents is due to gunshot wounds; for white adolescents, it is one in five. For 1986 to 1989 injuries resulting from the abuse of firearms increased 380 percent at major urban emergency centers. Many factors, including the social acceptance of violence, peer pressure, substance abuse, impulsive behavior, a belief in invincibility, and a perceived need for protection, account for this epidemic of largely preventable violent deaths and avoidable injuries.[67] What remains lacking is the overall social resolve to address the problem. Solutions are available, as they are for sexually transmitted disease and adolescent pregnancy, but society is unwilling to accept responsibility and initiate action.

As the end of the century of the child nears, it is appropriate to reflect upon the words of Anna Salvia, a Ukrainian immigrant who arrived in America in 1923. She recalled that as she and her brother were examined for exit from the Ukraine, the thoroughness of the process suggested that "in America, everybody must be so healthy."[68] The report of the Select Committee on Children, Youth and Families for 1989 provides some mixed confirmation of Anna's impression. The life expectancy for American children is now more than 75 years. In 1988 there were fewer than 2 cases of whooping cough or mumps among every 100,000 Americans, and only one-half as many cases of rubella or measles.[69] Yet only three-quarters of American children were immunized against measles, mumps, rubella, and polio, and less than 90 percent have received adequate protection against diphtheria or tetanus.[70] Accidents, many of which are preventable, are the leading cause of death for American children. In 1986 nearly 8,000 American adolescents died in motor vehicular accidents.[71] Nearly four million children have asthma, chronic bronchitis, or hay fever; two million have dermatitis; and one million children have a speech or hearing impairment.[72] In 1987 at least 1,489 children under 14 years of age were infected with the HIV virus.[73]

These statistics provide an ambiguous picture of children's health in America. Infectious diseases—measles, mumps, and whooping cough—are rare, yet significant numbers of American children are incompletely immunized against these easily preventable and potentially fatal conditions. In 1988 the nation spent more than $40 billion on health care, yet barely one-half (53 percent) of American parents rated their children's health as excellent.[74] Even more telling is the recognition that children compose the largest group among those living in poverty in the United States. One of every five American children lives in poverty, and nearly one-half of all black and Hispanic children reside below the poverty level.[75] Not surprisingly, black infants and children die more than twice as frequently as do white children. Unfortunately, the problem is not abating. In Illinois, from 1984 to 1988, the death rate for black children rose seven times faster than for white children. Clearly, many factors are responsible for the continuing health problems of children in America, but among the most important, in Illinois and throughout the nation, are the "complex mix of social, economic and health factors" that are bred by poverty.[76]

In September 1990 the United States joined 70 other nations in sponsoring the United Nations World Summit for Children. Yet, statistics about the health of American children show that their health is below the standards mandated by resolutions that President Bush endorsed at the UNICEF conference.[77] The problem was graphically defined by an eleven-year-old New York City girl named Liberty. She recalled it was "a very sad thing that little babies have to suffer the way they are. . . . There is a baby on the fourth floor that has scabies on her body. The baby is only five months old. I don't think any one is really trying to help. We have no place to cook a decent meal for a family with no kitchen, just a hot plate and washing the dishes in the bathroom."[78] At the same time that Liberty detailed the poverty of her life and the president reported his helplessness when seeing infants "addicted to cocaine, their tiny bodies trembling with pain," funding for children's services was reduced in the federal budget. The position of children's health in America is reflected in a New York schoolgirl's comment that "everything is upside down."[79]

The high frequency of infant death, the incomplete extent of immunization programs, and the increasing number of malnourished American children are all evidence that children's health in America is not what it should be. Medical care in America, as Rosemary Stevens has described in her study of American hospitals, is based in "sickness" and "wealth."[80] The treatment of disease, not its prevention, is emphasized; and, increasingly, only the rich can afford medical attention that is based upon expensive medical technology. Not only have the public health principles that eliminated smallpox and polio been forgotten, but limited financial resources have been expended for increasingly complex and expensive methods of diagnosis and treatment, like computerized tomography and liver transplantation. At the same time, little attention is given to the basic problem of children's health—poverty. Only by our "strik[ing] at the roots of [the] evil"[81] that is poverty and the social ills that face too many will more American children be healthy.

At a time when not only violence but also poverty and malnutrition are increasing, the cry for attention to the health of America's children could not be greater. Unfortunately the voices of children often remain unheard among their elders. Nonetheless the problems of sick and injured children in America and throughout the world call for the avoidance of preventable health and social problems. Parents and society must recognize that solutions to the problems of children's health in America are based, as members of the American Academy of Pediatrics were advised at the 1992 annual meeting, on understanding the "real causes of the crises of our times", and employing individual and organized efforts for their resolution.[82] Solutions, as the preceding pages amply demonstrate, are based as much on addressing poverty, limited education, and social disadvantage as they are on promoting the advance of medicine. American society must find the moral resolve that led previous generations to foster motherhood and cleanliness for the benefit of children, to ground present solutions to the problems of children's health on equity, accountability, foresight, and social justice.

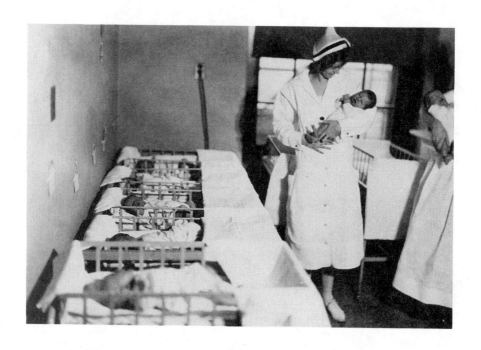

During the early twentieth century, giving birth in a hospital became standard. By the 1920s, in many urban hospitals the newborn nursery was often overcrowded. Hospital Archives, University of Kansas Medical Center, Kansas City, Kansas.

A Chronology of Children's Health in America

1587   The first white child, Virginia Dare, is born in the English colonies.

1617–19   Smallpox epidemic along the Massachusetts Bay Coast causes a 90 percent mortality among Native Americans.

1630   Dr. Samuel Fuller arrives in Massachusetts Bay Colony to find many sick and dead.

1647   Governor Winthrop records "epidemical sickness" among Native Americans and colonists in Massachusetts Bay Colony.

1684   Samuel Willard's *The Child's Portion* is published.

1689   Walter Harris, London consultant to the King, publishes *De Morbis Acutis Infantum*.

1692   Martha Carrier, whom Cotton Mather dubbed the "Queen of Hell," is executed for reportedly creating a smallpox epidemic and practicing witchcraft.

1693   Governor Andros of Virginia Colony declares a "Day of Humiliation and Prayer" when the colony experiences a fatal measles epidemic. John Locke's *Some Thoughts Concerning Education* is published.

1718   Cotton Mather publishes "Raphael. The Blessings of an HEALED SOUL" for the benefit of sick Bostonians.

1721   During a smallpox epidemic in Boston, Cotton Mather and Dr. Zabdiel Boylston urge inoculation against the disease.

1735–40 Epidemic diphtheria spreads from New Hampshire to New Jersey with thousands of deaths.

1736   John Tennent's *Every Man His Own Doctor* is published.

1740   Bethesda Orphan House, the first child care institution in America, is founded in Savannah, Georgia, by the evangelist George Whitefield.

1742   *The Compleat Housewife* by Eliza Smith is published.

1752   Pennsylvania Hospital is opened in Philadelphia.

1759   Benjamin Franklin and William Heberden publish "Some Account of the Success of Inoculation for Small-pox in England and America."

1763   First English translation of Rousseau's *Emile* is published.

1769   William Cadogan's "An Essay upon Nursing and the Management of Children" is published.

1773   Michael Underwood's *A Treatise on the Diseases of Children* is published.

1793   Yellow fever epidemic occurs in Philadelphia with hundreds of deaths.

1794   Philadelphia edition of Mary Wollstonecraft's *Vindication of the Rights of Woman* is published.

1800   Harvard professor and physician Benjamin Waterhouse introduces the smallpox vaccination developed by the English physician Edward Jenner to America.

1806   Orphan Asylum Society is established in New York City as an outgrowth of the Society for the Relief of Poor Widows with Small Children.

1809   William Buchan's *Advice to Mothers* is published.

1812   Peter Smith's *Indian Doctor's Dispensatory* is published.

1813   Eli Ives of Yale University begins first annual American series of medical school lectures on the diseases of children, which lasts 39 years. Federal legislation passed encouraging smallpox vaccination.

1817   American Asylum for the Education and Instruction of the Deaf and Dumb opens in Hartford, Connecticut.

1826   William Dewees publishes *Treatise on the Physical and Medical Treatment of Children,* the first medical textbook on children's diseases by an American physician.

1832   Samuel Howe opens the New England Asylum for the Blind in Boston.

1836   Thomas Hersey's *The Midwife's Directory* is published.

1843   Dorothea Dix reports to the Massachusetts Legislature on the care of the insane.

1845   *Nurse's Manual and Mother's Medical Adviser* is published in Philadelphia.

1853   Charles Loring Brace establishes the Children's Aid Society in New York City.

1854   Nursery and Child's Hospital opens in New York City, the nation's first children's hospital.

1855   Children's Hospital of Philadelphia opens.

1857   John Gunn's *New Domestic Physician* is published and is reprinted in more than 200 editions by the end of the century.

1859   Chicago Nursery and Half Orphan Asylum is established.

1860   Abraham Jacobi is appointed to the first university chair of children's diseases in America; subsequently Jacobi forms the first department of pediatrics at an American medical school— the College of Physicians and Surgeons in New York City.

1866   New York City becomes the first American city to establish a municipal health department.

1868   Boston Children's Hospital opens.

1869   Massachusetts becomes the first state to systematically collect statewide vital statistics.

1871   Jacob Abbot's *Gentle Measures in the Management and Training of the Young* is published. Harvard University catalog first lists coursework in the diseases of children.

1873   American Public Health Association is founded. Section on Obstetrics and Diseases of Women is founded within the American Medical Association.

1874   The first child abuse trial in America begins when Mary Ellen appears in a New York City courtroom.

1875   New York Society for the Prevention of Cruelty is founded.

1880   American Medical Association organizes a section on the Diseases of Children.

1881   Clara Barton organizes the American Association of the Red Cross. Silver nitrate prophylaxis for ophthalmia neonatorum is developed. Evidence is presented that milk-borne infections result from bacterial contamination of fresh milk.

1884   The medical journal *Archives of Pediatrics* begins publication.

1888   American Pediatric Society is founded. Charles Chapin establishes the first American health department laboratory in Providence, Rhode Island. Thomas Morgan Rotch becomes first professor of pediatrics at Harvard University.

1889   Dr. Henry Koplik establishes the first infant milk station in New York City. Hull House is founded by Jane Addams on Chicago's West Side.

1890   John Keating's *Cyclopaedia of the Diseases of Children* is published.

1893   Dr. Henry L. Coit of New Jersey founds the nation's first medical milk committee.

1893–94 Smallpox epidemic occurs in conjunction with the Chicago World's Fair; despite the administration of 1,084,500 doses of vaccine, more than 1,000 die.

1894   L. Emmett Holt of New York City publishes *The Care and Feeding of Children*. Milwaukee health department establishes free diphtheria treatment stations. Boston introduces a system of school medical inspection.

1896   The first edition of L. Emmett Holt's *The Diseases of Infancy and Childhood* is published.

1897   New York Health Department begins compulsory smallpox vaccination for schoolchildren. National Congress of Mothers is formed. Minnesota establishes first state hospital for crippled children.

1902   First school nurse in America is appointed in New York City.

1904   National Child Labor Committee is founded.

1905   Samuel Crumbine develops the fly swatter.

1908   Chicago becomes the first city in the world to require a pasteurized municipal milk supply. Clifford Beer's *A Mind That Found Itself* is published. New York City Department of Health establishes the nation's first Division of Child Health. The American Association for the Study and Prevention of Infant Mortality is founded by physicians and laypersons.

1909   Clifford Beers founds the National Committee for Mental Hygiene. Ellen Key publishes *The Century of the Child*. President Roosevelt holds the First White House Conference on the Care of Dependent Children. Sigmund Freud delivers a series of five lectures at Clark University.

1910   New Jersey becomes the first state to mandate physical examination before school attendance.

1911   *American Journal of the Diseases of Children* begins publication. Arnold Gesell founds the Clinic for Child Development at Yale University.

1912   The Children's Bureau is established, with Julia Lathrop as first director.

1914   The Children's Bureau publishes the first edition of *Infant Care*.

1916   Poliomyelitis epidemic spreads across 26 states with more than 27,000 cases and 6,000 deaths. A collection of Sigmund Freud's completed works is published in an American edition.

1918   Pandemic of Spanish influenza occurs, with tens of thousands of deaths nationwide.

1920–25   Commonwealth Fund–sponsored child health demonstration project begins in selected American cities.

1921   Congress passes the Sheppard-Towner Act, and within six months matching funds become available for state programs.

1922   American Child Health Association is formed by the merger of the American Child Hygiene Association and the Child Health Organization; Herbert Hoover proclaims the Child's Bill of Rights at the inaugural meeting.

1924   May Day is first promoted as national Child Health Day.

1928   John B. Watson's *Psychological Care of the Infant and Child* is published. "Cheerio," a children's health radio program sponsored by the American Child Health Association, begins.

1929   Refunding of the Sheppard-Towner Act is defeated.

1930   Third White House Conference on Child Health and Protection is held.

1931   First annual meeting of the American Academy of Pediatrics is held.

1935   Enactment of the Social Security Act provides federal aid to states for maternal and children's health programs.

1936   Congress provides funding for the Social Security Act. Sulfa drugs are found effective against bacterial infections, including pneumonia, tonsillitis, scarlet fever, and impetigo.

1937   More than 500,000 children are reported as recipients of aid to dependent children.

1939 Federal funding is first made available for state programs for the treatment of children with rheumatic fever.

1940 White House Conference on Children in a Democracy is held.

1942 Children's Bureau establishes Commission on Children in Wartime.

1943 Congress approves funding for Children's Bureau Emergency Maternal and Infant Care Program.

1946 Childhood nutrition is promoted by passage of the National School Lunch Act. Benjamin Spock publishes *The Common Sense Book of Baby and Child Care.*

1950 The National Association for Retarded Citizens is formed. Mid-century White House Conference on Children and Youth is held in Washington.

1951 Federal funding for regional centers for research and care of children with amputations is started. The first clinic for adolescent patients is established at Boston Children's Hospital.

1954 Poliomyelitis vaccination test program begins.

1955 Congress approves $30,000,000 for assistance to state poliomyelitis vaccination programs.

1958 More than 1,000,000 doses of Salk polio vaccine is administered in Chicago.

1959 Declaration of the Rights of the Child is endorsed by the United Nations and the White House Conference on Children and Youth.

1961 Clinical recognition of the battered child syndrome is reported.

1962 The tranquilizer thalidomide is recognized as a cause of birth defects.

1963 The National Institute of Child Health and Human Development is established as a part of the National Institutes of Health. Measles vaccine is licensed for commercial production.

1965 Congress extends Medicare benefits to children in low-income families.

1966 Economic Opportunity Act provides neighborhood comprehensive health centers for low-income families.

1967 Infant care, family planning, and dental care programs are funded under the Child Health Act.

1970 The Center for Disease Control reports no poliomyelitis deaths in America.

1971   White House Conference on Youth is held.

1975   Special Supplemental Food Program for Women, Infants and Children (WIC) is started.

1978   Louise Brown, the world's first test tube baby, is born in England.

1979   Global eradication of smallpox is achieved.

1981   *Report of the Select Panel for the Promotion of Child Health* urges more governmental and medical attention to the health problems of American children. The first cases of AIDS (acquired immunodeficiency syndrome) are reported.

1986   The number of cases of measles doubles from the previous year; because of incomplete vaccination, this trend continues into the 1990s.

1989   *Report of the Select Committee on Children, Youth and Families* confirms that the health and life expectancy of minority children lags behind that of white children.

1990   UNICEF Conference on Children reports the health of American children has not kept pace with that of children in many other developed countries.

Notes and References

Introduction

1. Edmund Morgan, *The Puritan Family*, rev. ed. (New York: Harper, 1966), 64.
2. John Locke, *Some Thoughts Concerning Education* (New York: Oxford, 1989), 83.
3. Cotton Mather, *The Diary of Cotton Mather* (Boston: Massachusetts Historical Society Collection, 1911), 179.
4. Samuel Sewall, *Diary* (New York: Farrar, Straus & Giroux, 1973), 350.
5. Michael Underwood, *A Treatise on the Diseases of Children with General Directions for the Management of Infants from the Birth*, rev. ed. (Philadelphia: T. Dobson, 1773), vii.
6. Mather, 252.
7. Charles R. King, "Dr. Franklin, I Presume? The Medical Side of Benjamin Franklin" (paper delivered at the Fellows Colloquium, Newberry Library, Chicago, Ill., January 1991).
8. Jean Jacques Rousseau, *Emile, On Education* (New York: Basic, 1979).
9. Mary Wollstonecraft, *The Works of Mary Wollstonecraft* (New York: New York University Press, 1989), 459.
10. Tombstones, Copp's Hill Burying Ground, Boston, Massachusetts.
11. Sylvia D. Hoffert, *Private Matters: American Attitudes toward Childbearing and Infant Nurture in the Urban North, 1800–1860* (Urbana: University of Illinois, 1989), 15.

12. Linda Pollock, *A Lasting Relationship: Parents and Children over Three Centuries* (London: Fourth Estate, 1987), 180.
13. Pollock, 175.
14. Thomas E. Cone, *History of American Pediatrics* (Boston: Little, Brown, 1979), 69.
15. Abraham Jacobi, "History of Pediatrics and Its Relation to Other Science and Arts," *American Medicine* 8(1904):804.
16. *New York Times*, 2 July 1876, 12.
17. Barbara Rosenkrantz, *Public Health and the State, Changing Views in Massachusetts, 1842–1936* (Cambridge, Mass.: Harvard University Press, 1972), 77.
18. Nancy Cott, *The Grounding of Modern Feminism* (New Haven: Yale, 1989), 168.
19. Molly Ladd-Taylor, *Raising a Baby the Government Way. Mother's Letters to the Children's Bureau, 1915–1932* (New Brunswick: Rutgers, 1986).
20. Ladd-Taylor, 2.
21. Charles E. North, "Milk and Its Relation to Public Health," in Mazyck Ravenel, *A Half Century of Public Health* (New York: American Public Health Association, 1921), 236–89.
22. Benjamin Spock, *Baby and Child Care*, rev. ed. (New York: Pocket Books, 1968); Sigmund Freud, *The Standard Edition of the Complete Psychological Studies of Sigmund Freud* (London: Hogarth Press, 1959).
23. *Mid Century White House Conference on Children and Youth. A Healthy Personality for Every Child* (Washington, D.C.: Government Printing Office, 1950), 1.
24. Brian Birch, "Possessed of a Restless Spirit: A Young Girl; Memories of the Southern Iowa Frontier," *Palimpsest* 66(1985):183.

Chapter 1

1. John Winthrop, *Journal, A History of New England* (New York: Barnes & Noble, 1966), vol. 1, 266–68.
2. Samuel Sewall, *Diary* (New York: Farrar, Straus & Giroux, 1973), 730.
3. E. Brooks Holifield, *Era of Persuasion: American Thought and Culture, 1521–1680* (Boston: Twayne, 1989).
4. Ross W. Beales, Jr., "The Child in Seventeenth Century America," in Joseph M. Hawes and N. Ray Hiner, *American Childhood: A Research Guide and Historical Handbook* (Westport, Conn.: Greenwood, 1985), 18–20.
5. Peter Slater, *Children in the New England Mind in Death and in Life* (Hamden, Conn.: Archon Books, 1977), 93.
6. Robert Pernell, *De Morbis Puerorum, or A Treatise of the Diseases of Children* (London: F. Legatt, 1653), 6.

7. John Duffy, "The Passage to the Colonies," *Mississippi Valley Historical Review* 38(1951):23.

8. Ibid., 31.

9. Holifield, 34.

10. Karen Ordahl Kupperman, "The Puzzle of the American Climate in the Earlier Colonial Period," *American Historical Review* 87(1982):1262.

11. Maris A. Vinovskis, "Angels' Heads and Weeping Willows: Death in Early America," *Proceedings of the American Antiquarian Society* 86(1976):273–302.

12. Vinovskis, 289.

13. Darrett B. Rutman, *Winthrop's Boston Portrait of a Puritan Town 1630–1699* (Chapel Hill: University of North Carolina, 1965), 27.

14. Beales, 20.

15. Sewall.

16. Constance B. Schulz, "Children and Childhood in the Eighteenth Century," in Hawes and Hiner, 67.

17. Darrett B. Rutman and Anita H. Rutman, "Of Agues and Fever: Malaria in the early Chesapeake," *William and Mary Quarterly* 33(1976):31.

18. Cotton Mather, *Diary of Cotton Mather* (Boston: Massachusetts Historical Society Collection, 1912), vol. 8, 187.

19. Matthew Hebron, "Diary," Matthew Hebron Papers. Library of Congress, Washington, D.C. (no date, unpaginated).

20. Wyandham Blanton, *Medicine in Virginia in the Seventeenth Century* (Richmond: William Byrd Press, 1930), 65.

21. Thomas Cone, *History of American Pediatrics* (Boston: Little, Brown, 1979), 56.

22. Linda Pollock, *A Lasting Relationship: Parents and Children over Three Centuries* (London: Fourth Estate, 1987), 97.

23. Winthrop, vol. 2, 72.

24. Sewall, 482, 640.

25. Mather, 293.

26. Winthrop, vol. 2, 209–210.

27. Mather, 250–54.

28. Robert H. Bremner, *Children & Youth in America: A Documentary History, Vol. 1, 1600–1865* (Cambridge: Harvard University, 1970), 292.

29. Cited in Rose Lockwood, "Birth, Illness and Death in Eighteenth Century New England," *Journal of Social History* 12(1978):118.

30. Michael Shute, "A Little Great Awakening: An Episode in the American Enlightenment," *Journal of the History of Ideas* 37 (1976): 590.

31. Ernest Caulfield, *A True History of the Terrible Epidemic Vulgarly Called the Throat Distemper, Which Occurred in his Majesty's New*

England Colonies Between the Years 1735 and 1740 (New Haven: Beaumont Medical Club, 1939).

32. Caulfield, 12.
33. Morris C. Leikind, "Colonial Epidemic Diseases," *Ciba Symposia* 1(1940):372.
34. Jonathan Dickinson, *Observations on that terrible Disease vulgarly called the Throat-Distemper with Advice as to the Method of Cure* (Boston: S. Kneeland & T. Green, 1740), 27.
35. Helen Duncan Behnke, "Colonial Theories Concerning the Cause of Disease," *Medical Life* 41(1934):72.
36. Blanton, 62.
37. Mather, 304–5.
38. Winthrop, vol. 2, 326.
39. Rutman and Rutman, 45.
40. John B. Blake, "The Compleat Housewife," *Bulletin of the History of Medicine* 49(1975):30.
41. Charles R. King, "Dr. Franklin, I Presume? The Medical Side of Benjamin Franklin" (paper delivered at the Fellows Colloquium, The Newberry Library, Chicago, Ill., January 1991).
42. Jonathan Butler, *Awash in a Sea of Faith, Christianizing the American People* (Cambridge: Harvard University, 1990), 78–80.
43. Wayland D. Hand, *Magical Medicine. The Folkloric Component of Medicine in the Folk Belief, Custom, and Ritual of the Peoples of Europe and America* (Berkley: University of California, 1980).
44. Edmund S. Morgan, *The Puritan Family*, rev. ed. (New York: Harper, 1966), 64.
45. William J. Bouwsma, *John Calvin: A Sixteenth Century Portrait* (New York: Oxford, 1988), 30.
46. Cotton Mather, *Angel of Bethesda*, (Barre, Mass.: American Antiquarian Society, 1972), 6.
47. Shute, 594.
48. Butler, 70.
49. David E. Stannard, *The Puritan Way of Death: A Study in Religion, Culture and Social Change* (New York: Oxford, 1977), 51.
50. David E. Stannard, "Death and the Puritan Child," *American Quarterly* 26(1974):472.
51. David E. Stannard, "Death and Dying in Puritan New England," *American Historical Review* 78(1973):1312.
52. Mather, *Diary*, 187.
53. Slater.
54. Mather, *Diary*, 20.
55. Mather, *Angel of Bethesda*, 6.
56. Lockwood, 111.

57. Mather, *Diary*, 297.

58. Mather, *Angel of Bethesda*, 37.

59. Butler, 70.

60. Mather, *Diary*, 294.

61. Ibid., 635.

62. Ibid., 252.

63. Ibid., 520.

64. Issac Kramnick, "Republican Revisionism Revisited," *American Historical Review* 87(1982):629.

65. Patrick Romanell, *John Locke and Medicine: A New Key to Locke* (Buffalo: Prometheus, 1984), 114.

66. John Locke, *Some Thoughts Concerning Education* (New York: Oxford, 1989), 79.

67. C. John Somerville, *The Rise and Fall of Childhood* (Beverly Hills: Sage Publications, 1982), 121.

68. Arthur W. Calhoun, *A Social History of the American Family from Colonial Times to the Present* (New York: Barnes & Noble, 1945), 106.

69. Pollock, 33–34.

70. Kenneth Dewhurst, *John Locke, Physician and Philosopher: A Medical Biography* (London: Wellcome Historical Trust, 1963), 259–60.

71. Locke, 84.

72. Locke, 103.

73. Locke, 178.

74. Linda Kerber, *Women of the Republic: Intellect and Ideology in Revolutionary America* (Chapel Hill: University of North Carolina, 1980), 243.

75. Jean Jacques Rousseau, *Emile, or on Education* (New York: Basic, 1979).

76. Rousseau, 55.

77. Rousseau, 28.

78. Jacques Derrida, *Of Grammatology* (Baltimore: Johns Hopkins, 1976), 247.

79. David Lundberg and Henry F. May, "The Enlightened Reader in America," *American Quarterly* 28(1976):262.

80. Janet Todd and Marilyn Butler, *The Works of Mary Wollstonecraft*, vol. 4 (New York: New York University Press, 1989), 459.

81. Paul Merrill Spurlin, *Rousseau in America, 1760–1809* (University, Ala.: University of Alabama, 1969), 133.

82. Ronald L. Numbers, *Medicine in the New World* (Knoxville: University of Tennessee, 1987).

83. John Ruhrah, *Pediatrics of the Past* (New York: Paul Hoeber, 1925), 365.

84. Walter Harris, *A Treatise on the Acute Diseases of Infants* (London: Thomas Astley, 1742), 1.

85. Michael Underwood, *A Treatise on the Diseases of Children with gener-*

al directions of the Management of Infants from the Birth, rev. ed. (Philadelphia: Dobson, 1773), vi.

86. Underwood, 6–7.
87. Judy B. Litoff, *American Midwives, 1860 to the Present* (Westport: Greenwood, 1978), 4.
88. Laurel Thatcher Ulrich, "'The Living Mother of a Living Child': Midwifery and Mortality in Post-Revolutionary New England," *William and Mary Quarterly* 46(1989):27.
89. Laurel Thatcher Ulrich, *A Midwife's Tale: The Life of Martha Ballard, Based on Her Diary, 1785–1812* (New York: Random House, 1990).
90. Ulrich, *A Midwife's Tale,* 40–43.
91. Carol F. Karlsen, *The Devil in the Shape of a Woman: Witchcraft in Colonial New England* (New York: Vintage, 1987), 99–100.
92. Cited in Bouwsma, 77.
93. Gail S. Murray, "Rational Thought and Republican Virtues: Children's Literature, 1789–1820," *Journal of the Early Republic* 8(1988):159.
94. Stannard, "Death and the Puritan Child," 462.
95. Kenneth A. Lockridge, *Literacy in Colonial New England: An Enquiry into the Social Context of Literacy in the Early Modern West* (New York: Norton, 1974).
96. Alice Judson Ryerson, "Medical Advice on Child Rearing, 1550–1900," *Harvard Education Review* 31(1961):309–11.
97. Spurlin, 74.
98. Cone, 56.
99. Margaret Hope Bacon, *Mothers of Feminism: The Story of Quaker Women in America* (New York: Harper & Row, 1986), 57.
100. Paula A. Treckel, "Breast Feeding and Maternal Sexuality in Colonial America," *Journal of Interdisciplinary History* 20(1989):25.
101. Winthrop, vol. 2, 268.
102. Ernest Caulfield, "Infant Feeding in Colonial America," *Journal of Pediatrics* 41(1952):683.
103. William Cadogan, *An Essay upon Nursing and the Management of Children from Their Birth to Three Years of Age* (London: Robert Horsfield, 1769), 5.
104. Donald R. Hopkins, *Princes and Peasants: Smallpox in History* (Chicago: University of Chicago, 1983).
105. Cited in Stannard, "Death and the Puritan Child," 464.
106. Hopkins, 241–42.
107. John B. Blake, "Smallpox Inoculation in Colonial Boston," in Gert Brieger, *Theory and Practice in American Medicine* (New York: Science History Publications, 1976), 111.
108. Thomas H. Brown, "The African Connection: Cotton Mather and the Boston Smallpox Epidemic of 1721–1722," *Journal of the American Medical Association* 260(1988):2248.

109. Mather, *Diary*, 620.
110. Ibid., 632.
111. Ibid., 655.
112. Ibid., 635.
113. Blake, 114.
114. Edward Jenner, "Vaccination Against Smallpox," in Charles B. Eliot, *The Harvard Classics Scientific Papers* (New York: Collier, 1960), 153.
115. Hopkins, 141.
116. Ibid., 265.

Chapter 2
1. *New York Times*, 12 May 1918, 8.
2. Ibid., 11 May 1913, 2.
3. Ibid., 10 May 1909, 18.
4. Mary Wollstonecraft, *Vindication of the Rights of Women* (New York: Norton, 1975), 152.
5. Linda Kerber, *Women of the Republic: Intellect and Ideology in Revolutionary America* (Chapel Hill: University of North Carolina Press, 1980), 11.
6. Nancy Cott, *The Bonds of Womanhood: "Woman's Sphere" in New England, 1780–1835* (New Haven: Yale University Press, 1977).
7. Linda Kerber, "The Republican Mother: Women and the Enlightenment —An American Perspective," *American Quarterly* 28(1976):191.
8. Mary Beth Norton, "The Evolution of White Women's Experience in Early America," *American Historical Review* 89(1984):593.
9. Mary Cable, "Bringing Up Baby," *American Heritage* 24(1972):58.
10. Nancy M. Theriot, *The Biosocial Construction of Femininity: Mothers and Daughters in Nineteenth Century America* (Westport, Conn.: Greenwood, 1988), 27.
11. Ruth H. Bloch, "American Feminine Ideals in Transition: The Rise of the Moral Mother, 1785–1815," *Feminist Studies* 4(1978):115.
12. Peter Gregg Slater, *Children in the New England Mind in Death and Life* (Hamden, Conn.: Archon Books, 1977), 100.
13. Benjamin Rush, *Thoughts Upon Female Education, Accommodated to the present state of Society, Manners, and Government in the United States of America* (Philadelphia, 1787), 28.
14. Wollstonecraft, 177.
15. J. C. Abbott, *Mother at Home: Or, the Principles of Maternal Duty* (New York: American Tract Society, 1833), 12–13.
16. Sylvia D. Hoffert, *Private Matters: American Attitudes Toward Childbearing and Infant Nurture in the Urban North, 1800–1860* (Urbana: University of Illinois, 1989), 15–16.

17. Linda Pollock, *A Lasting Relationship: Parents and Children over three Centuries* (London: Fourth Estate, 1987), 175.
18. Anne C. Kuhn, *The Mother's Role in Childhood Education, New England Concepts 1830–1860* (New Haven: Yale University Press, 1947), 72.
19. Ibid., 35.
20. Anthony M. Platt, *The Child Savers: The Invention of Delinquency,* 2d ed. (Chicago: University of Chicago Press, 1977), 78–79.
21. Barbara Welter, "The Cult of True Womanhood," *American Quarterly* 18(1966):151–74.
22. Kuhn, 74.
23. Pollock, 179–80.
24. Arthur W. Calhoun, *A Social History of the American Family from Colonial Times to the Present* (New York: Barnes & Noble, 1945), vol. 2, 62.
25. Catherine E. Beecher and Harriet Beecher Stowe, *American Woman's Home or, Principles of Domestic Science* (New York: J. B. Ford, 1869), 104.
26. Ibid., 263.
27. Catherine Beecher, *Suggestions Respecting Improvements in Education* (New York: J. B. Ford, 1874), 8.
28. Robert H. Bremner, *Children and Youth in America: A Documentary History, Vol. 1, 1600–1865* (Cambridge: Harvard University Press, 1970), 801.
29. Kuhn, 22.
30. William G. McLoughlin, "Evangelical Child Rearing in the Age of Jackson: Francis Wayland's Views on when and how to Subdue the Willfulness of Children," in Joseph M. Hawes and N. Ray Hiner, *American Childhood: A Research Guide and Historical Handbook* (Westport, Conn.: Greenwood, 1985), 89.
31. Charles Strickland, "A Transcendental Father: The Child Rearing Practices of Bronson Alcott," *Perspectives on American History* 3(1969):22.
32. Jacob Abbot, *Gentle Measures in the Management and Training of the Young* (New York: Harper, 1871), ii.
33. Kuhn, 21.
34. Barbara Finkelstein, "The Reconstruction of Childhood in the United States, 1790–1870," in Hawes and Hiner, 118.
35. Eliza Smith, *The Compleat Housewife or the Accomplished Gentlewoman's Companion* (Williamsburg, Pa.: William Parks, 1742).
36. John C. Abbott, *The Mother at Home; or The Principles of Maternal Duty* (London: John Masen, 1834), 17.
37. Hoffert, 149.

38. Harriet Connor Brown, *Grandmother Brown's Hundred Years 1827–1927* (Boston: Little, Brown, 1919), 96.

39. Clarence Meyer, *American Folk Medicine* (New York: Crowell, 1973), 4.

40. Ibid., 6.

41. Peter Smith, *Indian Doctor's Dispensatory, Being Father Smith's Advice Respecting Diseases and Their Cure* (Cincinnati, 1812).

42. William Buchan, *Advice to Mothers, on the Subject of their own Health; and of the means of Promoting the Health, Strength, and Beauty of their Offspring* (Boston: Joseph Bumstead, 1809), 3.

43. John C. Gunn, *New Domestic Physician, or, Home Book of Health* (Cincinnati: Moore, Wilstack & Keyes, 1862).

44. Thomas Hersey, *The Midwife's Practical Directory* (Baltimore: Hersey, 1836).

45. John Abbott, iii.

46. David Wark, *Private Information for Mothers, Wives and Daughters. A Practical Home Doctor for Women and Children* (New York: Interstate, 1882), vi.

47. *Nurse's Manual and Mother's Medical Adviser: A Guide to the Inexperienced by a Practicing Physician* (Philadelphia: Lindsay & Blakiston, 1845), 21–22.

48. Kuhn, 134.

49. Jane Censer, *North Carolina Planters and Their Children 1800–1869* (Baton Rouge: Louisiana State University, 1984), 35.

50. Pollock, 214.

51. *Nurse's Manual,* 22.

52. *Leavenworth Medical Herald* 1(1867):292.

53. Sally McMillen, "Mothers' Sacred Duty: Breast Feeding Patterns among Middle and Upper-class Women in the Antebellum South," *Journal of Southern History* 51(1985):351.

54. Hoffert, 149.

55. L. Emmett Holt, *The Care and Feeding of Children: A Catechism for the Use of Mother's and Children's Nurses* (New York: Appleton, 1894), 79.

56. McMillen, 352.

57. *Kansas Medical Index* 4(1883):118.

58. Wark, 422.

59. Julie A. Matthaei, *An Economic History of Women in America* (New York: Schocken, 1982), 60.

60. Hoffert, 142.

61. John Clarke, *Commentaries on Some of the most Important Diseases of Children* (London: Longman, Hurst, Rees, Orme & Brown, 1815), 20.

62. Richard A. Meckel, *Save the Babies: American Public Health Reform*

and the Prevention of Infant Mortality 1850–1929 (Baltimore: Johns Hopkins, 1990), 29.

63. Arthur Abt, *History of Pediatrics* (Philadelphia: Saunders, 1965), 150.
64. Mary Cable, *The Little Darlings—A History of Child Rearing in America* (New York: Scribner's, 1972), 156–57.
65. McMillen, 341.
66. William Alcott, *Forty Years in the Wilderness of Pills and Powders; or the Cogitations and Confessions of an aged Physician* (Boston: John Jewett, 1859), 138.
67. Susan Cayleff, "Gender, Ideology and the Water-Cure Movement," in Norman Gevitz, *Other Healers: Unorthodox Medicine in America* (Baltimore: Johns Hopkins, 1988), 85.
68. William Dewees, *Treatise on the Physical and Medical Treatment of Children,* 6th ed. (Philadelphia: Carey, Lea & Blanchard, 1836), ix.
69. Ibid., iii.
70. Ibid., 217.
71. Ibid., ix.
72. Ibid., 216–17.
73. Ibid., 331.
74. Ibid., vii.
75. Ibid., iv.
76. J. Forsyth Meigs and William Pepper, *A Practical Treatise on the Diseases of Children,* 5th ed. (Philadelphia: Lindsey & Blakiston, 1874), 21.
77. Elizabeth Blackwell and Emily Blackwell, "Medicine as a Profession for Women," in Alice S. Rossi, *The Feminist Papers from Adams to de Beauvoir* (Boston: Northeastern University, 1988), 355.
78. Ibid., 350.
79. Ibid., 355.
80. Charles R. King, "An Empty Chair, Childhood Death on the Kansas Frontier," *Kansas History* 14(1991):26.
81. Gravestones, Copp's Burying Ground, Boston, Mass.
82. Hoffert,175.
83. Hoffert, 157–58.
84. Pollock, 130–32.
85. Hoffert, 175.
86. Kuhn, 88.
87. Pollock, 132.
88. Samuel Longfellow, *The Life of Henry Wadsworth Longfellow with Extracts from His Journals and Correspondence* (Boston: Houghton Mifflin, 1891), vol. 2, 136.
89. Pollock, 132.
90. Censer, 28.
91. Ibid., 29.

92. Ibid., 32.

93. Ibid., 30.

94. Ibid., 32.

95. Nancy Schrom Dye, "Daniel Blake Smith, Mother Love and Infant Death, 1750–1920," *Journal of American History* 73(1986):329.

96. Kenneth F. Kiple and Virginia H. Kiple, "Slave Child Mortality: Some Nutritional Answers to a Perennial Puzzle," *Journal of Social History* 10(1977):284.

97. Kenneth F. Kiple and Virginia Himmelsteib-King, *Another Dimension to the Black Diaspora: Diet, Disease and Racism* (New York: Cambridge University Press, 1981), 100.

98. Ibid., 136–37.

99. Todd Savitt, *Medicine and Slavery: The Disease and Health of Blacks in Antebellum Virginia* (Urbana: University of Illinois, 1978), 7.

100. Kiple and Himmelsteib-King, 42.

101. Elizabeth Fox-Genovese, *Within the Plantation Household: Black and White Women of the Old South* (Chapel Hill: University of North Carolina, 1988), 323–24.

102. John Boswell, *The Kindness of Strangers: The Abandonment of Children in Western Europe from Late Antiquity to the Renaissance* (New York: Pantheon, 1988).

103. Kiple and Himmelsteib-King, 96.

104. Censer, 137.

105. Glenda Riley, *Frontierwomen: The Iowa Experience* (Ames: Iowa State University, 1981), 82.

106. Glenda Riley, *The Female Frontier: A Comparative View of Women on the Prairie and the Plains* (Lawrence: University Press of Kansas, 1988), 52.

107. Sandra L. Myers, *Westering Women and the Frontier Experience 1800–1915* (Albuquerque: University of New Mexico, 1982), 130.

108. King, 26–27.

109. Elliott West, *Growing Up with the Country: Childhood on the Western Frontier* (Albuquerque: University of New Mexico, 1989), 38.

110. Lillian Schlissel, *Women's Diaries of the Westward Journey* (New York: Schocken, 1982), 58.

111. Gabriella Foster, Letter to Robert Foster, 24 December 1863. Broward Family Letters, Mahaffie Farmstead, Olathe, Kansas.

112. West, 218.

113. Ibid., 237.

114. Ibid., 232.

115. Ibid., 233.

116. Lillian Schlissel, Byrd Gibbens, and Elizabeth Hampsten, *Far From Home: Families of the Westward Journey* (New York: Schocken, 1989), 152–54.

117. Pollock, 99.
118. Ibid., 98.
119. Hoffert, 146.
120. Susan Groag Bell and Karen M. Offen, *Women, the Family and Freedom: The Debate in Documents* (Palo Alto: Stanford University Press, l983), 138.
121. Helen Watterson Moody, "The True Meaning of Motherhood," *Ladies Home Journal* 16(1899):12.
122. Rima D. Apple, *Mothers and Medicine: A Social History of Infant Feeding 1890–1950* (Madison: University of Wisconsin, 1987), 108.

Chapter 3

  1. Joyce Antler and Stephen Antler, "From Child Rescue to Family Protection: The Evolution of the Child Protective Movement in the United States," *Children and Youth Services Review* 1(1979):177–78.
  2. Marshall Spatz, "Child Abuse in the Nineteenth Century," *New York Affairs* 4(1977):80.
  3. Editorial, *New York Times,* 19 July 1876.
  4. *Wisconsin Humane Society Report for 1885,* Milwaukee. Special Collections, Newberry Library, Chicago, Ill.
  5. Michael Katz, *In the Shadow of the Poorhouse: A Social History of Welfare in America* (New York: Basic, 1986), 119.
  6. Antler and Antler, 187.
  7. Spatz, 80.
  8. Antler and Antler, 178.
  9. Carl N. Degler, *Out of Our Past: The Forces that Shaped Modern America* (New York: Harper, 1959), 312.
  10. Robert Bremner, *Children and Youth in America: A Documentary History, 1600–1865* (Cambridge: Harvard University Press, 1970–71), vol. 2, 808–809.
  11. *The Daily Democrat* (Chicago), 2 June 1849, 4.
  12. Paul Avrich, *The Haymarket Tragedy* (Princeton: Princeton University, 1984), 80.
  13. Lawrence H. Larsen, *The Urban West at the End of the Frontier* (Lawrence: Regents Press of Kansas, 1979), 69.
  14. Charles N. Glaab and Theodore A. Brown, *A History of Urban America* (New York: Macmillan, 1967), 87.
  15. Oscar Handlin, *Boston's Immigrants: A Study in Acculturation,* rev. ed. (Cambridge: Harvard University Press, 1959), 115.
  16. Geraldine Mineau, "Fertility on the Frontier: An Analysis of the Nineteenth Century Utah Population" (Ph.D. diss., University of Utah, 1980), 56–57.
  17. T. R. Noyes, *Report of the Health of the Children of the Oneida Community* (Oneida, N.Y., 1878), 67.

18. Handlin, 226.
19. Ibid., 330.
20. Robert Ernst, *Immigrant Life in New York City, 1825–1863* (New York: King's Crown Press, 1949), 53.
21. Hartment Keil and John B. Jentz, *German Workers: A Documentary History of Working-Class Culture from 1850 to World War I* (Urbana: University of Illinois Press, 1988), 62.
22. Judith Walzer Leavitt, *The Healthiest City: Milwaukee and the Politics of Health Reform* (Princeton: Princeton University Press, 1982), 124–25.
23. Odd S. Lovall, *A Century of Urban Life: The Norwegian in Chicago before 1930* (Chicago: Norwegian American Historical Association, 1988), 38–39.
24. Ibid., 41.
25. Paul A. Gilje, "Infant Abandonment in Early Nineteenth Century New York City; Three Cases," *Signs* 8(1983):580.
26. *New York Times,* 28 July 1874, 11.
27. Ibid., 21 July 1876, 3.
28. Linda Gordon, *Heroes of Their Own Lives: The Politics and History of Family Violence* (New York: Penguin, 1988), 43–44.
29. *Annual Report for the Nursery and Children's Hospital for 1879.* (New York: New York Hospital, 1880).
30. Robert Bremner, *Children and Youth in America: A Documentary History, 1866–1932* (Cambridge: Harvard University Press, 1971), vol. 1, 250–51.
31. *New York Times,* 28 July 1876, 2.
32. Charles E. Rosenberg, "Social Class and Medical Care in Nineteenth Century America: The Rise and Fall of the Dispensary," *Journal of the History of Medicine and Allied Sciences* 29(1974):48.
33. Gordon, 29.
34. Christine Stansell, "Women, Children, and the Uses of the Streets: Class and Gender Conflict in New York City, 1850–1860," *Feminist Studies* 8(1982):312.
35. Stansell, 326.
36. Anthony M. Platt, *The Child Savers: The Invention of Delinquency,* 2d ed. (Chicago: University of Chicago Press, 1977), 83.
37. Michael Grossberg, *Governing the Hearth: Law and the Family in Nineteenth Century America* (Chapel Hill: University of North Carolina Press, 1985), 11.
38. Roscoe Pound, "Individual Interests in Domestic Relations," *Michigan Law Review* 14(1916):182.
39. Homer Folks, *The Care of Destitute, Neglected and Delinquent Children* (New York: Johnson Reprints, 1970), 96.
40. Gordon, 62–3.

41. Priscilla Ferguson Clement, "Children and Charity: Orphanages in New Orleans, 1817–1914," *Louisiana History* 27(1986):337.

42. Thomas E. Cone, *History of American Pediatrics* (Boston: Little, Brown, 1979), 75.

43. Marion J. Morton, "'Go and Sin No More': Maternity Homes in Cleveland, 1869–1926," *Ohio History* 93(1984):129.

44. Paul Boyer, *Urban Masses and Moral Order in America, 1820–1920* (Cambridge: Harvard University Press, 1978), 89.

45. Susan N. Downs and Michael W. Sherraden, "The Orphan Asylum in the Nineteenth Century," *Social Science Review* 57(1983):277.

46. Folks, 5.

47. Ibid., 8.

48. Raymond Mohl, *Poverty in New York 1783–1825* (New York: Oxford, 1971).

49. Boyer, 94.

50. Miriam Langsam, *Children West: A History of the Placing Out System of the New York Children's Aid Society 1853–1890* (Madison: University of Wisconsin, 1969), 7.

51. Folks, 28.

52. *New York Children's Aid Society Annual Report for 1869.* Special Collections, Newberry Library, Chicago, Ill., 43.

53. Langsam, 25.

54. Donald D. Jackson, "It Took Trains to Put Street Kids on the Right Track Out of the Slums," *Smithsonian* 17(1986):94.

55. *New York Children's Aid Society Annual Report for 1868*, 79. Special Collections, Newberry Library, Chicago, Ill., 43.

56. Ibid., 63.

57. Ibid., 67.

58. *Nineteenth Annual Report of the Brooklyn Children's Aid Society, 1884.* Special Collections, Newberry Library, Chicago, Ill., 23.

59. Peter Romanofsky, "Saving the Lives of the City's Foundlings: The Joint Committee and New York City Child Care Methods, 1860–1907," *New York Historical Society Quarterly* 61(1977):59.

60. Ibid., 58.

61. Ibid., 59.

62. *Account of the Proceedings at the Dedication of the Children's Mission Home* (Boston, Mass., 27 March 1867).

63. Bremner, *Children and Youth, 1600–1865*, 785.

64. Gordon, 35–36.

65. Platt, 79.

66. Oscar L. Dudley, "Saving the Children: Sixteen Years' Work Among the Dependent Youth of Chicago," in *Story of Child Saving in the United States* (Boston: George H. Ellis, 1893), 103.

67. *Nineteenth Annual Report of Boston's Children's Friend Society* (Boston: John Wilson & Son, 1852), 6.

68. Anne B. Richardson, "The Mass System of Caring for State Minor Wards," in *Story of Child Saving in the United States,* 57.

69. Kathleen Schmeling, "Every Child Is Worthy of Kindness and Care," *Michigan History* 74(1990):24.

70. *Twenty-Third Annual Report of the Executive Committee of the Boston Children's Aid Society, 1887.* Special Collections, Newberry Library, Chicago, Ill., 17.

71. Records of Chapin Hall (Chicago Historical Society, Chicago, Ill.).

72. Abraham Jacobi, "An Address on the Claims of Paediatric Medicine," *Transactions of the American Medical Association* 31(1880):713.

73. Morris J. Vogel, *The Invention of the Modern Hospital, Boston 1870–1930* (Berkley: University of California, 1980), 23.

74. Janet Golden (ed.), *Infant Asylums and Children's Hospitals: Medical Dilemmas and Developments 1850–1920* (New York: Garland, 1989), 7.

75. Philopedos [pseud.]. *A Few Remarks about Sick Children in New York and the Necessity of a Hospital for Them* (New York: William C. Bryant, 1852), 12.

76. *Fourth Annual Report of the Nursery and Child's Hospital* (New York, 1858), 2.

77. *Eighth Annual Report of the Nursery and Child's Hospital* (New York, 1862), 5.

78. Ibid., 30.

79. Virginia A. Metaxas Quiroga, "Female Lay Managers and Scientific Pediatrics at Nursery and Child's Hospital, 1854–1910," *Bulletin of the History of Medicine* 60(1986):194.

80. *Annual Report of the New York Infant Asylum* (New York Hospital Archives, New York, N.Y., 1871).

81. James M. Brown, "Unwanted Children" (Address given to the American Humane Association, New York, September 1896, 5.

82. Brown, 20.

83. Abraham Jacobi, "Report on the Raising and Education of Abandoned Children in Europe, with Statistics and General Remarks," in Golden, 34.

84. Jacobi, "Report," 134.

85. Bremner, *Children and Youth, 1866-1932,* 831–32.

86. Clement A. Smith, *The Children's Hospital of Boston: "Built Better Than They Know"* (Boston: Little, Brown, 1983), 10.

87. Smith, 7.

88. Vogel, 15–17.

89. Smith, 7.

90. Sydney A. Halpern, *American Pediatrics: The Social Dynamics of Professionalization, 1880–1980* (Berkeley: University of California, 1988), 40–41.

91. Thomas Morgan Rotch, "The Development of the Hospital, with Especial Reference to the Medical Service," *Boston Medical and Surgical Journal* 170(1914):485.

92. Vogel, 75.

93. *Annual Report of the Maurice Porter Memorial Hospital for Children, 1895* (Chicago Historical Society, Chicago, Ill.), 7.

94. *First Annual Report of the Home for Destitute and Crippled Children, 1893* (Newberry Library, Chicago, Ill.), 5.

95. *Third Annual Report of the Home for Destitute and Crippled Children, 1895* (Newberry Library, Chicago, Ill.), 6.

96. William Gerhardt, "The Birth of Pediatrics: Children's Hospital in Its First Five Decades," *Queen City Heritage* 41(1983):4.

97. Marian Hunt, "Women and Child Saving: St. Louis Children's Hospital 1879–1979," *Missouri Historical Society Bulletin* 36(1980):71.

98. Richardson, 97.

99. Julia Lathrop, "Cook County Charities," in *Hull House Maps and Papers* (New York: Crowell, 1895), 147–48.

100. Alfred W. Crosby, *America's Forgotten Pandemic: The Influenza of 1918* (New York: Cambridge University Press, 1989), 68.

101. Hunt, 74.

102. Viviona A. Zelizier, *Pricing the Priceless Child: The Changing Social Value of Children* (New York: Basic, 1985), 22.

103. Susan Tiffin, *In Whose Best Interest? Child Welfare Reform in the Progressive Era* (Westport, Conn.: Greenwood, 1982), 113.

Chapter 4

1. Brian P. Birch, "Possessed of a Restless Spirit: a Young Girl; Memoirs of the Southern Iowa Frontier," *Palimpsest* 66(1985):183.

2. William Alcott, *Forty Years in the Wilderness of Pills and Powders; or the Cogitations and Confessions of an Aged Physician* (Boston: John P. Jewett, 1859), 12.

3. Robert M. Cruden, *Ministers of Reform: The Progressive Achievement in American Civilization* (Urbana: University of Illinois, 1985), 175.

4. John Abbott, *Mother at Home: Or, the Principles of Maternal Duty* (New York: American Tract Society, 1833), 19.

5. Edward Fitch, letter to his parents, 20 April 1859. Kansas Collection, University of Kansas Libraries, Lawrence, Kansas.

6. Judith Walzer Leavitt, *The Healthiest City: Milwaukee and the Politics of Health Reform* (Princeton: Princeton University, 1982), 180.

7. E. P. Stewart, *Letters of a Woman Homesteader* (New York: Houghton Mifflin, 1982), 190.

8. Cited in Thomas E. Cone, *History of American Pediatrics* (Boston: Little, Brown, 1980), 69.

9. Alfred Newman, "The Proper Constitution of the Food of Infants," *Leavenworth Medical Herald* 1(1867):1.

10. "Minutes of the Leavenworth Medico-Churgical Society for April, 1867," *Leavenworth Medical Herald* 1(1867):28.

11. Katie H. Armitage, "Elizabeth 'Bettie' Duncan: Diary of Daily Life," *Kansas History* 10(1987):285.

12. John C. Parrish, "My Most Interesting Cases." Parrish Papers. Western Historical Manuscript Collection, University of Missouri, Columbia, Missouri.

13. Sylvia Hoffert, *Private Matters: American Attitudes Toward Childbearing and Infant Nurture in the Urban North, 1800–1860* (Urbana: University of Illinois, 1989), 70.

14. Linda Pollock, *A Lasting Relationship: Parents and Children over Three Centuries* (London: Fourth Estate, 1987), 121.

15. A. B. McCandless, "The Doctor and Child," *Kansas Medical Journal* 9(1897):533.

16. T. W. Peers, "The Clothing of Infants and Children," *Kansas Medical Journal* 5(1893):327.

17. L. Emmett Holt, *The Diseases of Infancy and Childhood* (New York: Appleton, 1897), 47–81.

18. H. P. Bowditch, "The Relation Between Growth and Disease," *Transactions of the American Medical Association* 32(1881):371.

19. Sidney B. Finn, "A. Jacobi on Teething," *Alabama Journal of Medical Sciences* 10(1973):326.

20. Bowditch, 377.

21. Bayard Holmes, "A Study of Child Growth: Being a Review of the Work of Dr. William Townsend Porter of St. Louis," *New York Medical Journal* 60(1894):420.

22. Caroline Benedict Burrell, *The Mother's Book: Suggestions Regarding the Mental and Moral Development of Children* (New York: University Society, 1911), 163.

23. Abraham Jacobi, *Therapeutics of Infancy and Childhood*, 2d ed. (Philadelphia: Lippincott, 1898), 62.

24. Debra K. Longshore, "Infant Feeding," *Kansas Medical Journal* 2(1890):547.

25. Nathan Davis, *Clinical Lectures on Various Important Diseases* (New York: Woolworth, Ainsworth, 1873), 139.

26. John W. Kyger, "Treatment of Infantile Diarrheas," *Kansas City Medical Index* 14(1893):209.

27. C. P. Lee, "Cholera Infantum," *Leavenworth Medical Herald* 5(871):145.

28. Beverly Deslazo, "Cholera Infantum," *American Midwife* 2(1896):95

29. Rose Cheney, "Seasonal Aspects of Infant and Childhood Mortality: Philadelphia, 1865–1920," *Journal of Interdisciplinary History* 19(1984):561.

30. G. H. T. Johnson, "Prevention of Disease," *First Annual Report of the Kansas State Board of Health* (Topeka, Kan., 1885), 120.

31. Charles W. Earle, *Scarlatina in Chicago, Particularly the Epidemic of 1876–7* (Chicago: Chicago Historical Society, 1878), 21.

32. J. Lewis Smith, *A Treatise on the Diseases of Infancy and Childhood,* 7th ed. (Philadelphia: Lea Brothers, 1890), 41.

33. Harold K. Faber and Rustin McIntosh, *History of the American Pediatric Society* (New York: McGraw-Hill, 1966), 5.

34. *First Annual Report of the Kansas State Board of Health,* 101.

35. U. Potter, "Diphtheria," *Transactions of the Medical Society of the State of New York for 1861* (New York City), 63.

36. James H. Cassedy, *Charles V. Chapin and the Public Health Movement* (Cambridge: Harvard University, 1962).

37. Ibid., 113.

38. Ibid., 199.

39. Morris J. Vogel, *The Invention of the Modern Hospital: Boston, 1870–1930* (Chicago: University of Chicago, 1980), 62.

40. "The Cure of Diphtheria by Serum Injection," *Kansas City Medical Index* 15(1894):387.

41. Leavitt, 71.

42. Vogel, 63.

43. Harold K. Faber and Dustin McIntosh, *History of the American Pediatric Society 1887–1965* (New York: McGraw-Hill, 1966), 35–36.

44. R. L. Duffus and Emmett Holt, Jr., *L. Emmett Holt: Pioneer of a Children's Century* (New York: Appleton, 1940), 100.

45. Duffus and Holt, 38.

46. Henry F. Dowling, *Fighting Infection: Conquests of the Twentieth Century* (Cambridge: Harvard University, 1977), 38.

47. Charles R. King, *The Woman and Her Physician, Women's Medical Care on the Western Frontier, 1850–1900* (forthcoming).

48. M. R. Mitchell, "Practical Points as to the Attention to the Child at Birth," *Kansas Medical Journal* 7(1895):436.

49. J. P. Chesney, "Resuscitation of Asphyxiated Infants," *Leavenworth Medical Herald* 2(1869):449–51.

50. Mitchell, 436.

51. Chesney, 450.

52. Jacobi, v.

53. Smith, 35.

54. Ibid.
55. Clement A. Smith, *The Children's Hospital of Boston* (Boston: Little, Brown, 1983), 11.
56. Cone, 85–86.
57. Howard A. Pearson, *Lectures on the Diseases of Children: The First American Academic Course in Pediatrics by Eli Ives, M.D.* (New Haven: Yale University, 1986).
58. Ibid., 44–46.
59. "Medical Student Lecture Notes." Yale Medical School, 1826. National Library of Medicine, Bethesda, Md.
60. Pearson, 136.
61. "Medical Student Lecture Notes."
62. Pearson, 93.
63. Ibid., 142.
64. Ibid., 105.
65. Charles D. Meigs, *Obstetrics: The Science and the Art,* 3d ed. (Philadelphia: Blanchard & Lea, 1856), 719.
66. Noah Castle, "Cholera Infantum, A Dissertation for the Doctor of Medicine Degree at Washington University of Baltimore, 1845" (Toner Collection, Library of Congress, Washington, D.C.), 3–4.
67. Gunning S. Bedford, *Clinical Lectures on the Diseases of Women and Children,* 4th ed. (New York: Samuel S. and William Wood, 1856), 287.
68. Meigs, 709.
69. Bedford, 287.
70. Charles West, *Lectures on the Diseases of Infancy and Childhood,* 4th ed. (Philadelphia: Henry Lea, 1866), 18.
71. Edward Henoch, *Lectures on Diseases of Children: A Handbook for Physicians and Students* (New York: William Wood, 1882), iii.
72. Peter C. English, "Not Miniature Men and Women: Abraham Jacobi's Vision of a New Medical Specialty a Century Ago," in Loretta M. Kopelman and John C. Moskop, *Children and Health Care: Moral and Social Issues* (New York: Kluwer Academic, 1989).
73. Thomas Bonner, *American Doctors and German Universities: A Chapter in International Intellectual Relations, 1870–1914* (Lincoln: University of Nebraska, 1963).
74. Jacobi, v.
75. Abraham Jacobi, "History of Pediatrics and Its Relation to Other Sciences and Arts," *American Medicine* 8(1904):805.
76. Sydney Halpern, *American Pediatrics: The Social Dynamics of Professionalization, 1880–1980* (Berkeley: University of California, 1988), 83.
77. Abraham Jacobi, "An Address on the Claims of Pediatric Medicine," *Transactions of the American Medical Association* 31(1880):713.

78. Ibid., 709.

79. Ibid., 711.

80. Ibid.

81. Faber and McIntosh, 53.

82. Abraham Jacobi, "Progress in Knowledge of the Acute Contagious Diseases and Infections," *Transactions of the American Medical Association* 32(1881):351.

83. M. P. Guersant, *Surgical Diseases of Infants and Children* (Philadelphia: Henry Lea, 1873), iii.

84. Jacobi, "An Address," 711.

85. John M. Connoly, "Some Results of the Committee on Milk and Baby Hygiene on Behalf of Babies," *Boston Medical and Surgical Journal* 162(1910):131.

86. Jacobi, *Therapeutics*, vi.

87. Faber and McIntosh, 33.

88. Isaac Abt, *Pediatrics* (Philadelphia: Saunders, 1923–26).

89. Holt, v.

90. Duffus and Holt, 119.

91. John Ruhrah, *A Manual of the Diseases of Infants and Children* (Philadelphia: Saunders, 1905).

92. John Zahorsky, *Golden Rules of Pediatrics* (St. Louis: C. V. Mosby, 1906), 9.

93. Ibid., 17.

94. Abraham Jacobi, *Infant Diet* (New York: Putnam, 1885), 2.

95. Bryon A. Russell, *It Was Like This* (Sioux Falls, S.D.: Center for Western Studies, 1987), 81–84.

96. Faber and McIntosh, 9.

97. Ibid., 28.

98. Ibid., 80.

99. Frank Spooner Churchill, Frank Spooner Churchill Papers. National Library of Medicine, Bethesda, Md. (undated note).

100. Joseph Kett, *The Formation of the American Medical Profession, the Role of Institutions 1780–1860* (New Haven: Yale, 1968), 167–68.

101. Paul Starr, *The Social Transformation of American Medicine: The Rise of a Sovereign Profession and the Making of a Vast Industry* (New York: Basic, 1982).

102. Dorothy Pawluck, "Transitions in Pediatrics. A Segmental Analysis," *Social Problems* 301(1983):451.

103. Faber and McIntosh, 113.

104. Ibid., 117.

105. Thomas M. Rotch, "The Position and Work of the American Pediatric Society Toward Public Questions," *Transactions of the American Pediatric Society* 21(1909):7.

106. Ibid., 29.
107. Augustus Caille, "The Influence of American Pediatric Societies in Promoting the Welfare of American Children," *Transactions of the American Pediatric Society* 16(1904):6.
108. Jacobi, "History of Pediatrics," 805.
109. L. Emmett Holt, "American Pediatrics—A Retrospective and a Forecast," *Transactions of the American Pediatric Society* 35(1923):16.
110. Faber and McIntosh, 18.
111. H. L. K. Shaw, "The American Pediatric Society and Preventive Pediatrics," *American Journal of Diseases of Children* 38(1929):7.

Chapter 5

1. Robert Lewis Taylor, "Swat the Fly II," *New Yorker* 24(1948):29–31.
2. John Duffy, *The Sanitarians: A History of American Public Health* (Urbana: University of Illinois, 1990): 47
3. John M. Toner, "Boards of Health in the United States," *Reports and Papers of the American Public Health Association* 1(1873):499–500.
4. Naomi Rogers, "Germs with Legs: Flies, Disease and the New Public Health," *Bulletin of the History of Medicine* 63(1990):617.
5. J. L. Gilbert, "Municipal Medicine," *Kansas Medical Journal* 8(1896):483.
6. Alice Hamilton, *Exploring the Dangerous Trades* (Boston: Little, Brown, 1943), 79.
7. Hilda Satt Polacheck, *I Came a Stranger: The Story of a Hull House Girl* (Urbana: University of Illinois, 1989), 73.
8. Carl Sandburg, *The Chicago Race Riots* (New York: Harcourt, 1919), 2.
9. Gilbert, 487.
10. Ibid., 484.
11. Ibid. 487.
12. Richard L. Bushman and Claudia L. Bushman, "The Early History of Cleanliness in America," *Journal of American History* 74(1988):1218.
13. Richard A. Meckel, *Save the Babies: American Public Health Reform and the Prevention of Infant Mortality, 1850–1929* (Baltimore: Johns Hopkins, 1990), 16.
14. C. E. A. Winslow, *The Evolution and Significance of the Modern Public Health Campaign* (New Haven: Yale University, 1923), 25–26.
15. Bruno Latour, *The Pasteurization of France* (Cambridge: Harvard University, 1988), 123.
16. Judith Walzer Leavitt, *The Healthiest City in America* (Princeton: Princeton University, 1982), 30.
17. Jacob Riis, *How the Other Half Lives: Studies Among the Tenements of New York* (New York: Dover, 1971), viii.
18. Selma Berrol, "Ethnicity and American Children," in Joseph M. Hawes

and N. Ray Hiner, *American Childhood: A Research Guide and Historical Handbook* (Westport, Conn.: Greenwood, 1985), 344.

19. Florence Kelley, "The Sweating System," in *Hull House Maps and Papers* (New York: Crowell, 1895), 34.

20. Edward T. Devine, *Misery and Its Causes* (New York: Macmillan, 1910), 55.

21. Riis, 129.

22. Stuart Galishoff, *Safeguarding the Public Health: Newark, 1895–1918* (Westport, Conn.: Greenwood, 1975), 3.

23. Ibid., 10.

24. Ibid., 7.

25. Ibid., 55.

26. Harvey F. Dowling, *Fighting Infection: Conquests of the Twentieth Century* (Cambridge: Harvard University, 1977), 14.

27. Chicago Board of Health, *Report of the Board of Health of the City of Chicago, 1895,* 184.

28. Barbara Sicherman, *Alice Hamilton: A Life in Letters* (Cambridge: Harvard University, 1984), 145.

29. Edward Meeker, "The Improving Health of the United States, 1850–1915," *Explorations in Economic History* 9(1972):353.

30. Nancy Tomes, "The Private Side of Public Health: Sanitary Science, Domestic Hygiene, and the Germ Theory, 1870–1900," *Bulletin of the History of Medicine* 64(1990):523.

31. Ibid., 520.

32. Ibid., 514.

33. Mrs. Max West, *Infant Care* (United States Department of Labor Children's Bureau, Publication no. 8, Washington, D.C., 1914), 64.

34. Ibid., 75.

35. George Rosen, *Preventive Medicine in the United States, 1900–1975* (New York: Prodist, 1977), 17.

36. Galishoff, 122.

37. Robert Bremner, *Children and Youth in America, A Documentary History, 1866–1932* (Cambridge: Harvard University, 1970–1971), vol. 2, 886.

38. Ibid., 887.

39. Winslow, 52.

40. Galishoff, 125.

41. Samuel J. Crumbine, *The Frontier Doctor* (Philadelphia: Dorrance, 1948), 143.

42. Winslow, 53.

43. Naomi Rogers, "Dirt, Flies and Immigrants: Explaining the Epidemiology of Poliomyelitis 1900–1916," *Journal of the History of Medicine and Allied Sciences* 44(1989):486.

44. James H. Cassedy, *Charles V. Chapin and the Public Health Movement* (Cambridge: Harvard University, 1962), 190.
45. *Chicago Daily News,* 21 September 1968, 21.
46. Patricia Dean, "Children in Montana," *Montana* 34(1984):43.
47. William Carlos Williams, *Autobiography* (New York: Random House, 1951), 159.
48. *Chicago Herald Examiner,* 23 October 1918, 7.
49. W. L. Schenck, "Small-pox and its Prophylaxis," *First Annual Report of the Kansas State Board of Health,* 1885, 127.
50. J. H. Pulte, *Homeopathic Domestic Physician Containing the Treatment of Diseases; Popular Explanations of Anatomy, Physiology, Hygiene and Hydropathy, A Treatise on Domestic Surgery and an Abridged Materia Medica,* 7th ed. (Cincinnati: Moore, Wilstack & Keys & Company, 1859), 540.
51. Elizabeth Hampsten, *Read This Only to Yourself: The Private Writings of Midwestern Women, 1880–1910* (Bloomington: Indiana University, 1982), 101.
52. Leavitt, 95.
53. James H. Hannaford, "Report of the Marion County Health Officer," *First Annual Report of the Kansas State Board of Health,* 1885, 90.
54. Galishoff, 156.
55. Donald R. Hopkins, *Princes and Peasants: Smallpox in History* (Chicago: University of Chicago, 1983), 283.
56. Riis, 88.
57. Florence Kelley, *First Special Report of the Factory Inspectors of Illinois on Small-Pox in the Tenement Home Sweat-Shops of Chicago* (Chicago, 1894), 8.
58. Hopkins, 292.
59. Herman N. Bundesen, "One Hundred Years of Public Health in Chicago 1840–1940," *Illinois Medical Journal* 77(1940):427.
60. *Chicago Tribune,* 3 February 1901, 17.
61. Kathryn Sklar, *Notes of Sixty Years: The Autobiography of Florence Kelley* (Chicago: Charles H. Kerr, 1986), 87–88.
62. Kathleen W. Jones, "Sentiment and Science: The Late Nineteenth Century Pediatrician as Mother's Adviser," *Journal of Social History* 17(1983):79.
63. Thomas E. Cone, *History of American Pediatrics* (Boston: Little, Brown, 1979), 151.
64. George Rosen, *A History of Public Health* (New York: MD Publications, 1958), 167–69.
65. Rosen, 162–64.
66. Cassedy, 198.
67. Rosen, 342.

68. Josephine S. Baker, *Child Hygiene* (New York: Harper, 1925), x.
69. Emmett Holt, "Infant Mortality, Ancient and Modern: An Historical Sketch," *Archives of Pediatrics* 30(1913):913.
70. Leavitt, 175.
71. Galishoff, 112.
72. Raymond Pearl, "Biometric Data on Infant Mortality in the United States Birth Registration Area, 1915–1918," *American Journal of Hygiene* 1(1921):437.
73. Baker, 18.
74. Harold Ray Lentzner, "Seasonal Patterns of Infant and Child Mortality in New York, Chicago and New Orleans" (Ph.D. diss., University of Pennsylvania, 1987), 41.
75. Meckel, 119.
76. Riis, 129.
77. Ibid., 145–46.
78. John Zahorsky, *Golden Rules of Pediatrics* (St. Louis: C. V. Mosby, 1906), 11.
79. Riis, 130.
80. R. L. Duffus and Emmett Holt, *L. Emmett Holt: Pioneer of a Children's Century* (New York: Appleton, 1940), 172.
81. Elizabeth Lowell Putnam, Letter to the London Times, 8 November 1917, Putnam Papers, Schlesinger Library, Radcliffe College, Cambridge, Mass.
82. Samuel J. Crumbine, "Infant Mortality," 1914, speech manuscript, Clendening Medical Library, University of Kansas Medical Center, Kansas City, Kans.
83. J. Whitridge Williams, "What the Obstetrician Can Do to Prevent Infantile Mortality," *Transactions of the Annual Meeting of the American Association for the Study and Prevention of Infant Mortality* 1(1910):201.
84. Judith Walzer Leavitt, *Brought to Bed: Childbearing in America 1750–1950* (New York: Oxford, 1986).
85. Leavitt, *Brought to Bed,* 187.
86. Charles R. King, "The New York Maternal Mortality Study: A Conflict of Professionalization," *Bulletin of the History of Medicine* 65(1991):476.
87. Bremner, 876.
88. Holt, 885–86.
89. Sydney Halpern, *American Pediatrics: The Social Dynamics of Professionalization, 1880–1980* (Berkeley: University of California, 1988), 76.
90. Emmett Holt, *The Diseases of Infancy and Childhood for the Use of Students and Practitioners of Medicine,* 6th ed. (New York: Appleton, 1914), 9, 122.
91. Rima Apple, "'To be used only under the Direction of a Physician':

Commercial Infant Feeding and Medical Practice, 1870–1940," *Bulletin of the History of Medicine* 54(1980):402.

92. John Lovett Morse, "Recollections and Reflections on Forty-five Years of Artificial Infant Feeding," *Journal of Pediatrics* 7(1935):304.

93. Apple, 404.

94. Ibid., 402.

95. Jones, 86.

96. Mary A. Duns, *The Practical Care and Feeding of Children*, 2nd ed. (Chicago: Chicago Medical Book Company, 1901), ix.

97. Ibid., v.

98. Morse, 309.

99. Elizabeth Lowell Putnam, Address to the Massachusetts Legislative Committee on Public Health, March 1912, Putnam Papers, Schlesinger Library, Radcliffe College, Cambridge, Mass.

100. Elizabeth Lowell Putnam, "Milk-Borne Infectious Diseases," Putnam Papers, Schlesinger Library, Radcliffe College, Cambridge, Mass.

101. Ibid.

102. Putnam, Address to the Massachusetts Legislative Committee.

103. Putnam, "Milk-Borne Infectious Diseases."

104. Winslow, 53.

105. Charles E. North, "Milk and Its Relation to Public Health," in Mazyck Ravenel, *A Half Century of Public Health* (New York: American Public Health Association, 1921), 277.

106. Bremner, 871–74.

107. Ibid., 874.

108. Norman Shaftel, "A History of the Purification of Milk in New York, or, 'How Now Brown Cow,'" *New York State Journal of Medicine* 58(1958):911.

109. Leavitt, *Healthiest*, 164.

110. Elizabeth Lowell Putnam, undated letter, Putnam Papers, Schlesinger Library, Radcliffe College, Cambridge, Mass.

111. North, 265–66.

112. *New York Evening Post*, 4 November 1905, 24.

113. Henry L. Coit, letter to his sister, 22 May 1893, Coit Papers, National Library of Medicine, Bethesda, Md.

114. Manfred J. Wassermann, "Henry J. Coit and the Certified Milk Movement in the Development of Modern Pediatrics," *Bulletin of the History of Medicine* 76(1972):386–87.

115. P. H. Mullowney, "Milk Inspection Report," February 1912, Putnam Papers, Schlesinger Library, Radcliffe College, Cambridge, Mass.

116. North, 271.

117. Harold K. Faber and Dustin McIntosh, *History of the American Pediatric Society 1887–1965* (New York: McGraw-Hill, 1966), 4.

118. North, 238.

119. Linda Bryder, *Below the Magic Mountain: A Social History of Tuberculosis in Twentieth Century Britain* (New York: Oxford, 1988), 135.

120. Chicago Department of Health, *Report of the Department of Health of the City of Chicago* (1918), 827.

121. *New York Herald,* 20 April 1909, 5.

122. Ibid., 22 April 1909, 1.

123. Lina Straus, *Disease in Milk, the Remedy Pasteurization: The Life Work of Nathan Straus,* 2d ed. (New York: Dutton, 1917), 290.

124. U.S. Children's Bureau, "Baby Saving Campaigns: A Preliminary Report on What American Cities Are Doing to Prevent Infant Mortality" (Washington, D.C., 1916), 22.

125. The Milk Fund, records, Putnam Papers, Schlesinger Library, Radcliffe College, Cambridge, Mass.

126. Sinclair Lewis, *Arrowsmith* (New York: Harcourt, 1925).

127. Charles E. Rosenberg, "Making It in Urban Medicine: A Career in the Age of Scientific Medicine," *Bulletin of the History of Medicine* 64(1990):167.

128. Lewis, 37.

Chapter 6

1. Rochelle Beck, "The White House Conferences on Children: An Historical Perspective," *Harvard Education Quarterly* 43(1973):654.

2. Ellen Key, *The Century of the Child* (New York: Putnam, 1909).

3. L. R. DeBuys, "Conservation of Child Life: A National Responsibility," *Journal of the American Medical Association* 71(1918):240.

4. Henry Coit, "Factors in the Conservation of Child Life," Coit Papers, National Library of Medicine, Bethesda, Md.

5. Felix Adler, "The Attitude of Society Toward the Child as an Index of Civilization," *Annals of the American Academy of Political and Social Sciences* 29(1907):138.

6. Robert H. Wiebe, *The Search for Order* (New York: Hill & Wang, 1967).

7. H. H. Hart, "An Epoch in Child Helping," Russell Sage Foundation Papers, Rockefeller Archives, North Tarrytown, N.Y.

8. Henry B. Sigerist, *Civilization and Disease* (Chicago: University of Chicago, 1943), 7.

9. John Burnham, *Paths into American Culture* (Philadelphia: Temple University Press, 1988), 223.

10. Ibid., 228.

11. Richard P. Hofstadter, *Darwinism in American Thought* (Boston: Beacon, 1955), 125.

12. George Rosen, *Preventive Medicine in the United States 1900–1975, Trends and Interpretations* (New York: Prodist, 1977), 16.

13. Walter I. Trattner, *Crusade for Children: A History of the National Child Labor Committee and Child Labor Reform in America* (Chicago: Quadrangle, 1970), 12.

14. Caroline Benedict Burrell, *The Mother's Book: Suggestions Regarding the Mental and Moral Development of Children* (New York: University Society, 1911), 271.

15. Beatrice Forbes-Robertson Hale, *What Women Want* (New York: Frederick A. Stobes, 1914), 285.

16. Ida Tarbell, *The Business of Being a Woman* (New York: Macmillan, 1912), 198.

17. Kathleen W. Jones, "Sentiment and Science: The Later Nineteenth Century Pediatrician as Mother's Advisor," *Journal of Social History* 17(1983):86.

18. Joan G. Zimmerman, "The Jurisprudence of Equality: The Women's Minimum Wage: The First Equal Rights Amendment, and Adkins v. Children's Hospital, 1905–1923," *Journal of American History* 78(1991):197–98.

19. Viviana A. Zelizer, *Pricing the Priceless Child: The Changing Social Value of Children* (New York: Basic, 1985), 28.

20. Ibid., 44.

21. *New York Times,* 23 October 1908, 9.

22. *Bulletin of the Kansas State Board of Health* 3(1907):94.

23. Molly Ladd-Taylor, *Raising A Baby the Government Way. Mother's Letters to the Children's Bureau, 1915–1932* (New Brunswick: Rutgers University, 1986), 55.

24. Ibid., 4.

25. Samuel Pancoast, *Pancoast's Tokology and Ladies Medical Guide* (Philadelphia: Thompson & Thomas, 1901), 455.

26. Burrell, iii.

27. William Palmer Lucas, *The Health of the Runabout Child. The Journey from Mother's Lap to the School Gate* (New York: Macmillan, 1928), 80.

28. Ibid., 53.

29. John Lovett Morse, Edwin T. Wyman, and Lewis W. Hill, *The Infant and Young Child: Its Care and Feeding from Birth until School Age, A Manual for Mothers* (Philadelphia: Saunders, 1924), 11.

30. Ladd-Taylor, 163.

31. Frieda E. Lippert and Arthur Holmes, *When to Send for the Doctor* (Philadelphia: Lippincott, 1913), 13.

32. Ibid., 24.

33. W. McKim Marriott, *Infant Nutrition: A Textbook on Infant Feeding*

for Students and Practitioners of Medicine (St. Louis: C.V. Mosby, 1930), 7.

34. Steven Schlossman, "Philanthropy and the Gospel of Child Development," *History of Education Quarterly* 21(1981):275.

35. Schlossman, 296.

36. Judith Walzer Leavitt, *The Healthiest City in America* (Princeton: Princeton University, 1982), 217.

37. Zelizer, 26.

38. Hale, 147.

39. D. Clayton Brown, "Health of Farm Children in the South, 1900–1950," *Agricultural History* 53(1979):171–72.

40. Ibid., 187.

41. Frank Tannenbaum, "Race Theory and Negro Mortality," *Opportunity* 2(1924):132.

42. Ebner V. McCollum, "Nutrition as a Factor in Physical Development," *Annals of the American Academy of Political and Social Sciences* 98(1921):34.

43. Ladd-Taylor, 87.

44. Ibid., 118–19.

45. Ibid., 122.

46. Rosen, 3.

47. Barbara Rosenkrantz, *Public Health and the State, Changing Views in Massachusetts, 1842–1936* (Cambridge: Harvard University, 1972), 77.

48. L. Emmett Holt, letter to the Laura Spelman Rockefeller Fund, 4 December 1922, Rockefeller Archives, Tarrytown, N.Y.

49. Josephine Baker, "Preliminary Statement on the American Child Hygiene Association," Putnam Papers, Schlesinger Library, Radcliffe College, Cambridge, Mass.

50. Josephine Baker, *Child Hygiene* (New York: Harper, 1925), 308.

51. Leavitt, 72.

52. Carl Betz, *A System of Physical Culture*, 3d ed. (Kansas City: KC Presse, 1888), frontispiece.

53. John Duffy, "School Buildings and the Health of America: School Children in the Nineteenth Century," in Charles E. Rosenberg, *Healings and History Essays for George Rosen* (New York: Science History Publications, 1979), 168.

54. Baker, *Child Hygiene*, 306.

55. Stuart H. Rowe, *The Physical Nature of the Child and How to Study It* (New York: Macmillan, 1910), 7.

56. Lydia Roberts, "The Nutrition and Care of Children in a Mountain County of Kentucky" (Children's Bureau Publication no. 110, Washington, D.C., 1922), 39.

57. Baker, *Child Hygiene*, 255.

58. American Public Welfare Association, "Welfare Survey of Highland Park, Illinois, 1938" (Social Welfare Archives, University of Minnesota Libraries, Minneapolis, Minn.), 12.

59. James N. Giglio, "Voluntarism and Public Policy Between World War I and the New Deal: Herbert Hoover and the American Child Health Association," *Presidential Studies Quarterly* 13(1983):432.

60. Ibid., 439.

61. Ibid., 441.

62. Angelo Patri, radio script for "Our Children," 12 January 1925, Library of Congress, Washington, D.C.

63. Mrs. Campbell Forrester, speech to the Huron County Federation of Women's Clubs, 7 June 1924, Florence Baker Collection, Library of Congress, Washington, D.C.

64. Kate Barrett, untitled address to the Eighth Special Purity Congress, 1914, Barrett Papers, Library of Congress, Washington, D.C.

65. File memorandum, 1914, Russell Sage Foundation, Rockefeller Archives, Tarrytown, N.Y.

66. Jane Addams, "A Function of the Social Settlement," publication no. 25 of the American Academy of Political and Social Sciences, 16 May 1899, 40.

67. *Hull House Bulletin* 2(March 1897):1.

68. Addams, 49.

69. Ibid.

70. Leavitt, 199–200.

71. File memorandum, 1 February 1923, Laura Spelman Rockefeller Memorial Fund, Rockefeller Archives, Tarrytown, N.Y.

72. *Report of the Henry Street Settlement for 1926* (Social Welfare History Archives, University of Minnesota Libraries, Minneapolis, Minn.), 12.

73. Robert Bremner, *Children and Youth in America, A Documentary History, 1866–1932* (Cambridge: Harvard University, 1970–71), vol. 2, 843.

74. Ibid., 842.

75. Ibid., 843.

76. File memorandum on prenatal activities, Commonwealth Fund, Rockefeller Archives, Tarrytown, N.Y.

77. Alexander McKelway, "The Children's Bureau," unpublished speech, 1919, McKelway Papers, Library of Congress, Washington, D.C.

78. Bremner, 642.

79. Alexander McKelway, speech before the United States Senate, 1910, McKelway Papers, Library of Congress, Washington, D.C., 26.

80. Susan Tifflin, *In Whose Best Interest? Child Welfare Reform in the Progressive Era* (Westport, Conn.: Greenwood, 1982), 238.

81. Dorothy E. Bradbury, "Five Decades of Action for Children: A History

of the Children's Bureau" (Department of Health, Education and Welfare, Washington, D.C., 1967), 5.

82. Jacqueline K. Parker and Edward M. Carpenter, "Julia Lathrop and the Children's Bureau: The Emergence of an Institution," *Social Service Review* 50(1981):64.

83. Ibid., 67.

84. Grace Abbott, *The Child and The State: I. Legal Status in the Family, Apprenticeship and Child Labor* (Chicago: University of Chicago, 1938), viii.

85. Parker and Carpenter, 66.

86. Bradbury, 17.

87. Ladd-Taylor, 2.

88. Ibid., 175.

89. Ibid., 22.

90. Tarbell, 198.

91. Parker and Carpenter, 71.

92. James G. Burrow, *Organized Medicine in the Progressive Era: The Move toward Monopoly* (Baltimore: Johns Hopkins, 1977), 92.

93. *Topeka Capitol*, 21 May 1915, 1.

94. *Bulletin of the Kansas State Board of Health*, June 1917, 112.

95. Samuel J. Crumbine, *Frontier Doctor* (Philadelphia: Dorrance, 1948), 212.

96. *Kansas City Journal World*, 25 July 1915, 4.

97. *Topeka Capitol*, 3 July 1928, 3.

98. File memorandum, September 1921, Russell Sage Foundation, Rockefeller Archives, Tarrytown, N.Y.

99. Joseph B. Chepaitis, "Federal Social Welfare: Progressivism in the 1920s," *Social Service Review* 46(1972):216.

100. "The Sheppard-Towner Bill," *Medical Women's Journal* 28(1921): 13–14.

101. Ibid.

102. Ladd-Taylor, 25.

103. Thomas E. Cone, *History of American Pediatrics* (Boston: Little, Brown, 1979), 203.

104. Ladd-Taylor, 26–27.

105. Ibid.

106. Emmett Holt, letter to the Laura Spelman Rockefeller Fund, 4 December 1922, Rockefeller Archives, Tarrytown, N.Y.

107. Ladd-Taylor, 54.

108. Ibid., 28.

109. Bradbury, 25.

110. Testimony during Hearings before the Committee on Interstate and Foreign Commerce, House of Representatives, 70th Congress, 2d sess., 24–25 January 1929, 23.

111. Ladd-Taylor, 30.
112. Grace Abbott, *From Relief to Social Security: The Development of the New Public Welfare Services and Their Administration* (Chicago: University of Chicago, 1941), 164.
113. Ladd-Taylor, 31.
114. Sydney Halpern, *American Pediatrics: The Social Dynamics of Professionalism, 1880–1980* (Berkeley: University of California, 1988), 85.
115. Ralph E. Pumphrey, "Michael Davis and the Transformation of the Boston Dispensary, 1910–1920," *Bulletin of the History of Medicine* 49(1975):463.
116. Abbott, *From Relief*, 263.
117. *Third White House Conference on Children* (Washington, D.C.: U.S. GPO, 1930), 17.
118. Bess Furman, "Hidden Hunger in a Land of Plenty," unpublished manuscript, Furman Papers, Library of Congress, Washington, D.C.

Chapter 7

1. Graeme Mitchell and Walter H. Trachsler, "Report of the Use of Sulfanilamide and Its Derivatives at the Children's Hospital of Cincinnati," *Journal of Pediatrics* 11(1937):183–87.
2. Cotton Mather, *A Man of Reason* (Boston: John Edwards, 1718), 17–20.
3. Norma Selbert, *Child Health* (Philadelphia: Saunders, 1931), 17.
4. Nancy Potlishman Weiss, "Mother the Invention of Necessity: Dr. Benjamin Spock's Baby and Child Care," in Joseph M. Hawes and N. Ray Hiner, *American Childhood: A Research Guide and Historical Handbook* (Westport, Conn.: Greenwood, 1985), 285.
5. Selbert, 105.
6. Ibid., 80.
7. Louise Zabriskie, *Mother and Baby Care in Pictures* (Philadelphia: Lippincott, 1935).
8. Benjamin Spock, *Baby and Child Care,* rev. ed. (New York: Pocket Books, 1968), 10.
9. Dorothy Whipple, *Our American Babies: The Art of Baby Care* (New York: Barrows, 1944), viii.
10. Elizabeth Lowell Putnam, president's address, Ninth Annual Meeting, American Association for the Study and Prevention of Infant Mortality, Chicago, 5–7 December 1918.
11. Rima Apple, "'To Be Used Only under the Direction of a Physician': Commercial Infant Feeding and Medical Practice, 1870–1940," *Bulletin of the History of Medicine* 54(1980):406.
12. Ibid., 412.

13. Graves F. Powers, "Infant Feeding: Historical Background and Modern Practice," *Journal of the American Medical Association* 105(1935):759–61.

14. *Chicago Daily News,* 3 November 1947, 4.

15. Marjorie Gooch, "Ten Years of Progress in Reducing Maternal and Infant Mortality," *The Child* 10(1945):77.

16. Selbert, 35.

17. Leona Baumgartner, letter to Dr. Roderich Heffron, 5 October 1949, Commonwealth Fund, Rockefeller Archives, Tarrytown, N.Y.

18. *New York Times,* 28 August 1990, 1.

19. Catherine Dollfus, Michael Patetta, Earl Siegel, and Alan W. Cross, "Infant Mortality: A Practical Approach to the Analysis of the Leading Causes of Death and Risk Factors," *Pediatrics* 86(1990):176.

20. *Third Annual White House Conference on Child Health and Protection* (Washington: U.S. GPO, 1930), 3.

21. Grace Abbott, *The Child and the State: I. Legal Status in the Family, Apprenticeship and Child Labor* (Chicago: University of Chicago, 1938), 283.

22. Samuel J. Crumbine, letter to B. B. Armstrong, 17 April 1942, Commonwealth Fund Papers, Rockefeller Archives, Tarrytown, N.Y.

23. Edwin F. Daily, "Progress Report on Maternal and Child Health Services, 4 March 1940" (Social Welfare History Archives, University of Minnesota Libraries, Minneapolis, Minn.), 9.

24. Martha Eliot, "Statement to the Subcommittee on Wartime Health and Education" (United States Senate, Washington, D.C., 1 August 1944), 1.

25. *Mid Century White House Conference on Children and Youth* (Washington: U.S. GPO, 1950), 1.

26. Records of the Child Study Association, Social Welfare History Archives, University of Minnesota Libraries, Minneapolis, Minn.

27. Susan Tiffin, *In Whose Best Interest? Child Welfare Reform in the Progressive Era* (Westport, Conn.: Greenwood, 1982), 267.

28. Steven L. Schlossman, "Before Head Start: Notes toward a History of Parent Education in America, 1897–1929," *Harvard Education Review* 46(1976):436.

29. William James, *The Principles of Psychology* (New York: Dover, 1950), 1.

30. Richard Hofstadter, *Anti-Intellectualism in American Life* (New York: Knopf, 1963), 359.

31. John Dewey, *The Child and the Curriculum* (Chicago: University of Chicago, 1902), 31.

32. Alfred Binet and Theodore Simon, *The Development of Intelligence in Children* (Nashville: Williams, 1980), 9.

33. Ibid., 182.

34. David Elkind, "Essay Review: G. Stanley Hall: The Psychologist as Prophet," *Harvard Education Quarterly* 43(1973):423.
35. Schlossman, 443.
36. G. Stanley Hall, *Adolescence: Its Psychology and Its Relations to Physiology, Anthropology, Sociology, Sex, Crime, Religion and Education* (New York: Appleton, 1905), xiii.
37. John B. Watson, *Psychology from the Standpoint of a Behaviorist,* 2d ed. (Philadelphia: Lippincott, 1924), xi.
38. Ibid., 7–8.
39. John B. Watson, *Psychological Care of the Infant and Child* (New York: Norton, 1928), 87.
40. John B. Watson, "Psychology as the Behaviorist Views It," *Psychology Review* 20(1913):158.
41. Watson, *Psychological Care,* 9.
42. Ibid., 3.
43. Sigmund Freud, *The Standard Edition of the Complete Psychological Studies of Sigmund Freud,* vol. 11(London: Hogarth Press, 1959), 45.
44. Ibid., vol. 7, 173
45. Ibid., vol. 11, 48.
46. John C. Burnham, *Psychoanalysis and American Medicine 1894–1918: Medicine, Science and Culture* (New York: International Universities Press, 1967), 199–200.
47. Freud, vol. ll, 40.
48. Alfred Kazin, "The Freudian Revolution Analyzed," in Benjamin Nelson, *Freud and the Twentieth Century* (New York: World, 1957), 14.
49. Geoffrey Steere, "Freudianism and Child-Rearing in the '20s," *American Quarterly* 20(1968):759.
50. Arnold Gesell, "Normal Growth as a Public Health Concept," *American Child Health Association* 3(1926):48.
51. D. A. Thom, *Habit Clinics for Child Guidance,* Children's Bureau Publication no. 135 (Washington, D.C., 1938), 96.
52. Trustee's Confidential Monthly Report, 1 June 1953, Child Research Council Papers, Commonwealth Fund, Rockefeller Archives, Tarrytown, N.Y., 4.
53. Arnold Gesell, Report of the Committee on Mental Hygiene, American Academy of Pediatrics, November 1939, Gesell Papers, Library of Congress, Washington, D.C., 7.
54. Margo Horn, "The Moral Message of Child Guidance, 1925–1945," *Journal of Social History* 18(1983):26–28.
55. Dorothy Pawluck, "Transition in Pediatrics: A Segmental Analysis," *Social Problems* 30(1983):450.
56. Thomas E. Cone, *History of American Pediatrics* (Boston: Little, Brown, 1979), 229.

57. Borden S. Veeder, "Trend of Pediatric Education and Practice," *American Journal of Diseases of Children* 50(1935):1.

58. *Third White House Conference on Children*, 34–35.

59. C. Henry Kempe, F. N. Silverman, and B. F. Steele, "The Battered Child Syndrome," *Journal of the American Medical Association* 181(1961):17–21.

60. Albert J. Solnit, "Child Abuse: Least Harmful, Most Protective Intervention," *Pediatrics* 65(1980):170–71.

61. Samuel Levine, "Pediatric Education at the Crossroads," *American Journal of Diseases of Children* 100(1960):654.

62. Julius B. Richmond, "Child Development, A Basic Science for Pediatrics," *Pediatrics* 39(1967):656.

63. "Better Health for Our Children, A National Strategy," report of the Select Panel for the Promotion of Child Health, 1981, Washington, D.C., vol. l, 1.

64. Herbert L. Needleman and Richard L. Jackson, "Lead Toxicity in the 21st Century: Will We Still Be Treating It?" *Pediatrics* 89(1992):628.

65. Agency for Toxic Substances and Disease Registry, *The Nature and Extent of Lead Poisoning in Children in the United States: A Report to Congress* (Atlanta: Department of Health and Human Services, 1988).

66. Needleman and Jackson, 629.

67. Committee on Adolescence, "Firearms and Adolescents," *Pediatrics* 89(1992):784.

68. Anna Salvia, transcript of an interview (undated), National Park Service, Ellis Island, N.Y.

69. *Report of the Select Committee on Children, Youth and Families. United States Children and Their Families: Current Conditions and Recent Trends* (Washington: U.S. GPO, 1989), 183

70. Ibid., 195.

71. Ibid., 182.

72. Ibid., 203.

73. Ibid., 196.

74. Ibid., 207.

75. Ibid., x.

76. *Chicago Tribune*, 2 December 1990, 3.

77. *New York Times*, 26 September 1990, 1.

78. Ibid., 30 September 1990, 5.

79. Ibid., 1 October 1990, 11.

80. Rosemary Stevens, *In Sickness and in Wealth: American Hospitals in the Twentieth Century* (New York: Basic Books, 1989).

81. Leon Eisenberg, "Preventive Pediatrics: The Promise and the Peril," *Pediatrics* 80(1987):421.

82. David Werner, "Beyond Pediatrics: The Health and Survival of Disadvantaged Children," *Pediatrics* 91(1993):705.

Bibliographic Essay

As this work demonstrates, the condition of children's health in America is dependent on the daily life of individual families and the larger society. Consequently, letters, diaries, journals, and even fictional works are historical records of the nature of children's health in America. From the diaries and journals of Samuel Sewall and Cotton Mather to Sinclair Lewis's *Arrowsmith* (New York: Modern Classics, 1949), these primary sources about children's health are widely placed in archives, libraries, and state and local historical societies throughout the nation. It is not the purpose of this essay to cite these primary sources as the notes throughout the text adequately define many of these materials. Rather, this essay serves as a guide to the secondary literature about children's health in America.

From the colonial era to contemporary America, physicians have written widely on the health of the nation's children. Medical textbooks, medical journals, and volumes of family health advice are all examples of these commonly available professional sources. During the colonial era, the works of English authors were especially popular. These works, including Walter Harris's *A Treatise on the Acute Diseases of Infants* (London: Thomas Astley, 1742), Michael Underwood's *A Treatise on the Diseases of Children with General Direction of the Management of Infants from Birth* (Philadelphia: Dobson, 1773), and William Cadogan's *An Essay upon Nursing and Management of Children from Their Birth to Three Years of Age* (London: Robert Horsfield, 1769), were written for both parents and professionals and were regularly consulted by colonial parents, along with John Locke's

Some Thoughts Concerning Education (New York: Oxford, 1989). Throughout the nineteenth century popular manuals of domestic medicine like
William Buchan's *Advice to Mothers, on the Subject of Their Own Health;
and of Their Offspring's* (New York: Arno, 1972) and John Gunn's *New
Domestic Physician* (Knoxville, Tenn.: F. S. Heiskell, 1833) were published
in multiple editions and made available across the nation. Popular in the
twentieth century were Norma Selbert's *Child Health* (Philadelphia:
Saunders, 1931) and, more recently, Benjamin Spock's *Baby and Child Care*
(New York: Pocket Books, 1981). In addition, several publications of the
Children's Bureau, like the multiple mid-century editions of *The Mother's
Manual* (Washington: U.S. GPO) were distributed around the country by
federal, state, and local health departments. Beginning with William
Dewees's *Treatise on the Physical and Medical Treatment of Children*
(Philadelphia: Carey, Lea & Blanchard, 1838) in the mid-nineteenth century
and continuing with the works of Abraham Jacobi and L. Emmett Holt near
the end of the century, pediatricians readily consulted comprehensive manuals of professional advice. These efforts continue in the twentieth century with
popular medical works like Abraham Rudolph and Julian Hoffman *Pediatrics*
(Norwalk, Conn.: Appleton, 1987) and the regular issue of pediatric journals,
such as *The American Journal of Diseases of Children, Pediatrics,* and the
Journal of Pediatrics.

   Surprisingly few comprehensive considerations of children's health in
America have been written. *History of Pediatrics* (Philadelphia: Saunders,
1965) written by Arthur Abt in the early years of this century is now dated.
Thomas Cone, in a *History of American Pediatrics* (Boston: Little, Brown,
1979), presents the health care of American children largely from the perspective of the medical profession. The more recent *American Pediatrics: The
Social Dynamics of Professionalization, 1880–1980* (Berkeley: University of
California, 1989) by Sydney Halpern considers the subject as part of the
larger process of the professionalization of American physicians; but the larger social perspective on this subject remains largely unconsidered.

   In the absence of general overviews of American children's health, there
are broad-based historical perspectives on American children, especially the
important collections of essays edited by Joseph Hawes and Ray Hiner.
Both *American Childhood: A Research Guide and Historical Handbook*
(Westport: Greenwood, 1985) and *Growing Up in America: Children in
Historical Perspective* (Urbana: University of Illinois, 1985) contain essays
that raise issues and questions about children's health in America. The
works also have excellent bibliographies about all aspects of children and
American life. C. John Summerville's *Rise and Fall of Childhood* (New
York: Random House, 1990) is also very useful. *Growing Up in America:
Historical Experiences* by Harvey J. Graff (Detroit: Wayne State University

Press, 1987) offers more personal insights into the history of children in American life.

In each of the historical periods considered for this work, important secondary sources are available for further consideration. Since death was common for colonial children, works like *The Puritan Way of Death: A Study in Religion, Culture and Social Change* (New York: Oxford, 1977) by David Stannard, and Peter Slater's *Children in the New England Mind in Death and Life* (Hamden, Conn.: Archon Books, 1977) are important for the understanding of this fundamental personal, family, and social event. Consideration of common infectious conditions of the era, such as diphtheria and smallpox, are found in Donald Hopkins's *Princes and Peasants: Smallpox in History* (Chicago: University of Chicago, 1983) and Ernest Caulfield's *A True History of the Terrible Epidemic Vulgarly Called the Throat Distemper* (New Haven, Conn.: Beaumont Medical Club, 1939).

Throughout history mothers have played an important role in the health of their children. By the early nineteenth century the role of republican motherhood was believed to be increasingly essential for the health of the nation's children. This evolution of this role is reflected in Linda Kerber's *Women of the Republic: Intellect and Ideology in Revolutionary America* (Chapel Hill: University of North Carolina, 1980), and specific northern examples of this process are reported in Sylvia Hoffert's *Private Matters: American Attitudes toward Childbearing and Infant Nurture in the Urban North 1800–1860* (Urbana: University of Illinois, 1989), and southern examples by Jane Censer in *North Carolina Planters and their Children 1800–1869* (Baton Rouge: Louisiana State University, 1984). Linda Pollack extends the examination of mothers' roles into the twentieth century with *A Lasting Relationship: Parents and Children over Three Centuries* (Hanover, N.H.: University Press of New England, 1990), while Molly Ladd-Taylor emphasizes the role of the federal government in the promotion of children's health in *Raising a Baby the Government Way, Mother's Letters to the Children's Bureau, 1915–32* (New Brunswick: Rutgers University, 1986). *Brought to Bed: Childbearing in America, 1750–1950* (New York: Oxford, 1988) by Judy Leavitt points out the changes in both American medicine and society over two centuries as the medical care of birthing women evolved. This work provides important background for the analysis of infant care and the health problems of babies, as well as for the history of women and birthing.

By the second half of the nineteenth century child advocacy was a growing profession in America. The need for these efforts was defined by popular works cited in the text by Jacob Riis and Homer Folks. Miriam Langsam in *Children West: A History of the Placing Out System of the New York Children's Aid Society 1853–1890* (Madison: University of Wisconsin, 1969) defines the important social role of public and private efforts for the benefit of destitute, neglected, and delinquent children. Successful infant feeding, as described in Rima Apple's *Mothers and Medicine: A Social History of Infant Feeding 1890–1950* (Madison: University of Wisconsin, 1987), was essential for the success of public programs that promoted children's health and nutrition. Public health measures, which John Duffy describes in *The Sanitarians* (Urbana: University of Illinois, 1990) and James Cassedy emphasizes in *Charles V. Chapin and the Public Health Movement* (Cambridge: Harvard, 1962), formed the backbone of these efforts, which spread throughout the nation. The recent work by Richard Meckel *Save the Babies: American Public Health Reform and the Prevention of Infant Mortality, 1850–1975* (Baltimore: Johns Hopkins, 1990) nicely summarizes these developments.

Elliott West demonstrates how the expansion of the western frontier affected children, in *Growing Up with the Country: Childhood on the Western Frontier* (Albuquerque: University of New Mexico, 1989). As the edges of the frontier were reached, the nation witnessed the birth of the Progressive era and the furtherance of children's health care measures. Progressives from Boston to San Francisco promoted health and improved living conditions for the nation's children. These events are chronicled by Robert Crunden in *Ministers of Reform: The Progressive Achievement in American Civilization 1889–1920* (Urbana: University of Illinois, 1985) and Susan Tiffin in *In Whose Best Interest?: Child Welfare Reform in the Progressive Era* (Westport, Conn.: Greenwood, 1982). Ultimately, children were healthier and American society placed a greater value on children, as Viviana Zelizer notes in *Pricing the Priceless Child: The Changing Social Value of Children* (New York: Basic, 1985).

The professional and lay literature about children's health in America during the twentieth century is literally voluminous. This material reflects both the growth of pediatric science and the expanded study of the mind and body of the child. The works by Freud, Dewey, Hall, and Watson cited in the text are useful in this regard. The increasing role of the federal government in the health of the nation's children is reflected not only in wider services but also in more federal publications. The periodic White House Conferences on Children demonstrate the expanded emphasis on the biosocial model of health care for the children of the nation. Study of these government publications is suggested for a concise understanding of this subject.

Index

The Author

Charles R. King obtained his M.A. in history and his M.D. at the University of Kansas. He is currently on the Obstetrics/Gynecology faculty at the Medical College of Ohio. The recipient of numerous awards, grants, and fellowships, Dr. King is a frequent contributor to professional journals.